LIVING
WITH
DIFFERENCE

LIVING
WITH
DIFFERENCE

Families with Dwarf Children

JOAN ABLON

photographs by Daniel Margulies

PRAEGER

New York
Westport, Connecticut
London

Copyright Acknowledgments

Portions of Chapters 3 and 8 appeared in Ablon, Joan, "The Parents' Auxiliary of Little People of America: A Self-Help Model of Social Support for Families of Short Statured Children," *Prevention in Human Services*, vol. 1, no. 3, Spring 1982. Copyright © 1982 by the Haworth Press, Inc. Reprinted with permission; all rights reserved.

Portions of Chapters 2, 8 and Appendix C appeared in Ablon, Joan, *Little People in America: The Social Dimensions of Dwarfism*, Praeger Publishers, 1984, reprinted with permission.

Portions of Chapter 8 are reprinted with permission from *Social Science and Medicine*, vol. 15B, no. 1. Ablon, Joan, "Dwarfism and Social Identity: Self-Help Group Participation." Copyright © 1981, Pergamon Press Ltd.

Library of Congress Cataloging-in-Publication Data

Ablon, Joan.
    Living with difference.

    Bibliography: p.
    Includes index.
    1. Dwarf children—United States.   2. Dwarf children—United States—Family relationships.
I. Title.
HQ773.65.A34   1988   649'.151   87–32790
ISBN 0–275–92901–9 (alk. paper)

Copyright © 1988 by Joan Ablon

Library of Congress Catalog Card Number: 87–32790

ISBN: 0–275–92901–9

First published in 1988

Praeger Publishers, One Madison Avenue, New York, NY 10010
A division of Greenwood Press, Inc.

Printed in the United States of America

∞™

The paper used in this book complies with the
Permanent Paper Standard issued by the National
Information Standards Organization (Z39.48–1984).

10 9 8 7 6 5 4 3 2

For the memory of my parents
Dave and Bess Ablon

Contents

Preface

I have written this book for the many audiences who have personal or professional investments in learning about the lives and families of profoundly short children in American society. Doctors, nurses, genetic counselors, social workers, and other health and social service professionals who see families with dwarf children often know little about the kinds of life experiences that shape their patients' and clients' lives and may critically affect their mental and physical health and welfare. This book is written for them as well as for the many persons with generic interests in physically different children. The case of dwarf children provides the opportunity to explore similarities and differences between dwarfs and the varied populations often considered under the broad rubric of difference. Families with dwarf children are a primary audience for this book. These families have few resources to provide them with an understanding of the kinds of lives their children will lead. Only a small fraction of them will make their way to the organization of Little People of America (LPA), where the answers to many of their questions may be found.

I am very appreciative of the National Science Foundation for their support of the first two years of this research, from 1976 to 1978 (grant number BNS76–18402), and to the Medical Anthropology Program, University of California, San Francisco, the base of my research and teaching activities, which has provided both affective and practical support. I owe thanks to colleagues and friends who have read or heard selections or drafts of this work and have offered criticisms and suggestions: Gaylene Becker, Leonard Borman, Ann Johanson, Daniel Margulies, Jean Pumphrey, Al and Harriet Stickney, Sol Tax, and Joan Weiss. I am especially grateful to Gaylene Becker, who was consistently generous in giving of her time and suggestions. The manuscript has benefited greatly from her contributions. I am appreciative of Judith Barker and Linnea

Klee for their coding of data, and to Marisa Leto and Regina Garrick for technical assistance in preparation of the manuscript. Many persons over twelve years assisted in the typing of tapes and various drafts of the manuscript: Evie Barlow, Priscila Ednalgan, Joy Edstrom, Barbara Jordon, and Cassandra Schaffer. To Priscila Ednalgan, who conscientiously typed the final drafts of this manuscript, seemingly thousands of pages and some many times over, I owe my special thanks for her unending patience and industry.

I am deeply indebted to the many members of LPA Parents' Groups throughout the country who so generously shared with me their family experiences and so provided the materials for this writing. I owe my special appreciation to Harriet and Al Stickney and Daniel Margulies for their ongoing support and encouragement, ready counsel, and warm friendship over many years. Daniel Margulies took the fine photographs included in this book and arranged for their use. My life has been enriched and nourished immeasurably through my work and friendships within LPA over the past decade.

LIVING
WITH
DIFFERENCE

Chapter 1
Introduction

Leigh Harkins fed her baby, put him to sleep, and pulled down the shades. She then went to bed and slept until her husband, Paul, came home from work in the afternoon. It was thirty days following the birth of her child, Josh, an achondroplastic dwarf. Leigh had the phone disconnected and refused to talk to her family or friends. In retrospect, she realized she had been in an acute depression for the first year after Josh's birth. Hallie Janes on the thirtieth day following the birth of her child, Bryan, also an achondroplastic dwarf, hurried around the house, placing last minute touches of color in the living room. This day she and her husband, Greg, were having an open house to introduce the husky, laughing, little boy to their family and friends. Hallie decided that this introduction would hasten Bryan's acceptance by their loved ones.

Leigh and Hallie display two quite different responses of new mothers of dwarf children. Between these two extremes lie many individual modes of adaptation to unexpected difference. Dwarfism invariably is an unexpected and shocking difference that families absorb and adapt to in diverse and complex ways.

Expectant parents everywhere characteristically await the birth of the "perfect child"—a beautiful baby with all the attributes that their society values. The possibility of a physically or mentally different child, although a relatively common but little recognized statistical reality, is kept in the far reaches of the mind. In fact, one out of every fourteen infants born in the United States each year, or more than 250,000 infants are born with significant physical or mental differences (McIntosh et al., 1954; Bierman et al., 1963; Shapiro, et al., 1965; Christianson et al., 1981; March of Dimes, 1986).

The possibility of problematic conditions emerging increases as children grow older. At five years the incidence of "severe and moderate (but not trivial)" anomalies in one study totaled 15 percent (Christianson et al., 1981). Prevalence figures for the total number of children or adults with special health conditions vary widely depending on the definitions that are used. Mattsson (1972) reported that 30 to 40 percent of American children have some degree of disability and some 7 to 10 percent of these have physical disorders. A 1980 UNICEF report stated that "at least one-tenth of all children are born with, or acquire impairments—physical, mental or sensory—that will interfere with their capacities for normal development."

THE STUDY AND THE SAMPLE

This study examines the birth and early years of dwarf children, a category of physically different children. The material presented here has resulted from interviews with twenty-five member families of Parents' Groups (formerly called the Auxiliary) of Little People of America, conversations with several dozen others, and from my observations at local, regional, and national meetings of this organization, and in particular Parents' Group functions at these meetings over a ten-year period, from 1976 to 1986.[1] I was treated graciously by parents, who universally welcomed the opportunity to talk openly and candidly about their experiences. A subsample of six sets of parents were interviewed systematically over a six-year period, from 1977 to 1983. The use of the anthropological open-ended approach to interviewing allowed parents the opportunity to discuss the kinds of issues and detail that were of importance to them and their families. Clinical interest typically focuses on physical structure and function related to the child's body. Few professionals have shown interest in the personal, day-to-day, nitty-gritty issues that are paramount in parents' minds and lives. Yet it is these social and psychological consequences of physical difference that make up the reality issues that families live with on a daily basis and that impinge on their lives. One central goal of my study has been to interpret and discuss these issues. I have included many accounts in parents' own words. The philosophy and conventional wisdom of the Parents' Groups of Little People of America are also presented as a rich blueprint for the positive adaptation of families.

FAMILY RESPONSE TO PHYSICALLY OR MENTALLY DIFFERENT CHILDREN

Profound distress is usually experienced by parents at the birth of a physically or mentally different child. The initial impact of such difference begins when diagnosis and labeling occur and may continue to be felt throughout the child's and parents' lifetimes. The birth of a different child has implications for all members of the family. Special health conditions affect the entire family's emotional climate, behavior, and role expectations. Family members typically feel their whole life is engulfed in a crisis situation that may seem unique and unending.

A significant literature has been developed on family response to the birth of a "disabled" or "handicapped" child. (See Appendix B for a more detailed summary of this literature.) While a disability is usually defined by actual functional impairment that can be objectively measured, a handicap exists when a disability puts a person at a disadvantage in a particular environmental circumstance (Mitchell, 1977). Therefore handicaps are relative and may be created by society through physical barriers or by negative attitudes. So-called "handicapping" conditions vary dramatically.

Expectant parents often invest a wealth of dreams and expectations in the birth of the perfect child as their gift to each other and the symbol of their love and marriage. If the child is less than their expectation of perfection, a devastating psychological trauma may be precipitated (Mori, 1983). It was observed that "the psychological life space of most parents is profoundly affected by the attributes of their children" (Cummings et al., 1966, p. 595). Variations in physical or mental characteristics that are considered as deficiencies or handicapping conditions may seriously influence parents' perceptions of their own identity and self-worth. Parents experience anxiety, loss, and depression as a result. Thus, parents' expectations for fulfillment and their evaluations of themselves may be at stake in the persons of their children and the normalcy of their family group.

A variety of factors that influence parents' responses to their child have been identified. Some of these are the severity of the child's handicap and the degree of its visibility, the social acceptability of the handicap, the socioeconomic level and cultural values and attitudes of the family, personality characteristics of parents, the manner in which the parents are informed of the condition, and the age of the child when the diagnosis is made (Schell, 1981; Marion, 1981; Darling, 1979).

Researchers have proposed various stages of emotional reactions and acceptance experienced by parents. The variety, sequence, and number of stages vary. The most common responses are grief, shock, anger, shame, and fear. For example, Solnit and Stark and others (Solnit and Stark, 1961; Bristor, 1984) suggested that parents mourn the loss of the perfect child. This concept has been explored in considerable detail, examining the grieving process that occurs. Stages of action or behavior rather than emotions have also been proposed. Some of these are awareness of the problem, recognition of its nature, search for a cause, search for a cure, and acceptance of the problem (Rosen, 1955).

Mori (1983) and Fortier and Wanlass (1984) presented very useful summaries of this literature on emotional and behavioral responses. Mori suggested consistent themes that appear. The early stages of responses are characterized by severe psychological disorganization. Parents are overwhelmed by such emotions as shock, anguish, and sorrow. In the middle stages parents may overcome the initial shock but they may reject the diagnosis. They may deny their child's condition, precluding intervention or communication about the problem. They may engage in "shopping behavior," repeatedly seeking from various professionals the cause and/or cure of their child's condition. The final stage of acceptance is based on reality. In this period parents focus on interactions between themselves and with the child that make possible a "nurturing relationship with the child" (Mori, 1983, pp. 21–22).

In the case of average-sized[2] parents who learn they have a dwarf child, interviews with parents suggest that overwhelming shock is, indeed, the universal, initial response. Because most parents have seen only a few dwarfs in their lifetime, they have no knowledge about the nature of their lives. Statements of parents reiterate their immediate need for information about how their child will fit the normal expectations of family and society. What will they look like? Will they date? Will they marry? The parents I talked with found answers to these questions in most cases through their contacts with Parents' Groups of Little People of America, not through the assistance of clinicians or other professionals, for whom the social and even physical realities of dwarfism often are as much a matter of mystery as they are to the lay public. After parents found solid answers to basic questions about their baby's social development and future, they could then proceed to the task of acceptance and adaptation.

LITTLE PEOPLE OF AMERICA

Little People of America is a nonprofessional self-help or mutual-aid support group with a membership of some 4,000 persons—dwarfs and their families. LPA is a remarkably energetic organization that sponsors activities on local, regional, and national levels. A significant component of LPA is the Parents' Group, an organization to assist parents of dwarf children in understanding and dealing with physical, social, and psychological problems that their dwarf children might experience. The majority of parents are average-sized persons. However, the number of dwarf parents who attend meetings with their dwarf children is rapidly increasing.

This study reports on the perceptions and behavior of families belonging to LPA Parents' Groups. The study does not claim to represent the experiences of all families in the country with dwarf children. The difficulties in trying to locate systematically a statistically random or representative sampling of families with dwarf children make such a venture untenable. There is no way to locate the total population of these families. Children are diagnosed at different ages, and many families never accept a diagnosis of dwarfism throughout their child's lifetime. The logistic and attitudinal problems preclude an exhaustive survey of dwarf children without a massive outreach effort that would have to contact every school, hospital, and clinic throughout the country in a systematic fashion. It is unlikely that such an enormous and expensive endeavor will ever be attempted.

As a specialized peer support group, Little People of America draws families who have been referred by a broad range of medical facilities and such public and private organizations as various children's and Shriner's hospitals and the March of Dimes. Other families come who have seen programs on LPA on television or have read stories on LPA in the newspaper, or have heard of LPA from relatives or friends. Most families appear to be middle class, although families of varying socioeconomic classes and ethnicities are recruited for membership. There are few very rich or very poor families. Whether significant differences exist in the nature and attitudes of families who come to LPA and those who do not is difficult to determine. Many families never learn of the existence of LPA. However, it is possible that families who do come to LPA are particularly assertive in their problem-solving efforts. On the other hand, it could be argued that those who hear of LPA and do *not* choose to come are also assertive, in that they are determined to pursue a "mainstreamed" way of life for their child with no external recognition of physical difference. I asked professionals at institutions across the country who have frequent occasion to refer families to LPA about this issue. Their responses suggest that parents who choose not to come to LPA are likely to fit into one or more of the following categories: (1) they are denying their child's dwarfism, (2) they are ethnic or linguistic minorities, (3) they are families who because of their structure or the nature of their community are able to offer a particularly supportive and normalizing atmosphere for their child, (4) they may not be joiners and would avoid any group membership, or (5) they are pathological families. This subject will be discussed in more detail in Chapter 10.

ATTITUDES TOWARD DWARFISM

Differing cultural groups have expressed dramatic and variable attitudes toward persons of profound short stature in art works, folklore, and written historical materials. Representations of dwarfs are found in ancient Egyptian, Greek, Roman, and Pre-Columbian New World archeological remains. Dwarfs typically have been regarded as special persons, in some situations as deities, in others as persons of special talent or as jesters and objects of humor. The central roles of dwarfs in European courts have been documented in major art works, such as those of Velasquez. (For historical perspectives see Johnston, 1963; Roth and Cromie, 1980.) Today in our own society dwarfs still are often portrayed by the media as mystical or magical creatures, rather than ordinary individuals of the mundane world of our daily reality. The complexities associated with this special status will be discussed in this section.

Every society categorizes physical and social attributes as positive characteristics to be valued or as negative traits to be rejected. Goffman described this social process in his classic work, *Stigma: Notes on the Management of Spoiled Identity* (1963):

Society establishes the means of categorizing persons and the complement of attributes felt to be ordinary and natural for members of each of these categories. Social settings establish the categories of persons likely to be encountered there. . . .

While the stranger is present before us, evidence can arise of his possessing an attribute that makes him different from others in the category of persons available for him to be, and of a less desirable kind in the extreme, a person who is quite thoroughly bad, or dangerous, or weak. He is thus reduced in our minds from a whole and usual person to a tainted, discounted one. Such an attribute is a stigma, especially when its discrediting effect is very extensive; sometimes it is also called a failing, a shortcoming, a handicap (pp. 2–3).

Persons with differences labeled as negative in our society typically must struggle to "normalize" their existence, that is, to construct and maintain normal comportments and lifestyles as much as is possible within social environments that are curious, ridiculing, and sometimes even hostile (Ainlay et al., 1986). Anthropologists have provided naturalistic portrayals of some of the varied populations labeled as stigmatized by our society (Edgerton, 1967; Becker, 1980; Estroff, 1981; Ablon, 1984; Langness and Levine, 1986). Through these studies we come to understand the strategies for coping and adaptation developed by persons who bear the onus of stigma and its many consequences. Goffman spoke of a "courtesy stigma" shared by family and close associates of stigmatized persons. Few accounts are available of the attitudes or coping mechanisms developed and maintained by persons with a courtesy stigma. This study explores the responses and experiences of one such population.

DWARFISM AS A "DIFFERENT" DIFFERENCE

The literature on the psychosocial aspects of dwarfism is typically included within the larger rubric of studies of disabled or handicapped populations. Likewise, those who deliver services count dwarfs among these populations. Although the condition of dwarfism shares a social stigma with many other conditions, an understanding of the experience of dwarf children must take into consideration two factors that critically affect the nature of their stigma in very crucial ways.

First, in our cultural tradition dwarfs belong to the mythic world, not the mundane world of our daily experience or reality. Dwarfs carry with them the historical and cultural baggage of special and even magical status much more than do persons with various other physical differences. Persons in the general population thus exhibit great curiosity about dwarfs, stare at them often unbelievingly, and in some cases even try to photograph them in a chance encounter. Persons with other physical differences do not experience such an extreme response.

Secondly, although dwarfism is a dramatic, physically distinctive, and immediately identifiable condition, dwarfs are usually not physically disabled or handicapped in the general sense of these terms. The body parts are all present, with each part fitting into a harmonic, although different, whole. As one parent of a dwarf child said, "Their bodies are just packaged a little differently." The difference of smallness of size is, however, a crucial symbolic difference of attribute in American society where tall stature is prized.

DWARFISM AS A SOCIAL DISABILITY

Many studies in the literature on disability lump together children with many types of difference, thereby ignoring the unique features and implications of each. Disability or handicapped labels suggest an extreme physical or mental difference that imposes significant if not severe physical or mental limitations on behavior or thinking capabilities, and also related negative social responses to individuals who have these conditions. Dwarfism, although a shocking and unexpected condition, in the great majority of cases does not carry with it the logistic realities that turn family life upside down with physical demands, continual and severe emotional traumas, or potentially conflictive decisions that must be made. Life is not transformed into an exhausting daily trial to maintain the child physically nor does the projection of a similar trajectory into the future pose an unending ordeal for parents (for example, see Featherstone, 1980).

Thus, there are realistic differences that lighten the physical load, but the initial emotional reaction of parents is not lightened by a rational consideration of relative severity or pain. The negative societal response to dwarfism is mirrored in parental response and reverberates throughout family life. Parents project themselves into their expectations for the perfect child, and if that child is found wanting, they will themselves be diminished in their own eyes. Although the specific situation of the dwarf child differs in significant ways from that of many physically different children, the period of initial family response to the disclosure of difference and the early family career of help and information seeking have many similarities.

THE AMBIGUITY OF DIFFERENCE

There are basic ambiguities, uncertainties, or vagaries of meaning surrounding a physically different child that begin at birth and that may be interpreted in several ways. The reality of the presence of the "imperfect" infant creates numerous complications that a death would not. Rather than the absence of the child, there is the discordant presence of a child very different from what parents may have expected. Further, as Featherstone vividly pointed out, this child may provide severe challenges in the form of logistics and also in the "heavy responsibility of leading this child into life, and loving him as though he embodied all their dreams" (Featherstone, 1980, p. 234).

Roskies (1972) eloquently expressed the ambiguities experienced by mothers of thalidomide children:

[T]he existing child embodies a basic contradiction. To put it in its crudest terms, living children are taken home, cared for, loved, and identified with, while dead children are buried. The child who is living but defective is an unknown combination of the two. Thus, immediately, the mother is confronted by the dilemma of deciding whether her child is normal enough to induce the mutuality of mother and child, or whether he is so defective that he no longer arouses the emotions and responses habitually aroused by a child. . . .

In common with mothers of all children, the course of development exacts a continuous process of adaptation and readaptation of a changing mother to a changing child. In this sense the rearing of a disabled child resembles the rearing of a normal child. But for the mother of the disabled child, the normal developmental crises are intermingled with an additional continuous crisis. The unclear and constantly changing amount of normality and abnormality embodied in the handicapped child makes the mothering of such a child an adventure in two different cultures. At times, the rules of the culture of normality are most relevant, while at other times the rules have to be taken from the culture of abnormality (pp. 20–21).

Indeed, in the case of dwarf children, parents may find themselves operating within a culture of ambiguity. The ambiguities experienced by dwarfs and their families are magnified by the near normalcy of dwarfs, as well as by their mystique. All persons who are physically or mentally different must negotiate their lives along a continuum of "normal"/similar to "abnormal"/different. Every special population can claim particular or unusual features that affect the social response of others and the physical realities of their existence. The fact of displaying a difference that seems minimal in many situations, yet highly charged and crucial in relation to American values, results in the situation of dwarfs being a unique variation in the study of physical difference.

In the next chapter the social significance of height in American society, and normative height, short stature, and dwarfism will be discussed. In the chapters that follow, parents' responses to births of dwarf children will be described, and major issues dealing with physical development and health, logistics of life, school, social, and family life will be examined. The organization of Little People of America, its Parents' Groups, and the kinds of issues broached there will be described. Three cases of particular families with dwarf children will be presented to illustrate different modes of family adaptation. Finally, a number of salient issues central to family response and adaptation will be discussed.

NOTES

1. The study reported here was one dimension of a larger study of the membership and organization of Little People of America. Another dimension focused on the life experiences of adult dwarfs and the impact of participation in LPA on their social identity and life style (Ablon, 1984). For more on the sample, see Appendix A.

2. Most dwarfs prefer the use of "average" rather than "normal" when comparatively referring to nondwarf individuals in the general population.

Chapter 2
Stature and Dwarfism

THE SOCIAL SIGNIFICANCE OF HEIGHT

For most Americans who share an ethos of "the bigger the better," dwarfs represent persons whose abilities and worth will be inferior, or at best different or special. Common expressions in daily use denote a negative evaluation of shortness; for example, "falls short of," "comes up short," "paltry," "pint size." The word "little" is often used as a denigrating expression, even when it does not relevantly pertain to size. Thus, for most Americans, including dwarfs themselves who have internalized the values of their culture, large body size is a desired physical feature.

Keyes (1980) surveyed the effects and results of the import of physical height on personal life in American society. Keyes emphasized that people continually "size up" one another as part and parcel of every interaction and often adapt their posture, stance, and behavior to each: "Our daily lives are made up of so many such micro height adjustments that we're normally not even aware they're taking place. Yet the life of each one of us is churned into paths determined by the reactions of other people to our height and our reaction to theirs" (p. 11).

A number of studies have documented the psychological and social significance of height in our society (for example, Secord and Jourard, 1953, 1954; Hinckley and Rethlingshafer, 1951; Gunderson, 1965; Caplan and Goldman, 1981; Martel and Biller, 1987). Studies have demonstrated the American penchant to relate tallness to political and economic accomplishment and success. Americans tend to vote for taller political candidates and hire and pay taller men a better wage (Deck, 1968, Martel and Biller, 1987). Height also has been found to be near the top of the list of traits women value in choosing a spouse

(Keyes, 1980; Gillis, 1982). For a review of this literature, see Martel and Biller, 1987.

"NORMAL" AND SHORT STATURE

A large number of Americans are relatively tall people in comparison to most of the world's population. Brues (1977) stated:

A fairly recent sample of 18-year-old men in the United States averaged a little under 5 feet 9 inches, with less than two-tenths of an inch difference between whites and blacks. . . . This is about an inch taller than during World War I, at which time also, the two races averaged the same in height. A comparable sample of American women would be about five inches less, a height which is normal for *males* in many parts of the world (p. 168).

Other figures for the average eighteen-year-old American man's height range around 5 feet 9.7 inches and figures for the average eighteen-year-old woman's height range around 5 feet 4.3 inches (U. S. Department of Commerce, Bureau of the Census, 1986, p. 120; U. S. National Center for Health Statistics Percentiles, n. d.).

Estimates of the number of persons with short and profoundly short stature are difficult to find and vary significantly between sources. An unpublished report prepared by Kelly et al. for the Human Growth Foundation[1] (1978) proposed that a height of less than two standard deviations (SD) below the mean constitutes "short stature." Men who are 5 feet 3.75 inches or less and women who are 4 feet 11.5 inches or less would fall in this category. Kelly et al. provided a variety of figures for short-statured persons by differing age groups and by varying causes. They stated from a total U. S. population figure of 219,104,692 (1978) there are 5.5 million persons with a height of less than two SD below the mean. Some 2,150,000 of these persons are less than twenty-one years old. Another source, Rieser and Underwood (1986), also stated that there are about 2 million children in the United States who are shorter than 98 percent of children their age. Rieser and Underwood (1986 p.9) presented the following list of possible causes of short stature and growth failure:

1. Familial short stature—"heredity" (short parents are more likely to have short children)
2. Constitutional growth delay—delayed puberty, delayed growth spurt, normal adult height
3. Illnesses and diseases that affect the whole body (systemic diseases)
   A. Nutritional deficiencies—undernutrition or malnutrition
   B. Digestive tract disease—bowel disease
   C. Kidney disease
   D. Heart disease
   E. Lung disease
   F. Diabetes mellitus—"high sugar"

G. Severe stress and/or deprived environment
4. Endocrine (hormone) diseases
   A. Lack of thyroid hormone—hypothyroidism
   B. Too much cortisol (stress hormone)—Cushing's syndrome
   C. Lack of growth hormone (GH)—deficiency
5. Problems in the tissues where growth occurs (congenital conditions)
   A. Intrauterine growth retardation—slow growth before birth caused by infections, smoking, alcohol use during pregnancy
   B. Chromosome abnormalities—Turner syndrome, other genetic syndromes
   C. Skeletal abnormalities (bone diseases)—defects in size, shape, growth of bones
6. Idiopathic—no cause can be found (p. 9)

DWARFISM

Clinical definitions of dwarfism vary. Some clinicians would consider persons who are at least three SD below the mean and in the lowest 0.25 percent in height of the general population to be dwarfs (Kelly et al., 1978). Men in this category would measure 5 feet, ½ inches or less and women would measure 4 feet 8 inches or less (U. S. National Center for Health Statistics Percentiles, n. d.). According to Kelly et al.'s figures, some 547,000 persons of all ages would fit in this category. Of these, 208,000 are under age twenty-one years. However, a more conservative height standard of 4 feet 10 inches or less for both sexes is required for membership in LPA. The figure of 100,000 for the total number of dwarfs in the country is frequently cited (Weiss, 1977). Some professionals would consider all profoundly short persons to be dwarfs, while others would utilize this term only for persons with skeletal dysplasias or primary disorders of bone which result in disproportionate short stature. Persons whose limbs are not in the expected proportions to their heads and torsos are considered to be of disproportionate stature.

Most cases of profound short stature are caused by skeletal or endocrine disorders that fall into causal categories 4 and 5 above. The number of actual types of dwarfism has been revised and greatly enlarged through the years. More than eighty specific and well delineated primary disorders of bone or skeletal dysplasias alone that result in short stature have been defined (Rimoin and Lachman, 1983; Scott, 1977). These may differ in etiology and physical characteristics. For compendia and descriptions of varying types of dwarfism, the reader is directed to Spranger et al., 1974; Maroteaux, 1979; Rimoin, 1979; Rimoin and Lachman, 1983; Wynne-Davies et al., 1985; McKusick, 1986.

There is a broad range of types of dwarfism among members of Little People of America. The majority of members exhibit some type of skeletal dysplasia. More than half of LPA members are achondroplastic dwarfs who have average-sized heads and torsos and unusually short arms and legs. Achondroplasia, the most common type of dwarfism, is caused by a genetic mutation that may then continue to be an inherited condition. Figures on the incidence of achondroplasia vary; for example, from 1 in 10,000 births (Kelly et al., 1978) to 1 in

27,100 (Camera and Mastroiacovo, 1982). Among the LPA membership are also significant numbers of hypopituitary and diastrophic dwarfs. Hypopituitary dwarfs, who have a malfunction of the pituitary gland and a shortage of the growth hormone it produces, are of average proportions and appear as small men or women. These persons, commonly called "midgets,"[2] usually are adults who reached adolescence or maturity before the development of the growth hormone treatment, a regimen usually requiring about ten years of semiweekly injections. If the treatment is begun early, it results in a relatively normal growth range for patients. This treatment is widely available now with the development of commercial synthetically produced recombinant human growth hormone obtainable by prescription through pediatric endocrinologists (Kaplan et al., 1986). Hypopituitary dwarfs often have other endocrine or systemic complications and frequently do not enjoy the robust health of achondroplastics.

Diastrophic dwarfism involves considerable complications of the limbs, with frequent modifications of the hands and feet, although the skull is not affected as is true in many cases of achondroplasia (Langer, 1965). Foot and leg surgeries today for children with diastrophic dwarfism may begin as early as one month following birth and continue regularly through adolescence. Diastrophic dwarfs often ambulate with crutches or in wheelchairs; thus, their mobility is more limited than that of persons with some other types of dwarfism.

Other types of dwarfism such as pseudoachondroplasia and spondyloepiphyseal dysplasia congenita (SED) are increasingly found among the LPA membership. Pseudoachondroplasia is similar to achondroplasia with shortening of the limbs relative to the torso, but the skull is not affected (Cooper et al., 1973). SED is characterized by a disproportionately short trunk and spinal and limb irregularities. The skull is not involved, although eye complications are common (Spranger and Langer, 1970).

As medical knowledge has grown about the kinds of problems different types of dwarfs might expect in their lifetimes, varied health regimens, therapies, and early preventive and therapeutic surgeries are being carried out. For example, many children, teenage, and young adult members of LPA are having considerably earlier and more frequent surgeries than had older members in their youth. Health problems will be discussed in Chapter 4.

NOTES

1. The Human Growth Foundation is a voluntary, nonprofit organization dedicated to helping medical science better understand the process of growth, particularly dwarfism. It is composed of concerned parents and friends of children with growth problems and interested physicians. Human Growth Foundation, 4720 Montgomery Lane, Bethesda, Maryland 20814.

2. "Midget" is regarded by many little people as a derogatory label, reported by subjects to be related to the stereotype of "midget" performers in the circus or entertainment worlds, professions still commonly though inaccurately attributed to a large number of dwarfs. Likewise, curious or ridiculing comments directed to or about dwarfs in public and within their hearing often refer to them as "midgets."

Chapter 3
Family Response to the Birth of the Dwarf Child

I heard Dr. Edwards use the word "dwarf" outside the room when he was talking to a resident. When he came in I said, "Dwarf? Are you saying my child's a dwarf?" What dwarf meant to me was a leprechaun. Whatever would *that* mean? Would we have to send her to a circus? What kind of life would she have?

(Mother of dwarf child)

BIRTH OF THE CHILD

The birth of the child was a long-awaited event for many of the families. For example, three of the six couples in the subsample tried to conceive over a period of several years and had consulted physicians and fertility clinics about their inability to conceive. Only one of the mothers had a problematic pregnancy. Most had long labors and one had a Caesarian section.

Parents in the twenty-five families almost invariably talked in detail about the manner in which they were informed of their child's dwarfism. In most cases the diagnosis of dwarfism was made within twenty-four to thirty-six hours following the birth. It appears that the discovery of the infant's physical difference was often made by nurses rather than physicians. In some cases a nurse on the newborn unit had called the doctor's attention to the infant several hours after it was pronounced "normal" by the attending obstetrician. For most parents shock was the immediate response to the news of their child's dwarfism. Because most average-sized persons have seen few dwarfs in their lives, the possibility of a dwarf child is usually not within any anticipated range of expected difference. The trauma of the situation was often exacerbated by physicians' delays and awkwardness in telling parents. Parents considered procrastination on the part of professionals to have been a critical factor in their emotional upset. In several cases mothers were not allowed to see their babies for a day or longer while doctors conferred for a confirmation of the diagnosis. Nurses and doctors often pointedly avoided mothers' queries about their babies. Some parents felt the delay in being informed was due primarily to the doctors not wanting to confront parents about their child. Most parents stated that they feel that the earlier the diagnosis is made and the sooner the family is told, the better, because the family may then more quickly begin their adaptation to the birth and to the fact of their child's condition.

When parents were finally told about their child, it was often with considerable awkwardness and negativity. Some physicians often dealt with parents by being indirect. For example, several couples were told that their babies had short arms and legs, or that their baby would be short, but not that their baby was a dwarf. For many, the ambiguities that characterize their child's dwarfism may well have been fostered in the messages of professionals at this time of birth. Mothers presented vivid accounts of their experiences:

The obstetrician came in first and he was very awkward and really didn't say very much. He said, "She's going to be short, but it's going to be all right." He didn't tell us she was a dwarf. He was very embarrassed.

[You mean embarrassed that he hadn't made the correct diagnosis the first night?]

He was just embarrassed that the whole thing had happened at all. The pediatrician came in a bit later. He had never seen a dwarf child. He was very blunt and businesslike. He said, "Your child is a dwarf, and the condition is called achondroplasia. She's never going to be any taller than four feet, and there will be these kinds of problems. But she'll probably be all right." Still, he was really doing his homework. By the second morning he came in with a medical book—a textbook. He turned to a page and said, "This is what she's going to look like." There was a picture of a nude female adult dwarf, with only the face and eyes blackened out. I noticed the webbed fingers and the sway back. Frankly, it was shocking to look at.

Jamestown Institute is a teaching hospital, and that room was packed with doctors and nurses. It just seemed like everybody had their hand in the pie. When Robb was born, the doctor took him and put his feet on my face and said, "His feet turn in." And I remember thinking he was the cutest baby I'd ever seen, and while they finished up all their work I watched him in the little isolet. The doctor said, "You'll see him this afternoon." That was about 10:00 or 11:00 in the morning. About 4:00 in the afternoon the lady in the next bed got her baby. She said, "I wonder why they haven't brought your baby?" And I knew I was not going to raise my head off the bed because of the headaches that can occur with a block, so I said, "Well, I wonder why they don't come." And I had rung the bell, I had done everything. I even had to help myself to the bedpan and I laid on that for about an hour after I was done; they wouldn't even come and take it. Nobody. They avoided me. And my roommate got so mad, she got up and helped with that. She said, "I'll take it out."

Ed knew something was up because, when he went into the nursery to look, our baby wasn't in there, and there were a group of doctors in the back. Still I hadn't gotten the baby, and they didn't say anything. During that afternoon, this nurse and maybe two others would come in by accident when I'd ring the bell, and I'd say, "I want to see my baby," and they'd say, "Oh, is that the baby with the arms?" I'd say, "Well, yeah." And another would say, "Is that the baby with the feet?" And, "Is that the baby with the hands?" I think those are the three parts they mentioned, and by that time I was upset. I said, "Something is wrong." They would say, "I'll go see," and then I'd never see them again. They just avoided me, and every time I'd ring, the nurses would say, "Oh, I don't know," and they'd leave.

Well, I tried to call Ed about 9:00 that night on the switchboard, and they said, "I'm sorry, you can't use the switchboard at 9:00 at night." I said, "I want to talk to my husband," and I started to cry. So they put him through. I cried and told him I hadn't seen the baby and I wondered what was up. I couldn't get a doctor. Nobody would come. So he got on the phone and called the doctor and said, "Either we see the baby or you're going to have an irate person in the hallway."

Well, the pediatrician came in just before I saw Robb, not my own pediatrician, because he was gone. Here came this poor fellow, and I said, "What's the matter with my baby?" and I started to cry. He was going to tell me all the good things first. He had taken the class on what to tell the parent. So he said, "That's not just a hand hanging off his shoulder." Well I had seen a baby with arms and legs, I hadn't seen a baby with a hand hanging off his shoulder. I wanted to know, maybe they got the wrong baby. So he went on to explain, and I don't remember all he said, but I remember I was really upset. He couldn't stand the pressure of standing there with me, and he left.

It was about three minutes later that here came a nurse with the baby, all wrapped up the way they do, and I was so tickled. And she brought him in, and she said, "Oh, he's so cute," and she lay him beside me. She was a student nurse with one of those student caps on. She unwrapped the blankets and said, "The doctor said you could see the baby now." I thought, "Yeah, I was supposed to see him at 4:00 and here it is 10:00 at night." I unwrapped the blankets and his little feet turned in, but he was cute, and I thought, "Isn't he the cutest thing I ever saw." The nurse left the baby with me, and then she came tearing back in that room so fast. She said, "Oh, I'm not supposed to leave you alone with him." I mean everything they did and said was so negative that I thought, "What do they think; I'm going to kill him?" At least I knew that he did have arms, he did have legs, and he did have feet. Even though they were turned in and crooked. I thought he was the cutest thing. And if you'd seen a birth picture of Robb, you'd know he was not the cutest thing. He was one baby that was not very handsome, but I thought he was beautiful. Maybe that was blind mother's love or something, but I thought he was adorable. And I was glad he seemed to be OK. And he was a big baby. He was eight pounds eight ounces and nineteen inches long.

In another case the parents were told only thirty minutes before leaving the hospital. Said the father in recalling this situation:

Here everything looked all right, and the chief nurse told the doctor thirty minutes before we were leaving that she thought something was wrong with the baby; the proportions weren't right. So they sent her up to X-ray. Here I came to get Nancy and take her home, and I say, "Where's the baby?" She says, "I don't know; they're taking X-rays." The doctor comes back and says, "Well, we think maybe your baby has achondroplasia, but we don't know." I say, "What's achondroplasia?" "It's dwarfism, but we won't know for a year," and he has his arms out and hands us the baby. [Pause] We walk out, and Nancy's hands are shaking. Here they tell us we may have a dwarf. We don't even know what it means, nothing.

We weren't going to wait a year. We couldn't get much out of our hospital. We went to a private doctor, and that doctor said, "I don't know anything about dwarfism, but there is a doctor, a radiologist at Children's Hospital who would know." We got the X-rays with great trouble and the doctor looked at them, and he said he was 99 percent sure that our child was an achondroplastic dwarf. Who knew what that meant? We were really in a state of shock totally. This was the real problem—what would our life be like? What should we do? There we were, just cast loose. We went to the library at Bailey Center, we went to the county library, and we went to libraries all over, and all we could find would be one paragraph on dwarfism. I read everything, and after I read that we knew more than any doctors did. We thought this was very shoddy. Talk about trauma! What do you do with such a thing?

Patrick really looked awful when he was born, and they told me that he would just be nothing but a vegetable and that we should just put him away. In fact, I did not see him for three weeks. My husband saw him at birth and just fainted on the floor. Most diastrophics have club feet, and his feet were very clubbed and bent up all the way to his testicles. He really did look very strange. He was diagnosed first as achondroplastic with some complicating features, a totally wrong diagnosis.

The kinds of negative medical experiences that many older parents reported suffering through a decade or more ago unfortunately still continue to be reported by new parents. For example, one new mother at a recent LPA Parents' Group meeting stated that she had no anesthesia at the birth of her child and was very alert. She heard her obstetrician exclaim loudly, "My God, it's a dwarf!" She said, "That was very shocking to me, as you may imagine. Of course, it went down from there." Another mother spoke of her memories of being shunned by the nurses who would not talk to her. She also felt her doctor handled it poorly. He said their child was going to be short and would not grow. She immediately asked, "Do you mean he's a dwarf?" She had known a dwarf who was a business acquaintance of her father's. The doctor said, "You know, modern medicine does wonderful things. We'll see what we can do." She told him, "If he's a dwarf, there won't be anything you can do. He's going to be short and that will be that."

Another mother reported a recent situation reflecting the general lack of knowledge exhibited by many doctors. After taking two days to diagnose her child, her physician told her abruptly that he had never seen a dwarf child before and really did not know much about dwarfism except that the child, a little girl, would never be able to have children. When she asked to be referred to a specialist, he would not give her a referral. This woman also reported that nurses came in from all over the hospital to stare at her child (in her presence) because they had never seen a dwarf.

A father described the recent birth of his son:

I knew on some level there was something happening. You know, the first day or two when I'd come in, the nurses would say, "Oh, *he's* the father." On some level you can tell when you come in a room and people point you out that there is something going on. I didn't know what it was, but I knew it was something going on. Also, when the doctor came in, they were measuring Noah, and they said his head is so many inches around and his chest is so many and whoever wrote down the measurements said, "WHAT? Are you sure of that? Redo it." That was the first real indication, but I didn't think anything about it at the time.

One average-sized woman who was married to an achondroplastic man talked of her shock at the birth of their dwarf child: "It's always a shock, even though you're married to a dwarf. And then the way the doctor did it: He came in and said, 'I regret to tell you that your child is a dwarf.' Here with my husband, a dwarf, standing right there."

Although the great majority of experiences were remembered to be negative, several parents described situations in which their doctors explained the situation in a sound, businesslike, and helpful way. Although acute shock was nonetheless exhibited by these parents also, the supportive communications of doctors in these instances tempered this shock, and in some cases ended it.

The obstetrician recognized he had a problem and called in a special pediatrician relatively knowledgeable about dwarfs. He told us very soon. He had done a lot of reading; he gave us things to read. He'd come in and talk to us, and he was so helpful. He essentially said to us, "This isn't something terrible; it's something that has dimensions, and has a history."

[What do you mean by dimensions?]

Well, that you haven't given birth to a freak. There's something known about it; it's a known quantity. You know how the child's going to be, and he's going to be a person, but he's going to be short and packaged differently.

And another mother:

My regular pediatrician was out of town, and this doctor did the routine exam. It was about the third day, and he came in there and, of course, Harold was with me. He said to us, "I want to tell you, your baby is going to be a little different." And I thought, "Oh my God." And he said, "Now she is never going to be as tall as the other children, and she may have short arms and legs, but she is very bright, and she is going to be just as lovable as the others. She is going to be a very lovable child. Remember, how you treat her is how the rest of the world is going to treat her. Everyone will love her." I was terribly shocked, and I just started crying, and I said, "Are you telling me I've brought a freak into the world?" He said to me, "Don't you ever use that word again. She is going to need more love, but she will give it back." I was just totally distressed.

And another father:

We had a wonderful pediatrician. He knew quite a bit about dwarfism. You know, he knew how to break it to us. He didn't just come in and say you have a dwarf. The doctor told me, "The measurements are a little short on his arms and on his legs, but he is in fine condition. He is very healthy and bright. I'm not sure what this means, but we'll let you know." We were very shocked. The next day he came in with a book. He thought that he might be hypochondroplastic, and he brought in a picture of a family that were hypochondroplastic.[1] Nothing looked terribly strange about this except that they were short. The doctor said, "Statistically, there are many more achondroplastics than there are hypochondroplastics. So, the chances are that he is probably achondroplastic just because of the sheer number. But he has a lot of personality, and he is just fine." You know, that's when the shock ended, right there.

Parents described various responses that followed the initial shock. Depression was the most common. One mother described her feelings in this way:

I just was in such a depressed state over this that they gave me some kind of drugs, and they just doped me up. I came home in about a week, but they kept my daughter at the hospital because I was so weak after my Caesarean. My mother called after a couple of weeks and said, "Why aren't you bringing that baby home? You don't want her home. You're just putting it off." I guess I really was thinking, "How can I deal with a child this different with these special problems. How can I see that she's loved in this world?"

Another mother described the birth of her diastrophic son:

Life was so hard. Just getting through the day was enough. I still feel that way sometimes. If I can just get through the day. At that time I had all those diapers and then surgeries and casts and then more surgeries. I had nervous problems for a while. I would wake up with a terrible depression in the morning and cry. I went to a psychologist, and he was just horrible. He didn't say a word, and I sat there for forty-five minutes, but it worked. I got so angry I felt that I didn't need his help, and I turned around and left. I was much better after that.

Of all of those interviewed, only three mothers reported extreme distress that lasted beyond the initial weeks or months following childbirth or, in the case of those diagnosed years later, after they were told about their child. A mother who experienced the greatest difficulty accepting her child gave this account of the first year:

I rejected the baby. I would not nurse him. I made all the preparations for nursing him, but no way could I nurse this baby. I told them, and they gave me pills to dry me up. I didn't want him. If I could have gotten rid of Josh, I would have, but I couldn't. What could I do? Here were my family and friends. What would they think of me getting rid of this baby? I had to bring him home. My mother came and stayed for a month, and she's the one who took care of him. I didn't do anything. Nothing. After my mother left, I would get up in the morning and bathe him and feed him and then put him to bed. And then I would go back to bed myself. You know, I just slept all day. Sometimes Paul would come home in the afternoon and I would still be sleeping. I didn't know it then, but that was a sign of a profound depression. I just slept all day. I guess I was up during the night. Josh had the colic, and we had to give him this medicine, and he cried a lot, and he wasn't an easy baby. That didn't help either. That was all we needed.

This mother sought psychiatric help and was told that she was mourning the loss of her normal child and that the process would take from one to two years, but that she would get over it. Another mother described a similar initial period of depression:

I was very shocked at first, but then I became angry and depressed, and that's what I remember most vividly. I was angry because we had done all the right things—we went to college, we got married in the church, then we waited three years to have our first child—and then *this* happened! It wasn't fair. When I came home from the hospital, I just did the essentials. I just sat around and didn't feel like doing anything. Sometimes Nick would come home from work and I'd still be in my nightgown. I guess this lasted about six months. After nine months I forced myself to go back to work, and that really helped because it gave me something else to think about. And then in another six months, I was pregnant again. When I had Sue I was fine. Then I knew I could have a normal child.

The cases of these mothers illustrate a number of research findings reported in the literature. In both instances severe depression accompanied the mourning of the loss of the expected perfect child. Both mothers were able to work through their depression within a year, a typically normative time for accomplishing grief work. Also both mothers stated that they really felt they got beyond the event and could adjust to the fact of their child's dwarfism after the birth of their second child, a normal baby. Both finally had the perfect child they had longed for.

Other mothers reported what apparently was a common response—ongoing anxieties and depression that lay beneath exteriors of very effective coping patterns. While often family, friends, and even spouses thought the mother had accepted the birth and was adapting to the new situation, her own private world was still in disarray.

I'm sort of ashamed to say this, and I haven't told it to people. I could only share it at first with my sister—the feelings I had really weren't nice feelings; I'm not proud of those feelings. I felt like *I* was the dwarf. I saw *myself* as being abnormal and stared at for the rest of my life. I put myself in her place, and instead of Carol, I had become the dwarf. That was going to be me, and I was ashamed that my whole life I was going to be this ill-formed person, this freak. I was going to be stared at. I guess that sounds really crazy. Those were really awful feelings.

Well, I couldn't believe it at first. I just said, "Oh, no!" I guess you could call that denial. But then for about two years I was in a funk—not all the time. I looked good. But I'd just sort of go in and out of a funk. I don't know whether you'd call that a melancholy thing or what.

I had a year of shock. It hurt; it really hurt. Nobody knew. Nothing helped, just the Good Lord.

Two mothers talked about their relatively rapid adjustments to the birth of their dwarf children, and in both cases attributed this to previous exposure to children with other physically or mentally different conditions.

We went to a volunteer bureau for five years, and we worked with blind and different kinds of handicapped children. People who have everything should really learn how people live who really do have problems. When our son was born, I adjusted to it immediately. I didn't have to be sedated; I didn't have terrible problems; I didn't cry. What I had to adjust to was the reaction of people around me. They looked at me like it was something awful, and then when they heard it was genetic [making a face] they looked like they were going to catch something. A friend of mine said that when she had hepatitis, people looked at her like they were going to catch something horrible from her, and I said, "Well, now you know how it is to be handicapped."

The second morning the doctor came in, and I was just sitting up writing cards telling everybody about it, and he said, "What are you doing?" He couldn't imagine I'd be in such good spirits.
 [Did you talk to anyone?]
 Just Hal. He was so supportive. The only other person I talked to was my mother. I told her and then said, "Go to church and light a candle for him. Then come back and tell Dad. Explain it to him." She was the only one I told. I just decided we'd have to get used to it, and we did.
 [How did you adapt so quickly to the news?]
 One thing maybe helped me in not being so shocked. When I was in high school I used to babysit for a doctor. He had three children, and one was Mongoloid. Another one's intestines were all messed up, and he had to go to New York or Chicago for an operation. So I knew he had those problems. He said to me once, "You just don't know what is going to happen, and you have to go ahead and try." Here was a doctor even, soul searching, with these problems. So I was used to taking care of these kinds of children. Maybe that was something that helped prepare me for this situation.

FATHERS' AND MOTHERS' REACTIONS

Men and women's reactions typically differed. In most cases men reacted more stoically than women. Although men acknowledged their shock, they did not show their distress in the same emotional manners as did their wives. Most men appeared to express a determined "get on with it" attitude. For example, these are the statements of one couple:

Mother: My husband was wonderful because where I couldn't function and was so depressed, he carried on and was always optimistic and tried. This went on for months and months.
Father: I put on a front, and I looked better than I felt inside. You know, it was like I'd walked into a room and someone closed the door, and I was in there by myself. If

I'd had someone in there to show me around, it would have been better. I wasn't happy about it. This isn't what I wanted, but I felt like I couldn't walk away from him. He was my child. When the doctor told us about the baby, he said, "You will come to love him." I felt like we would love him.

And another father:

She was more shook up than I was. You know, she was really very depressed for about two weeks, but I wasn't. It just didn't bother me. You can't just collapse with things; you have to take what comes. I could have the biggest disaster; the whole world could fall in, and I could stand it, but it's little things that make me furious. Like the guys that I work with, they make mistakes because they're not aware. They're thinking of something else. I don't believe in that; I like everything to be just right. Little things like that can really upset me, but the biggest thing in the world I can rock with. It didn't bother me when this happened. I accepted it. OK, we've got a dwarf, and that's it.

The realities of parental roles and time allocations ordinarily resulted in men working outside of the home in contrast to the new mother who was at home on a full-time basis and focused on the child. This tended to mandate who would be the primary caretaker and worrier for the child. One father's statement illustrated this: "She was really worried and ran around to all these doctors. She thought I wasn't worried because I didn't react like she did, but I was worried also. But she was the one who had to go around to all the hospitals and clinics with him because I was working."

Observations and interviews reflected the obvious concern of fathers about their dwarf children, yet they rarely expressed this concern in the same emotional manner as did their wives. In fact, a number of parents, both men and women, spontaneously brought up the differences in emotional expression permitted to men and women in this society. Typically, men are expected to maintain a tough exterior despite pain and sorrow. Fathers are often as affected as mothers, yet they are not permitted to express this. Stated one father, an active LPA Parents' Group member who often goes to hospitals to visit with new parents of dwarf children: "I've found that fathers are usually just devastated. But, the man has to play the macho and not show his feelings while the woman breaks apart. Fathers won't come to meetings either. They say they are too busy, but it's really too hard for them to face it, and they can't express their feelings. In fact, I found that I seemed to have taken it harder than my wife."

These differences appear to be congruous with differing styles of problem solving in general as related by spouses during the interviews. Both spouses tended to agree that wives react to problems in general more emotionally than their husbands, who often were more matter of fact and practical in the same situations.

While mothers dramatically showed their concern and anxieties about their dwarf children of either sex, men appeared to have special concerns about male children. Undoubtedly, each parent can more vividly understand and anticipate the many pitfalls in the future for a dwarf child of their own gender. The special problems of fathers in relation to their sons were reflected in these statements of a mother and a father:

I think LPA has been more important for my husband than for me.
   [Why is that?]
Because he hurts for Jacob. His heart hurts for him. I might hurt for him or for any child if they're sick, or if they have a problem, or if there's something they can't physically do, but you've got to learn how to sit back. I don't just hurt for him because he's got this ongoing condition. But my husband does.
   [Can you explain it?]
Men see things differently. They have an image of what their son should be, and Jacob's not that way, and he can't do these things. My husband wishes he had an average-sized son.

A father began a poignant revelation with a question about a child who has the same condition as his son:

Did you notice if the Wilkenson girl is on crutches? You know, this is very important to me. I don't want my kid to be on crutches. I know he's going to have a lot of problems, but I look at him and I just ache thinking about him on crutches, and that's why I'm so concerned about these surgeries. If they can just flatten out his foot. The doctor told us the kind of club foot he has is particularly difficult to work with. I haven't even talked to my wife about this. I guess sometimes you talk to someone else and things come out that you don't talk about to the people closest to you. Being an anthropologist, you'd know that in this society men come into their maturity and their manhood later than in other places. I'm just coming into mine. My mother used to wave my hair and my brother's hair. I think of what my mother did, and the problems I had, you know things like that. When I think of that, I'm just coming into my own maturity. So I'm looking at my son and his problems and thinking of his coming into his maturity, because it's a reflection of me coming into mine.

SECOND THOUGHTS

For some, the birth of a dwarf child had the potential for bringing guilt and regrets. Some parents described second thoughts or disagreements over the issue of having the baby who then turned out to be a dwarf infant. This situation in some cases proved to be a potential cause for recrimination: "He didn't want another child. We had one normal child, and he didn't want any more children. I was just dying to have another child, and I talked him into it. As soon as he said OK, that minute [snapping her fingers] we conceived. When the baby came, he said, You know we didn't have to have this child. I told you I only wanted one. We didn't have to have this happen to us."
And another husband:

Let me tell you in candor. When they told Helen that she was pregnant, she said, "Oh great! [sarcastically] Wait till my husband hears this." And the doctor said, "Look, you just have a D and C²; you don't even have to tell your husband." As close as we are, she couldn't consider something like that without telling me. When she told me, I said, "Run, don't walk." But there is more complexity to these matters. There are some things where you have one reaction from your heart and another from your head. It's like the death of an aged, sick parent. Your head tells you one thing, "It's better," and your heart says, "No, don't go." We're both practical people. Look here, we've got two children already. Everything's fine. Let's not do something that's going to cause us more problems. But her heart won out over her head, and the day came for her to have the abortion, and she just couldn't go through with it. Then when we found out we had a dwarf child, she had some remorse and said, "Oh, God, I didn't have to have this child." But I don't look back. You make a decision, and you go with it.

INFORMING FAMILY AND FRIENDS

Couples varied as to when and how they wished to inform their relatives and friends about their dwarf child. A number of factors entered into their decisions. Some couples were too shocked to be able to deal with issues of communication. For many the element of stigma affected their decisions. Since they could not themselves absorb the fact that their baby was a dwarf, they had real concerns about how their relatives and friends would accept such news. Some husbands already had called relatives and friends with the news of a normal birth before the diagnosis of their child was given to them. The task of recalling presented problems for some of these. Many couples stated that at the immediate time of the birth they either did not wish to report the news of the birth or they did not have the psychic energy to do so.

All of our friends are fairly well educated and broad-minded people, but we just didn't tell anybody right then. We just didn't have the emotional energy to spread out and tell people at that point.

When Bob got home after the baby was born, he called a number of people and told everybody we had a fine baby. After we knew, when I got home I wouldn't call anyone. I didn't write anyone. I even had the phone disconnected. Some people might think this was terrible, but I couldn't deal with any of this.

However, others felt the need to share the information immediately: "Ray had been calling people all night, and now he was having to call them all back." ["Why did you feel the need to call them again?"] "Well, we wanted everybody to know right from the start."

One couple sent out the following letter explaining their child's condition to friends and family nine days after her birth. The mother had seen a model of the letter used by a family whose child had Down's syndrome.

Dear Friends and Loved Ones:

On January 4, 1976 at 10:40 p.m., Susan gave birth to our long awaited first child. Sara Ann Barker was born by Cesarean Section after seventeen hours of labor which we shared together, using the LaMaze method of prepared childbirth.

First indications were that both mother and baby were fine. However, during the night as mother and father rested, our Doctor was checking Sara. On January 5, the Doctor came to us and indicated that X-Rays had shown that Sara was born with a genetic defect called Achondroplasia. Achondroplasia is a form of dwarfism caused by the improper development of cartilage and long bones of the body. The Doctor explained that this malfunction causes a disproportionate growth of the arms and legs leading to a very short stature. Sara will grow to be about four feet tall. She will have a normal size trunk; her arms and legs will be quite short.

Apparently Achondroplasia is caused by a mutation in the genetic structure of the sperm or egg. Sara's problem will be limited to the dwarfism. Her intellectual and emotional development should be normal.

We have had Sara with us only a week now, but we are already in love with her. She is a beautiful baby, good natured and happy. We believe that she can have a full and rewarding life built on love and acceptance. Accepting Sara's problem was difficult and painful at first, but we are coping well and looking forward to the joys and frustrations of parenthood.

We hope that you can, someday soon, come and see the Barkers and share with us the joy of new life exploring itself and the world.

Love,
Ron and Susan Barker

Ron Barker said about this letter: "I just decided early on, because that's about the time we looked at the model letter, that we had to get on with it. This was a situation we were going to work with, and we were going to let everybody know that Sara is Sara. She is a lovely person, and they're just going to have to get used to it."
Susan Barker added:

We really did it mostly to save ourselves from telling each person, as they came along and asked us. It just made it a little easier for us and also for others to deal with it and to deal with the initial shock. This way we didn't have to put up with this constant sympathy from those people who are trying to make us feel better. You know, saying things like, "God never gives you more than you can handle," and, "Oh, if anyone could handle this, you and Ron can," and so on. You know, at the time, you don't feel that God had very much to do with it, and *you're* not the ones that should handle it. We just didn't want to have to put up with that. So we did feel that it would make things easier, both for ourselves and our friends. The letter was not original with us. When I first saw it, it never occurred to me that we would need it, but it touched me so deeply that I cut it out and put it away. And then when we had Sara, we pulled it out and we modified and personalized it and we sent it out. We never regretted it. It really does force you out in the world to acknowledge what this is going to be.

This letter and the energies and foresight that went into sending it out well reflect the basic optimism and drive of this couple, both energetic problem solvers. Their subsequent child-rearing experiences have been very positive in keeping with this early auger of their problem-attacking and -solving abilities.

Another couple stated that they also wrote a letter to family and friends, and after their explanation they essentially said that if people did not take a positive attitude toward their child, they did not want to see them. One couple stated they decided to invite people to come over to see their new baby rather than "scramble their minds" if they found out by chance encounter.

RESPONSE OF FAMILY AND FRIENDS

The response of significant others varied considerably, and the amount and nature of support given to the parents also varied. The nature of the situation determined that they had to deal with their shock and initial acceptance of the situation by themselves. Parents' accounts reflect that their shock and distress during the first days and weeks following the birth of their child was not directly correlated with positive support or lack of support from significant others. Parents had to come to terms with the situation in their own minds. In some cases the reactions of the parents to their child's condition was negative, yet there was strong positive support from family and friends. In contrast, in some instances of relatively little emotional upset of the couple, both sets of grandparents reacted very negatively. Grandparents often exhibited negative reactions and essentially rejected their newborn grandchild. In some cases this rejection extended over a period of months. In other cases, although grandparents expressed initial shock, they quickly became supportive. One couple looked back on their parents' response with considerable humor:

Father: My father wouldn't believe it. [Imitating German accent] "Oh, vas does that doctor know? She looks all right to me, she looks just fine." When the doctor told me it was genetic, I told my father there must be some dwarfs in our family, and my father went into a rage and he said: "You come from an Aryan family. We are an Aryan people. [Pounding on the table] There are no dwarfs."
Mother: And my father kept saying that they had made a mistake and given us the wrong baby [laughing].

And another mother:

I'll never forgive our families. Neither of our parents called the first week or two. They were so shocked they couldn't bring themselves to call. It changed after that when they saw Lee. I guess I can excuse my parents more, because when my sister had her first child, she was very defective, and she died in about five days. She was very deformed. My mother did see that child, so she was quite shocked that her second grandchild was different also. This was the first grandchild for both of the grandparents. But their attitude changed, and they all dote over Lee now.

In contrast were the accounts of others:

When I called my mother-in-law to tell her we had a dwarf child, she said, "What?" That was the last thing she said with a shocked tone in her voice. She was very upset at first, as we were, but she handled it very well.

My sister was just great. She is seven or eight years younger than I am, so I guess at that time she was twenty-four. She really got right on it. She called the medical school and asked everybody what to do, and she called us and said that she found this and this and this, and you can do all these things.

Friends tended to be more predictably supportive of the situation. This could be in part because their physiological investment in the situation is less. They cannot be genetically "blamed" for contributing to the birth, and further, the birth has no implications for future children or grandchildren of *theirs*.

Our friends were just fabulous. They did something that I wouldn't have the guts to do. When they heard about this they called the hospital and told me, "Congratulations, aren't you very happy?" They really didn't know what kind of shape I'd be in, or whether I'd be happy, just finding out I had a dwarf child. They were wonderful, because of the fact that they called and were excited and congratulated us. This made us really feel good. All of our friends were wonderful, and they just love Bobbie for what he is.

However, fears and anxieties were often exacerbated by the well meaning but frequently fanciful predictions of relatives, friends, and even professionals about the child's alternatives for living and future possibilities. As in any situation, the rarer the condition and the less known about the lives of those who share it, the more fanciful might be the predictions. For example, the parents of a newborn dwarf daughter were told by one of her doctors that there was a "midget village" somewhere in Florida that they might want to send her to. They wondered, would this sort of banishment be her future?

As in the case of the Barkers, well wishing friends and relatives often tried to make parents feel better through such statements as: "Just think how much worse it could be. You should tour some of the state institutions and see how lucky you are" or "At least she's not mentally retarded." Some resorted to religious aphorisms such as "God chose you for this because you're so good [or strong]" or "God never gives us more than we can bear." Mothers reported they were not helped by such statements and in fact usually resented such gratuitous comments. It should be noted, however, that a number of mothers who came to such realizations *themselves* reported they were assisted by them. For example, two mothers stated their most serious concern was that their babies would also be mentally retarded. When they knew for sure that their babies had normal intelligence, they were very grateful. Others commented that in later years when they had occasion to visit pediatric wards, they concluded their children were fortunate to be healthy dwarfs.

THE MYSTIQUE OF DWARFISM FOR PARENTS

Parents state that much of their initial upset was due to their lack of knowledge about what the condition of dwarfism would mean for their child and themselves. Most average-sized parents remember seeing no more than one or two dwarfs previous to the birth of their own child, thus they had little impression of the nature or the quality of their lives. Concrete questions about how their child would negotiate fundamental life tasks and social activities plagued them. For example, some parents remembered their first concerns were about who their child would date and marry, even though the child was a newborn infant only one day old. Such questions seemed to be of more concern if the baby were a girl. These reality questions are illustrated by the following statements of parents:

Mother: My mind immediately jumped ahead to how she would do certain things. How would she ride a bicycle?
Father[quickly]: Your mind went to the prom.
Mother: That's right. Will she go to the prom? Will anyone ask her out? Will she have friends?

And other parents:

We wanted to know about the future. When you're a parent you have an image—not just a baby—an image of what this kid is going to be like in five years, ten years, fifteen years. Can he date? Can he marry? What's his life going to be like? Can he get a job? What are the kinds of things you're going to need to know to help him?

The problem is, we wanted to know too much. When you have a normal kid, you don't sit and anticipate everything that's going to happen to him for the next eighteen years. You don't say, "He's going to get busted for smoking pot, and he's going to misuse the car, and he's going to have problems dating!" You don't worry about all that ahead. But this was our problem after Sid was born. We were worried about everything. We anticipated all the problems and all the agonies, and everything he was going to have in his life. We just had to stop doing it, since you wouldn't do it for normal kids and we shouldn't do it for him.

I was very anxious at first. I just worried and worried and fretted and fretted. I think the best thing was when I started working, because then I didn't sit home and worry. Like I would sit here and worry about what was going to happen when she was in the sixth grade, and then in junior high, and that she wouldn't be popular. And I would worry about this and worry about that, and that something was going to happen to her that day, and all these things. But once I went back to work, that really helped.

I worried and worried. I am the world's worst worrier. When he was in grade school I worried about junior high. Then in junior high I worried about high school. Now in high school I'm worrying about college. Oh, did I have nightmares! And the funny thing is that most of the things I worried about never happened! Worrying never helped.

Indeed, in ongoing interviews with parents over the research period, almost every family I spoke with repeatedly brought up their concerns about their child's dating and marrying. They expected that LPA would offer the most feasible pool of prospective mates and mentioned the fact that so many attractive and educated young people are now available through the organization.

The kinds of questions parents expressed reflected their concerns about their children realizing and experiencing the normative, expected social and economic achievements of our society—dating, marriage, and occupational success. Although medical problems in some types of dwarfism loom large, these rarely are critical considerations at birth. The most overriding concerns of parents seemed to focus on those future life experiences that would legitimize their child as a normal person in American society.

The first major concern of some parents was that their child might also be mentally retarded. When their fears about this issue were allayed, they would then begin their adaptive problem solving.

Someone told us that we should put her in an institution, and the doctors told us there would be a fifty-fifty chance she would be mentally retarded. That was all I was really interested in, the mental side of it, whether she'd be mentally OK. But we were just determined to keep her.

You know, when I saw her chart there was something on it about Down's syndrome. I was really worried about that because she was so placid. She wasn't like our other children. She would just wake up and eat and then just go right back to sleep. My first concern wasn't that she was just a dwarf, but that everything wasn't right upstairs, because you know, I was thirty-eight when she was born; I was concerned about this.
 [Do you think that would have been worse if she were retarded?]
 [Immediately] Oh, yes!
 [What would have been the worst?]
 Oh, that would have been the worst.

THE EFFECT OF THE BIRTH ON THE MARITAL RELATIONSHIP

The birth of a dwarf child has the potential for greatly affecting the relationship between spouses. Parents reported varying accounts of how the birth of their child and early attendant complications of this event had affected their relationship, that is, either bringing them closer together or thrusting them apart. Some families felt that the experience brought them closer together because of the immediate crisis and ongoing joint problem solving entailed. Of the six couples whose experiences were followed in detail, three said they talked or "rapped" continually for days on end immediately following the birth, because they really needed one another then.

We spent a lot of time lying in bed and just sort of holding each other, trying to figure out what to do.

This brought us closer together because we needed one another. We could just sit up and talk all night. We could talk till 2:00 or 3:00. We rap a lot.

My husband was wonderful, and we shared in this together. He had never been open before. I realized that I was learning about him as well as about myself and our baby. But this really helped us. We didn't talk like that before Kevin was born.

One couple talked about the particular dimension the experience had brought to their relationship: "It increased our objective relationship rather than our romantic relationship. Rather than dealing with our romantic relationship, which was taking care of itself, we were driven into adulthood. We were able to discuss problems objectively and go through this together. Because if we split, this child would have additional trauma with having a broken home. We didn't feel that this was right."

Two couples of the six felt the crisis had no effect on their relationship. In one instance both spouses stated that each was totally miserable in their own way. The husband said, "I just felt totally alone, totally by myself." Another couple markedly disagreed between themselves in their joint interview about this issue, and in doing so brought up a number of differences in their respective perceptions of their problems in child rearing:

[Could you evaluate how Claire's being in your family affected your relationship?]
[Looking at me very strangely and then at each other.]
Father: Maybe it has brought us together. It gave us a common problem to work on together, and it gave us something that was different. It wasn't the same kind of problem that the others of our married friends had to work on. It was something that was strange and unusual.
Mother: [laughing] I'd say just the opposite. I think that it bothered you that I spent this much time with Claire. If she had not been a dwarf, I wouldn't have spent this much time with her, hovering over her. I think you sort of resented that. If she had been a normal child, then we would have had more time to do things together and to do things ourselves.
Father: No. That's disproven, because you hover over Janie [the most recent child], too. You hover over her in the same way. So you can't say that.
Mother: I guess that's true.

One family commented that they have seen a number of couples with physically different children divorce. They suggested the importance of the blame factor that husband or wife might be feeling.

People say, "Well, you're a special family and God doesn't give this to anybody, you know," but that's not true, because there are people in the mental hospitals and in the bars. And a lot of the families we met early are split. I think LPA has really helped keep families together.
[Why do you think these divorces occur?]
I don't think they can take the pressure. But I think more than that, there's an element of blame—whose fault is it. In fact, this one friend of ours who had a severely retarded

boy years ago told me that they went in to see a psychologist at one time to talk about their son. She said as they got up to the door she noticed her husband combing his hair. She thought, "That's OK. I'll take the blame. You want to make sure that you look OK so they won't think that you're the one." She just was very perceptive in a lot of little ways. I think the blame factor has a lot to do with why people split.

The experiences of parents illustrate the variety of potentially positive and negative effects the birth of an exceptional child may have on the relationship between spouses. If effective communication or the possibility of effective communication is present, the crisis that ensues with its need for problem solving may operationalize this communication. The crisis may have a productive maturing effect, bringing spouses close or closer together and more resolved in their planning for their child, and ultimately for the ways in which they work together.

However, also apparent is the heightened risk to the spousal relationship that the birth may bring. Existing dissensions may be exacerbated. If each partner has a way of viewing situations or problem solving that is too distinctive, both may be miserable in their own separate ways and even be pushed toward a permanent separation by the tensions of this crisis.

The birth also brings to the fore a number of generic issues faced by all parents and prospective parents. Both mothers and fathers have significant needs for bringing into the world a "perfect child." Their own ego investments are reflected in their identity with their child. They may unconsciously expect their child to fulfill unattended, unfinished, or frustrated needs of their own. They may wish to legitimate themselves as mature, productive human beings to their parents, siblings, family, and to society at large. The issue of the perfect child particularly looms largest at the time of the first birth. Other issues emerge as prospective or retrospective concerns. Should they have more children? Could this or another "imperfect" birth occur?

Retrospectively, some parents deal with regrets at having had the baby at all. For some the conception occurred relatively long after their initial child or cluster of children were growing up. They may have considered abortion, but did not act on it. If one parent has recriminations concerning the fact that now, unnecessarily, they have a dwarf child with all of the unknown problems which might accompany this, serious and permanent friction can develop in the relationship. Some parents suggested that the availability of the Parents' Groups of LPA and the sharing of information, experiences, and affective support have helped to defuse some of these problematic issues.

NOTES

1. Hypochondroplasia is a relatively tall form of dwarfism and is characterized by less dramatic differences in body proportions than achondroplasia. The cranium is not affected and there are fewer orthopedic and neurological problems than in achondroplasia.

2. Dilation and currettement is a common surgical procedure that entails dilation of the cervix and scraping of the endometrial tissue from the inner surface of the uterus.

Chapter 4
Developmental, Logistic, and Medical Problems

DEVELOPMENTAL PROBLEMS

Differing types of dwarfism carry with them their respective developmental problems. Medical specialists have developed revised chronologies for expected developmental milestones that are appropriate for dwarf children. For example, early motor differences between average and achondroplastic children appear in holding the head upright, rolling the body from a supine to prone position, and moving the body to an upright position to crawl. Achondroplastic children usually do not begin to walk until they are two to two and a half years of age— sometimes after their younger siblings have begun to walk. Parents comment on how children learn modes of standing upright and getting around:

We're really learning a lot about biology, because he invents things as he goes. This is what all the achondroplastic children do.

Sue couldn't start walking. But what she began to do when she could move, was to push herself by her head and feet around on her back. She would zoom around under tables and chairs even though she couldn't get up to walk. Then she could walk, but she couldn't stand up from a lying position, since her legs weren't usable for that leverage. We wondered how she was going to do it, and she did it like every other dwarf does it. They bend like an arch from head to foot and then just push themselves upright by their heads. They just learn to do it. We don't know how they learn to do these things, but they do.

She refuses to sit on the booster seat, but she can't reach the table. So she sits on her knees. I watch the things she does, and it's really occurring to me that the things that seem so simple require so much effort. She really has to jump up and down ten times to do some things. For example, she's seated on her knees to eat, and she has a coke with a straw in it, and the straw's way above her. So when it is time for her to take a sip, she jumps up and stands up, sips the straw, and then gets back down to her knees again. She manages these things very well.

Parents often comment on the problem of distinguishing between the things a child can realistically do and the things he cannot do. Experienced parents note that the children themselves will weed out the latter kinds of things.

Achondroplastic children's heads are often large in proportion to their bodies, and this causes them to be off balance. In some cases there is actually a condition of hydrocephalus, but more frequently the head size and growth patterns give rise to a false similarity to this condition.[1] Nonetheless, pediatricians tend to monitor these children closely. Ordinarily, the head growth will stop by itself, but in some cases a shunt is required. With or without shunts, for some the problem may continue beyond early childhood. The mother of a ten-year-old boy commented on this problem:

I've had him swimming for years. His head is so large and heavy that I didn't think he'd ever be able to get it out of the water. Now he has finally started swimming with his head out of the water—he doesn't have to have a bubble. I can't tell you what a great accomplishment that was. He does fall down a lot when he walks; when he wears sandals he doesn't, but when he wears leather shoes he does. I was very glad I was able to get him some new leather shoes at Macy's that fit his feet. But he does fall down a lot because of his head.

Some of the earliest problems that dwarf children experience in nursery schools or in child-care situations are that they cannot run as fast as other children and thus cannot keep up with their peers, and that they are inadvertently knocked down by others. Many children appear early on to develop differing strategies for either fitting in with the activities of their peer group or getting the others to change to activities in which they are able to participate. It appears that parents whose general attitudes are toward action and problem solving influence their children accordingly. For example, one father observed:

I've watched her carefully, and what she does is look at what's going on and she somehow works her way into it in a way that she can fit in. If the other kids are doing things that she can't do, she will go worry them enough to make a few of them stop and play with her in a way that she can function and play. I've noticed from the time she was an infant, she was very patient; she would watch what was going on, and then she would figure how she would fit in. She keeps trying and trying.

I guess I've grown up with values. We grow up with values of trying hard, of being independent and working and struggling. I was a football player. I always played football. I liked it, and I really believed in being physical and trying to do things. I think she's trying a little quickly, even though she's not really a physical, tough child.

The exchange of information at LPA Parents' Group meetings is invaluable for educating new and also experienced parents in developmental issues—what realistic expectations should be for their child, and what professional resources are available for preventive measures and problems that may occur. The combined experiences of parents and of adult dwarfs provides a wealth of information and options unavailable from any one person or treatment or service resource.

LOGISTICS OF LIFE

Parents and adult dwarfs also provide a unique source of information about practical necessities of life for dwarf children, such as mechanical aids for assistance with daily problems. Most dwarfs are able to manage the normal logistical problems of daily living through the use of relatively simple but clever gadgetry. Special stools, automobile extensions, and other devices allow most dwarfs to work and play in a normative fashion. Issues surrounding general household logistics, personal hygiene, and age appropriate clothing are of enduring interest to parents.

Some parents cut down the furniture in their child's room to be compatible with the size of the inhabitant. Other parents question if this equips a child for living in the real world. One parent stated his opinion on this issue: "Everyone should have a place to hide. The child should at least be able to be comfortable at home." Parents typically adapt toys and vehicles to fit their child's height. One parent described cutting down his son's ten-speed bicycle. The boy's peers made fun of him because the bicycle was so little; however, they soon became accustomed to it, and the teasing ceased. Most parents make numerous ingenious physical adaptations that easily simplify their child's life.

Issues of personal hygiene are very real concerns for dwarf children and their parents. A common question that parents ask is, "How can our short-armed child wipe him/herself efficiently after bowel elimination?" Many little people use a stick with disposable sponges that may be clamped on the end or other arrangements for this purpose (O'Donnell, 1977). Many adults and children attempt to have bowel movements only at home to avoid complications. Some children may have to undress almost completely to toilet. If school bathrooms do not have stalls, they may be able to get permission to use the bathroom in the nurse's room or in the office.

Our society places enormous importance on appropriate and stylish dress for persons of all ages. For children and teens dress typically is a critical marker of conformity and belonging. Parents have the least problem with finding commercially made clothes that fit dwarf infants and children. During the teen-age years, the disparity emerges between the need for conformity to the newest styles worn by average-sized peers and the availability of ready-made clothes. For disproportionate dwarfs with short limbs relative to longer, sometimes stocky torso length, or for those with particularly short trunks, problems in finding acceptable clothing may be acute. Frequently, mothers make their children's clothes or carry out major alterations on ready-made garments. Happily for many young people today, new lines of stylish clothing and shoes are increasingly available for shorter-, smaller-, and heavier-than-average children and teens. In some areas boutiques now specialize in modish clothes for profoundly short people.

An invaluable resource for convenience ideas for short-statured persons in the areas of home management and housing, daily living, clothing, work, recreation, and transportation is *The Idea Machine* (O'Donnell, 1977), available through LPA.

MEDICAL PROBLEMS

Most dwarfs share certain potentially problematic physical conditions or predispositions to conditions that are common to differing types of dwarfism. For example, most achondroplastics, who constitute the largest number of the dwarf population, tend to be robust and hearty, yet they also share propensities for back and leg problems, problems of the ears and upper respiratory system, and less commonly, hydrocephalus. Diastrophic dwarfs share common problems of hands, feet, and limbs. Most of these conditions can be significantly assisted by various surgical procedures. Specialty medical care is imperative, and early referral to specialists may determine successful or unsuccessful treatment. While few conditions of achondroplastics need to be treated at birth, in contrast, many diastrophic infants should begin a regimen of surgeries within weeks following birth.

Most physicians have seen few or no dwarfs in their practice; thus, they know very little about the physical, psychological, or social complexities of dwarfism. In fact, clinicians sometimes have significantly contributed to the problems of their patients and families by either ill-advised statements to the families or by not referring them to more specialized facilities or resources when indicated. In many major urban centers today, there are at least one or two doctors knowledgeable about many of the potential problems of dwarfism. The names of these persons are available through LPA, and referrals for specific problems are available by contacting members of the LPA Medical Advisory Board (Appendix D). Also available from Advisory Board members or from professional genetics organizations (Appendix D) are names of genetic counselors across the country. Following a child's diagnosis of dwarfism families should consult a genetic counselor (usually hospital based) to learn about their patterns of family inheritance for themselves and their children in relation to future family planning.

Families varied greatly in their assessments of the medical care their children received at birth and in their early years. Rarely did families feel they had a pediatrician who knew something about dwarfism. Some pediatricians quickly learned enough to be helpful, but most families soon moved on to specialists at local Children's or Shriner's hospitals. One parent commented on these early years: "Of course, there is a shock period where you keep saying, What can we do? and Isn't there something to do? and you run around looking for the miraculous cure. I think we spent about a year or two doing that. But there just wasn't anything to do."

Five of the six families who were repeatedly interviewed had significant complaints about the general medical experiences of their children. The negative attitudes and experiences of these five families reflect those of the larger sample. All of these families took their dwarf children to local pediatric centers where they expected they could get expert diagnosis and treatment. Three of these also took their children to one of several major national centers for research and treatment of dwarfism. Five of the six families felt they were given conflicting advice and recommendations by doctors in both local and national centers. Such conflicting advice often reflects the differential experiences of doctors with dwarf patients and also the difficulties in keeping up with rapid advances in medical science. For example, parents were sometimes caught between the diametrically opposite views of specialists in relation to surgeries and special procedures. In one case one physician insisted that a young child be given an angiogram to examine the heart function, and another forcefully persuaded the family against it. These parents, like most Americans, expect doctors to give them a consistent authoritative opinion on an appropriate procedure or regimen of treatment. When this opinion is not forthcoming, as it is not in many complex cases, the resulting uncertainties breed anger and frustrations in patients and their families who do not feel they have the appropriate knowledge to choose between alternatives.

Problematic Clinical Experiences

When parents of dwarf children come together, the conversation quickly turns to their children's medical problems. While on the one hand families are grateful for many aspects of medical technology and the remarkable skills of specialty physicians who have cared for their children, on the other hand, parents frequently bring up a variety of negative experiences they have had with physicians and hospitals. Diagnostic procedures to determine even the type of dwarfism of their children frequently have proven frustrating to families. Several children were given a myriad of tests and varied diagnoses, some bearing frightening prognoses for their futures. Said one parent:

For two years we went from doctor to doctor and were given different diagnoses. First, they thought it was Hurler's syndrome. Later, one of the things they thought was that he had cystic fibrosis, and those children usually don't live long. This was a terrible time because in those days they didn't tell you anything. Now, they have social workers. The doctors then wouldn't talk to you. Finally, they just gave me some medical books and articles to read, and I was reading this article and it said that children with cystic fibrosis didn't live beyond twelve years old. I called the doctor immediately and said, "What does this mean? That my son is not going to live?" Yet, he didn't have some of the symptoms like retardation or heart failure.

And another: "You know, we were in a period of thinking that whatever it was, it could be fixed. We still believed in doctors then.[Laughing] I just kept thinking the secret was in finding the right doctor. Then I finally realized that there was nothing that could be done for him. But I was *still* looking."

The Cliffords, parents of a twenty-one-year-old dwarf son, talked about their years of experiences with doctors. They expressed reactions common to many parents whose children have less common forms of dwarfism. The lack of certainty of supposed experts about even his type of dwarfism perplexed them. Further, the fact that doctors differed greatly in their opinions about what to do about his condition once it was determined further heightened their desperation and made them angry.

Mother: We've had him to every doctor. For years we would go to Newport [teaching hospital]. It wouldn't cost us anything. He'd be in the hospital a week, and they'd run all these tests. They couldn't do anything.

Son: I just lived on the hope that they could operate on me and straighten out my body. They claimed they could.

Mother: Yeah, but the doctors started arguing about it.

Son: They claimed that if they did a surgery on my back, I'd stop growing. Because what they wanted to do was to cut the tendons. Now I have stopped growing anyway.

[Did you go back?]

Son: No, I didn't go back.

Father: Well, they had an argument about whether to do the surgery, and some of them didn't want to do it.

Mother: That's what I don't like. Here we got our son in there, and they've learned all this stuff about us. They even sent reports on him to the Growth Center, to Johns Hopkins, and to Germany. And they just couldn't decide what to do. Some were afraid it would cripple him and make him worse for life, and others said it wouldn't. I don't know why these doctors are arguing. They come in and they just argue and argue, and this is my son in there, and they don't seem to come to any decision. You know, we had him in there time after time, and they had to retake every test. Every time I'd go, I had to fill out these forms. I can't remember his childhood now. When he was ten, I could remember his childhood. But now that he is twenty, all I can remember is back to ten. They have all those X-rays and blood tests and things. And they have to take them all over again, and start all over again. We're just fed up with doctors. All the promises, and there was nothing.

The father, Mr. Clifford, told the researcher that he had "grasped at any straws." One day he was talking to a fellow passenger on his commuter train. They passed some heavy equipment, and he said something about it. A nearby passenger said he knew a friend who got his hand crushed in heavy equipment, and there was a doctor in Houston that completely restructured his hand in "iron or something." Mr. Clifford said, "I traced it down. It took me days and days to find that doctor, and I traced him down. I called him to see if he might do something for my son. He couldn't do anything. I've grasped at any straws."

This family was hostile to the medical profession because of many years of encounters that they perceived as very negative.

One mother spoke angrily about her experiences with the many surgeries her diastrophic son needed. She particularly was outraged at an incident she felt was perpetrated on her son at a local children's medical center:

We've really had terrible medical attention at Children's: When anybody says Children's, I just go up the wall. Dr. Brown [specialist in dwarfism] has tried to get them to send the X-rays of my son, and they wouldn't do it. I'm sure they didn't do it because once they operated on the wrong leg. It was supposed to be the right, and when I came and pulled down the covers, here was the left leg with this cast, and the right also had a cast. I said, "Why is it on the left?" And they sputtered around and said, "Oh well, we decided to do both." I'm sure they did the wrong one at first and then had to do the other. They were all residents under a senior doctor. The nurse told me these residents were all vying to see who could take the most bone out of his leg.

Most parents found doctors in institutions specializing in dwarfism gave them far sounder advice than those outside such institutions. And indeed, families have far fewer complaints about specialty medical centers. Specialists, such as those on the Medical Advisory Board of LPA, are well respected, liked, and sometimes even idolized by patients and families.

The negative experiences of those families who have taken their children to renowned centers typically have centered around interpersonal issues rather than clinical treatment. For example, one mother described how they had taken their achondroplastic daughter to a well-known pediatric center. She echoed the feelings of seven other parents (every one who was known to the researcher to have gone there) who remarked on the rudeness of the specialist there (not a member of the LPA Medical Advisory Board). "He treated us terribly, and he treated my daughter like she was just a specimen, just a little creature." Said one usually soft-spoken father about this same physician: "He's a famous doctor. He might be known for his work, but frankly, he is arrogant. His manner was such that we couldn't stand him, and we're now going to another medical center."

Parents often felt that their child was treated impersonally and experimentally and that the chief physicians were much more concerned with the teaching value of their child's case for the residents and trainees clustering around them than with imparting specific information to them about their children. A dilemma of this situation is that the major centers for specialty treatment tend to be teaching hospitals, and specialists in those hospitals have central responsibilities for research and education of medical trainees as well as for clinical treatment. Thus, senior physicians are confronted by oftentimes conflicting priorities.

These statements of parents reflect their frustrations: [With some resentment] "That's just a one-way street. They just took a lot of tests and gathered data. They didn't give us anything. What we went there for was just to have her in

their records so that if any miracle cures or good things happen, they'll be able to call us and let us know. But essentially, we didn't get anything from them. We felt like we were just guinea pigs."
And another:

What really bothered me was that two doctors in white coats came and took Sue away into a distant room, and we could hear her screaming while they were doing all these X-rays. I didn't like the idea that they X-rayed her from head to foot, either.
[Did she already have X-rays?]
Yes, she had X-rays here.
[Could they have used these?]
I don't know. They wanted to have their own X-rays. They did several hours of tests on her. Then they talked to us for about ten minutes. The teaching thing I didn't like either. The doctor who was talking to us was some kind of doctor from Europe. He could hardly speak English, and essentially all they did was tell us that our child was an achondroplastic dwarf. We knew that. They took us into a room, and there were about seven or eight doctors, and they put her X-rays up. They talked to each other, and the chief told them about the X-rays. Then they turned to us and said, "Your daughter is an achondroplastic dwarf." We felt that it was just pure research, and we weren't getting anything out of it.

We were somewhat disappointed when we went to the Growth Center because we thought we could actually sit down with the doctor and talk. That's not what happens. The first time they spent hours taking X-rays and measurements. Then Dr. Green spent five minutes with us telling us there are only a few cases like his known in the world, and that's all he could tell us, and that we should bring him every year. Well, we can't go through that expense and take the children out of school. It takes a lot of time, and we're not getting that much out of it because they don't even know that much. Actually the doctors here disagreed with their diagnosis. The radiologist certainly disagreed with it, though he's more inclined toward it now. The orthopedist still does not agree with it.

In these cases, the parents left dissatisfied. In general, parents found no consideration given to their psychological, emotional, and social concerns.

However, despite parents' frequent bitterness at the way they perceived they and their children were treated, it appears that taking children for expert diagnosis is a necessity for peace of mind to know that they have done all that is possible for their children's conditions. For example, said one father whose wife had been quite critical of how they had been treated at a prominent growth career: "We're really glad we took our daughter there, because although we didn't learn anything new, we found they confirmed everything we had heard. That's what we wanted, at least. We urge other families to go there because they'll find out everything known. But we felt like we had to go. Also we felt like if somebody else had brought their child before her, then they'd have known more and could have better helped us. So we're helping others by bringing her in now."

Hydrocephalus

Hydrocephalus is not uncommon among achondroplastic dwarfs. Six parents from around the country with achondroplastic children described their dilemmas in deciding whether their child had this condition, which requires the insertion of a shunt to draw off fluid from the head. In almost every case the physicians involved disagreed among themselves about whether the child needed a shunt and the appropriate course of action to take. For example, two children were followed closely by their pediatricians, who suspected that they might need a shunt. The heads of both children appeared to be growing more rapidly than usual, and they had problems balancing and fell down frequently. In one case in which the shunt was later implanted, the pediatrician followed the child's charts closely, and as the boy's head grew larger, he feared brain impairment might result. After many tests that frightened his parents, three doctors evaluated his case: one opted to put in a shunt, one said he did not need it, and a third said he possibly needed it. The parents were forced to make the final decision based on these three evaluations, and they decided to have the shunt put in. The child's head stopped growing immediately. The doctors and the parents acknowledged that growth might have stopped at that time even without the shunt. Other families whose children either had a shunt put in or who were followed to determine the necessity for this procedure also reported conflicting opinions from their doctors, and accompanying periods of parental anxiety about the decision.

Our child was borderline. The doctor at Children's Hospital was not sure that our child needed a shunt. They had to take five or six tests, which spanned five months. One of them was a nuclear test and there were other tests. Each of the tests showed that there was something wrong. It wasn't severe, but every single test ended showing up something wrong. But when do you know what to do? Claremont Hospital is now saying they think there are too many shunts that are being put in. Parents are sometimes the best judge.

We had to make the final decision. I just love it the way these surgeons tell *you* to make the decision about whether to have surgery.

Surgery

Many types of dwarfism require surgery to assist or allow normal functioning of limbs or back. Trajectories plotting expected times for surgery for differing types of dwarfism have been developed, and families find these useful for planning for their children's needs. Yet, the types and timing of surgeries for legs and hip straightening for dwarfs still are perennial areas of disagreement among physicians. Persons with diastrophic dwarfism typically have as many as twelve surgeries or more, beginning only weeks after birth. Surgeries are much more common among child and young adult LPA members today than they were among more senior members in their younger years. Many surgical procedures were not even possible at that time.

A central issue for many parents is whether the necessary surgeries can be carried out at hospitals in their local areas, or whether the parents should take their child to a specialty medical center, such as Johns Hopkins, where there are surgeons with special expertise in operating on dwarfs. While most orthopedic or neurosurgeons in the country have never operated on a dwarf individual, specialists at Hopkins or other specialty centers have treated dozens or in some cases hundreds of dwarf patients. This unique consideration is a significant one for parents of dwarf children and adult dwarfs in their decision making about surgery.

Some orthopedic or neurological problems of achondroplastics may be sufficiently generic that surgeries can be accomplished in local areas. However, parents of achondroplastic children with special problems or of children with rarer types of dwarfism may have little choice but to seek out specialty centers. Parents who are deciding whether their children may need surgery and where they should have it are advised to get evaluations at specialty clinics or at LPA national conventions, where renowned medical specialists congregate to offer such consultation at no charge.

Significant economic, social, and psychological issues surround travel to a site several thousand miles away from home for surgery. For example, the researcher knows of at least a dozen instances in which the mother and dwarf child were obliged to spend two weeks to several months at a distant medical center. The situation of both child and mother being uprooted from home and stranded in a strange city without social support systems to meet their emotional and logistic needs typically constitutes a trying ordeal. At the same time the remaining family members are left to carry on their own lives with one parent absent. The stress on parents and other siblings can be enormous in these situations. Said one mother: "These doctors just don't understand the problems. They may tell you it will take six weeks, but it could take many months. It always takes a month longer. I had to move across the country for four months with my daughter. My husband had to take care of our other children and run the household and work. This was a real threat to our marriage."

Many surgeries require an extended period, that is, two weeks to two months, in the hospital for the initial surgery and then, some months later, another period of several weeks for physical therapy after healing begins and after casts and pins are removed. Experienced parents now often vehemently urge others to try to arrange for the physical therapy in their own local area even if the surgery has been done at a distant center.

Children typically undergo special emotional problems of their own at the time of surgery. The special needs and fears of child and teen patients are often discussed at LPA Parents' Group meetings. Some adult dwarfs have vividly recalled their own frightening experiences with surgery when they were children or teens. A major concern is the desire of many young patients to have their friends around them while they are hospitalized.

Logistic problems that exist during long recuperations are also significant issues. For example, one mother stated: "I live with two kids who are having leg straightening surgery, and they have been in wheelchairs almost a year. I'm not an RN, but I know a little bit after this. How do you deal with family life when you've got wheelchairs all over the place and two children with heavy casts at home?" Another asked plaintively, "How do you tell the doctors, No more surgeries!? We have had sixteen surgeries in fourteen years. That's enough!"

PARENTS' REACTIONS TO PHYSICIANS' SUGGESTIONS FOR TREATMENT

Many parents have developed considerable independence of thought from years of dealing with medical establishments. One mother at a recent Parents' Group meeting warned parents that they should learn about their child's specific dwarfism condition because they might have to educate their doctors about any unusual dangers of that condition that nonspecialists would not know. For example, she cited an instance in which she warned the doctors who were giving her child a spinal tap that they should first find out if this procedure could be of particular danger to an achondroplastic child. She was asked to leave the hospital area because she was "making too much noise." Her child did undergo an uneventful procedure, but after questioning specialists later, she determined that such a procedure might indeed lead to paralysis in the case of an achondroplastic person and should be administered only advisedly. This mother urges parents to choose local doctors who will be sensitive to their children and open to hearing about special problems to which dwarf children might be prone. They should shop around for doctors, if necessary, until they find the right one.

In recent years parents have been more forceful in resisting treatment suggestions that sound illogical to them. As one mother stated: "I knew that sounded like a ridiculous thing to do, and I've heard quite a bit at LPA that made me suspicious and hesitant to do those kinds of things. But it's hard to know because the doctors are so insistent, and then they tend to tell you ridiculous things. You go to a prestigious place like Newport Center and then get very poor treatment." And another: "You really have to push. When they tell you things should be slow, don't just accept what the doctors tell you. You have to assert yourself." ["How do you know how to do this?"] "I guess I do know how to talk to doctors. I've got moderate epilepsy myself, and my brother has partial epilepsy. I've always talked a lot to doctors. I'm critical of them, and I know you have to do this." And others:

I think that we don't believe everything that doctors tell us because we've learned that they're not the greatest experts. So we've learned that we have to make some of our own decisions. I think if we were just poor people who weren't educated, we'd believe more of what doctors tell us.

Once we moved here four years ago, we began going to Houston and have gotten much better surgery. In fact, Dr. Brown told me he picked out one of the doctors that could deal with me because I've gotten so feisty. Oh, I used to think there was such a mystique about doctors, and I was so passive. Now I just go in and I rant and rave.

Medical science has developed many forms of specialty treatment for the improvement of general health and mobility of dwarf children. Nonetheless, many families have had negative experiences at local and national medical centers. These experiences often are related to treatment that is perceived as technically excellent but impersonal. Likewise, families find divergence of professional opinions on specific procedures to be a source of anxiety and anger for them. Interactions with the medical world will be further discussed in Chapter 10.

NOTES

1. Hydrocephalus is characterized by an accumulation of cerebrospinal fluid within the skull and accompanied by enlargement of the head, prominence of the forehead, brain atrophy, mental deterioration, and convulsions. It may be congenital or acquired, of sudden onset or slowly progressive (Dorland, 1981, p. 622).

Chapter 5
School Experiences

Most parents spent considerable time in searching for a congenial beginning school situation for their dwarf child. Parents often put their children in special schools, for reasons spanning psychological, physical, and academic considerations. For example, one of the six families in the subsample took their two-year-old child to a school for orthopedically handicapped children, which, in retrospect, they felt was not a great help. Another had their child in a nursery school for visually handicapped children with the child of a friend because they felt the tempo of the school was better paced and more supportive for their child than a regular nursery school. This child also attended a neighborhood cooperative nursery. One family sent their child across town to a public kindergarten program where they knew there was a demanding teacher who would prepare her well academically for beginning school. Children who go to regular community or public nursery schools and kindergartens may encounter special problems. Some mothers noted that in the cooperative nursery schools where they enrolled their children, other mothers were afraid to stay alone with dwarf children, fearing some situations might occur that they could not handle.

Parents recount their searches to find the best public school option for their children:

We called several school districts that were supposed to be good and said, "I have a dwarf child. What would you do?" And they said, "We would put her in the educationally handicapped or special education program." We said, "Well, what's that?" And it always had retarded children, and we just didn't want that. We finally called this one school district, and they said that they were trying to start an orthopedically handicapped program and that they would welcome her. She was in kindergarten at that point, and we went out and found a house and moved to that district specifically for the reason of her education. When we went to Johns Hopkins two years ago, the school wanted a complete report on what they suggested at Hopkins, and they followed it out completely. For example, they suggested we might want to get her an automatic typewriter. The school had already built some steps for her for the water fountain. They worked it out so kids help her go to the bathroom, and in gym she keeps score.

I went to the school ahead of time when Tina was little. I told them she was going to be a small child. They said, "Oh, we'll have no problem." We didn't say "dwarf" because we really didn't know then. But when we came with Tina, they just couldn't believe it. The principal immediately phoned a number of other principals and was told that a dwarf child just didn't work out in a regular school because there were so many problems. If the kid got a chip on her shoulder, then they just couldn't deal with it. So they told us we should send her to the special school for the handicapped. We just absolutely wouldn't have it. We said no. We did start her in the regular school, and it worked out very well.

The most common issues spontaneously brought up and discussed at Parents' Group meetings deal with school—the introduction of the child into school, logistical problems the child will encounter in school, attitudes of classmates and teachers, and problems encountered in sports and varied school activities. Most parents advocate approaching the school administration before the child enters school and discussing potential problems. As one parent stated, you can expect some kind of exaggerated response of teachers and students, and then there is the personality of the dwarf child who brings on and encounters this response. Parents agree that it is most important to prepare their child with the poise and abilities that will allow them to deal with the response. As one mother said, "You know, kids today have much more mentality than we did years ago. They know so much. They are so sophisticated." Said one parent who is an eighth-grade teacher: "The best thing for a child is if he knows his parents think he is capable and he is all right and can do things. Then that child is going to be capable. By the time I see kids in the classroom, it's too late. I think kids know by the third or fourth grade whether they are going to do well in school or not. If they come with an attitude that they are going to do well, they are. It is not physical attributes or other things."

Logistic problems loom large for dwarf children, yet often simple solutions are able to take care of these. For example, some schools will modify desks or furnish blocks to place under childrens' seats for their feet. Said one parent: "When she went to the first kindergarten, they didn't have a block of wood for her, so she couldn't go to the toilet. Once we got a block of wood for her, there was no problem. She just worked things out herself." Another mother described the door modification her husband made at her son's schools: "Of course, at each of the schools he's been to, Bob immediately went to the school and took the heavy weight off the hinge of the school door and modified the handle. When the teacher first opens the door and it's unlocked, that makes it fairly easy for the children to open the door."

School buildings today are often very spatially dispersed. Thus, it helps if dwarf children have several lockers and several sets of books so that they do not always have to carry books from one end of the school to the other. Coats and boots can be left in the locker nearest the door to the exit area or bus stop.

Many dwarf children need personal assistance to go to the bathroom and for actual toileting. Bathroom doors are often too heavy for them to push or pull open. Because of hand and arm problems, some cannot lower or raise their clothing. Some schools will allow companions for children if they can tolerate the assistance. Parents sometimes express their concerns about their children's limitations in regard to toileting at school. Said one parent: "She still can't pull up her pants. I'm a Girl Scout counselor, and I know this is an age where girls become curious about other girls. The way things are now at school, it's sort of a prize for the best one to get to accompany her to the bathroom and help her undress and dress. I don't like this situation, and I don't want it to stay that way. That's why I am anxious to have the surgery on her hands completed."

Schools are now obliged by law to provide individual programming for children defined as handicapped (Public Law 94–142). Many parents do not realize that under this law their child is entitled to certain logistic and procedural advantages in schools. If parents know the law and what their child is entitled to, they will have an easier time in dealing with school officials. One family whose child had some unusual physical problems was told that their child could not be accommodated in that school district because no school was equipped to deal with his problems. This family was forced to sue the school to provide for the special care he needed and to which he was entitled. The school then approached the state to provide them with the expenses involved for his necessary care and the physical modifications needed. As one parent noted, "You have to be your child's advocate until the child is able to be their own advocate."

An LPA parent who is also a professional educator published this informational statement on legal rights in *LPA Today*, the LPA newsletter (March-April, 1985, p. 4). [*]

Do you know your child's education rights?

By R. Helen Ference, R. N., Ph.D.

Co-chairperson, Parent Committee

Do you know your child's education rights?

In 1978, Congress passed Public Law 94–142 which ensures that children with physical handicaps and those with other exceptionalities (gifted, mentally retarded, visually and hearing impaired, socially and emotionally disturbed, learning disabled, and speech and language impaired) receive a free, appropriate public education.

What is the procedure?

When a request is made, the schools conduct a free evaluation. Such an evaluation should include testing by a school psychologist and input from many professionals from within and outside the school. If the determination is made that the child is exceptional,

*Reprinted with permission from *LPA Today*, March-April, 1985.

parents are instructed to attend a planning meeting where an Individual Education Program (I. E. P.) is developed. At such a meeting, plans are made for your child, such as any physical adjustments to be made in the school environment (Example: use of stools), or any problems related to size—being slow with written work, etc. Throughout the process, parents have access to due process procedures if they disagree with the evaluation or type of program offered for the child.

Some states have specific handbooks for parents. Inquire at your State Department of Education, Bureau of Special Education.

THE SOCIAL DIMENSIONS

Despite the frequency of logistic problems at school, in interviews parents tend to emphasize their concerns about their children's social life rather than logistics or academic achievements or deficiencies. And in fact, researchers have suggested that in many cases dwarf children often put their energies into social rather than academic achievements in school. Relatively few parents stated their dwarf child was excelling in their grades at school. Parents' concerns about their children's grades were practically related to their worries about their children being able to have economically successful occupations as adults. In fact, parents were reassured when their children had good social lives, reflecting that they had good social skills and were accepted by their peers despite or partly because of their dwarfism.

The social complexities encountered by dwarf children typically begin the first day children enter school and continue through high school graduation. Parents find that teachers are often able to prevent or alleviate initial teasing or comments from young peers. For example, one parent noted that her child was picked on from the minute he entered school. She finally asked the teacher to talk to all of the classes in the school about dwarfism and the fact that her child is a dwarf. Some parents have talked to classes themselves. In some instances, teachers will talk to their classes about general differences such as size and color that occur among all people. This generic approach has value and usefulness for all children.

Some parents expressed their concerns about being an ambassador for their child. Parents have stated that it is important to emphasize to the child's teachers and schoolmates that although the child is different, he/she is not "special." Some teachers tend to baby or overprotect a dwarf child which often leads to his/her problems with peers. Parents who have negotiated the complexities of this situation feel comfortable about their children's school experiences. Said one parent: "This school has worked out well. When he goes to a school we have to educate the teachers and principal and tell them this kid is like all other kids, but there are a few things he can't do because of physical limitations. However, by and large, he has to be treated just like all the other kids are treated. And you just have to do this. We really haven't had any problems and he's done very well."

Participation in sports is often a problem, particularly for boys. When there is a heavy emphasis on winning in sports events, dwarf children may be chosen last by their peers for team positions. However, dwarfs are able to excel in some sports activities, such as wrestling or racketball. Also many children are active in sports events as referees or scorekeepers. Parents' statements reflect the range of sports and physical activities in which their children take part.

They didn't have gym in school before, they just had the recess. Jacob has the gymnasium period now, and he does what he can. He did fifty pushups, and his teacher was astounded. He can't play football, but the things he can do he does and the ones he can't he doesn't.
[Does that create any problems?]
Oh no.
[They don't razz him?]
No one says anything.

Jim has been in little league and he has played well. He's a good catcher and he's a good hitter, but he'll often be out on first base because he can't run.
[Do his teammates resent this?]
No. At first, they used to walk him because they couldn't figure out how to pitch to him, but during the first seven or eight games, he just walked all the bases. After that they learned how to pitch to him. He can hit. It's worked out well.

She does have problems with things like the gymnasium. They are starting to do the calisthenics with bars. She said, "I just can't do that." You know, she works out a way, and the teachers usually work out a way. For example, she keeps score or something else.

She will not let herself be excluded! She just makes a point to fit in a lot of things and make a place for herself. For instance, in the swimming tournaments where the boys were swimming this summer, she took this job running the cards back and forth from the judges. When we would go places, people we didn't even know would come up and say, "How's Sara?" When she was in the hospital, they sent a giant card that had all the names of the swim team signed on it from the town nearby. People seem to know her everywhere.

The problems children experience moving from elementary schools to the larger, heterogeneous contexts of junior high and then high school with new and changing populations are also a frequent topic of discussion. For example, one mother said: "Oh, what I really dread is the middle school. In high school the kids don't tease as much, but the middle school is terrible, and all those new kids. You know, this school she is in now is fairly small, and they all know her. She's popular; she has friends."

Many parents believe that children do better if their childhood years are sedentary and they live in one locale and grow up in one familiar community where they are known, as opposed to moving to new locations and having to confront new and questioning peers and neighbors. One mother whose children moved four times before high school presented an alternative point of view.

Some people in LPA say, "Don't change schools," that you should try to live in the same house in the same neighborhood so that your child is always in the same environment. When I looked at those parents' children, I didn't see anything particularly desirous. So I didn't feel like that was something I needed to do for the purpose of protecting my kids. We lived in Rochester six years. Then we moved for a year and a half to Harristown, and they went to two schools up there. They went to the public school and then a parochial school. It was fine. I read an article about kids that had transfers, like military families. A survey said there's no real difference between kids that move or don't move. The only difference is if they're in families that love them. If you blame the move, you're blaming something external for what's really an internal problem. So we decided moving would be an adventure, and they always got excited about it.

Many other parents would no doubt argue with this point of view. And in fact, the life histories of adult dwarfs indicate that those persons who grew up in relatively unchanging environments felt they had benefited from the security of constant and familiar social contexts (Ablon, 1984). This issue is discussed further in Chapter 8.

Chapter 6
The Social World of the Dwarf Child

SOCIAL ATTRIBUTION OF DIFFERENCE

The neighborhood tends to be a familiar and comfortable social field for the dwarf child. Actual feelings of difference often begin when the child ventures out to nursery school or kindergarten and he/she first encounters the stares and comments of other children. Most parents stated that they have attempted to respond to their child's reports of negative experiences in a realistic manner. Fathers were more blunt than mothers in their responses.

Father: Once in kindergarten, Robb came home and said, "A kid down the street called me a dwarf." I think our philosophy started to come through when we said "So what? You are a dwarf. That kid's got a good set of eyeballs." . . . I think at that point if we had gotten indignant or something like that or put a negative connotation to it, it would have been bad. . . . Later on he would answer, "I'm just as big to me as you are to you."

Father: Lisa came in one day and said, "The kids called me a midget, and they said I had a big head." I said, "Look at it. You are a dwarf. Face it. You do have a head bigger than normal. So what? You go back and you tell them to go to hell." [Everybody in the discussion group laughed.] She's going to have to face the world. The fact is, she is a dwarf. She does have a big head. She's going to be top-heavy. She's going to have to learn about this. That's it. They shouldn't be coddled.

Mother: It seems that her best friend all through school has been a girl much taller. In fact, an unusually tall girl. Sometimes I wonder if this was protective. Sometimes I would hear the kids call her things outside. In those early years there were several kids that were quick to protect her. She didn't mind the term "dwarf," she talked of herself as a "dwarf," but she always hated "midget" and "shrimp"—particularly "shrimp." She came home crying from nursery school once. A boy called her a "shrimp." I tried to explain to her that everybody's got something; everybody's got a defect. I wear glasses, this person has this, and this one has that, and you're going to be a little shorter. That's it.

Mother: We just haven't run into bad things. There's always a couple of kids that will say nasty things. Like if there's someone who is overweight in the class, those kids would call that person "fatty" or whatever. But I tell her there will always be those kinds of people. You just have to get beyond that. She's been able to do that. She's really done very well.

Parents frequently discuss their own and their children's responses to the stares and comments of the public:

One of the first things you have to adjust to is people staring. If you have normal kids you don't have to worry about people staring at you. But I remember the first time the staring began—boy, you really have to get used to that. And that changes you, too. That makes a big difference in you.

We were at Denny's and my husband was walking with the two kids. These women said, referring to my daughter, "Look at that child. Just look at that child." I turned around and said, "That's my child." This woman said, "Oh, isn't she a lovely child." I gave her a look and said, "Yes, she is a lovely child." I really got mad.

Whenever we would go out to shopping centers, you couldn't believe it. Sometimes ten people would come up to us in an hour and say, "Oh, that's the most darling child I've ever seen." And they'd hug Shana and kiss her. She's always been that cute. Once when she was ten months old, I was standing in line somewhere and the woman behind me asked, "How old is your baby?" and I said, "Ten months old," and she said, "Oh, she couldn't be." And I said, "Yes she is." And she said again, "Oh no, she couldn't be!" I wasn't going to give her the satisfaction of saying why she was small, but I felt like saying, "Lady, I ought to know how old my kid is."

[When people stare, or say things to him, does he come back and tell you about it?]
    No, he used to sometimes, but I think that he doesn't want us to know that people stare at him. But I know they do, particularly when we go new places where they don't know him.

A small number of parents described their children's negative or denial reactions to their short stature:

Jenny is quite aware of being small, but she is handling it like she is normal. She's gone through periods when she says, "I'm not little." But I tell her, "You're little. You're a dwarf, and you're going to be little." And she says, "No, I'm not. I'm big. I'm *that* big. I'm very big, and I'm not going to be little. Why am I little?" And I say, "Because God made you little," and Jenny says, "Why would God do that to me?"

When my daughter was six, she, my husband, and our ten-year-old were at a pizza parlor. My daughter said, "Daddy, when I grow up will my feet touch the ground?" He said,

"No, they won't." And she said, "Well, why don't you just kill me right now?" Her brother immediately said, "What are you talking about? You have a brother who loves you, a father, a mother, and friends, and you're bright," and so on. But that didn't seem to help. The fact is, there will always be these difficult times that come up when we may need professional help.

One mother noted at a Parents' Group discussion that her daughter frequently shares with her and her husband bad experiences or bad things that other children say. Several adult dwarfs said, "Oh, I never went home and told my parents." In fact, children often do not report negative incidents to their parents. Parents typically feel that it is good to bring these situations up and let children know that it is all right to be mad, and that they should learn ways to deal with situations and with their anger. Some parents encourage children to reply to teasing with humor.[1]

We found that our daughter who is four was having these problems. I went to her nursery school and in a ten-minute period I heard about four different slurs. One kid came up and said, "Oh, you can't do that because you're too short," and somebody else said, "Yeah, why are you so short, shrimpo?" and something else. She really had these problems. When she came home, I said to her, "Do you like what this person said?" She said, "No, I don't like it, and I don't like being short." I said, "I bet it makes you mad, doesn't it." "Yes, it does make me mad." We let her know that it's all right to be mad.

A number of parents mentioned the fact that as babies or small children their dwarf children were perceived as particularly "cute" and evoked a lot of public comments in this regard. The parents talked about their concerns as to what public response would be as the child physically matured and this "cuteness" was replaced by the aspect of visible difference. Said one parent: "My parents and older friends just lavish everything on her now. What scares me is that she is just a darling baby, a cute lovable little bundle. When she gets to nine or ten, she may be a very unattractive child. What's going to happen then? Will they just dump her?"

Parents typically found that these anxieties were not realistic and that the love and attention of family and friends tend to stay with their children as they grow older.

PARENTS' PERCEPTIONS OF THEIR CHILDREN'S PERSONALITIES

Most parents characterized their dwarf child as "outgoing" with an attractive personality. Some parents connect their child's personality with their dwarfism, while others state his personality is independent of it.

We didn't have a problem with our child being retiring. And in fact, she made herself very outspoken and was very well known at school. What God didn't give her in height, he gave her in a big mouth and nerve to talk—a very outgoing personality. So it was good for her to be at the convention because there she's known for herself, not just as "the dwarf."

I have often thought how Bob might be different if he weren't a dwarf. You know, what if he were one of these big-footed, slathering things, like his friends. Bob is a very nice guy. I wonder, if he weren't a dwarf, maybe he wouldn't be so nice.

[What do you mean?]

He wants to be liked. You know, it's not typical of these teenagers to say, "I'm a nice guy. I want you to like me. What can I do to make you like me?" That's not what these kids are like. Bob has always been this way. He's overcompensated very well for his size. He's very outgoing. He can hold a conversation. He can come into a room full of adults and start a conversation or go out somewhere and we just exchange conversation like he was an adult. He's always been able to do that.

[How is Kevin doing in school?]

Oh, he does wonderfully. Everyone looks up to him. He has always been a leader. He has this wonderful outgoing personality, and the rest of the children look up to him.

[He has always been that way?]

From birth he was that way.

[How do you account for that?]

Just that he was that way. Also, he was our first child, and my husband and I just cherished him. We wanted to spend a lot of time with him. I think that helped.

[How is the other child's personality?]

Oh, he is much shyer. I think it's because Kevin is always in the limelight, and when we go out, people stare at us, and I believe that really bothers him.

[Well, what about Kevan?]

Oh no, it doesn't bother him; he loves it! Nothing seems to bother him.

Although an occasional parent describes a lonely, unhappy child, most children have been socially successful in their parents' eyes as defined by the fact that they have what is considered a usual or even greater number of friends. Several children have been very popular throughout school. For example, one twelve-year-old boy was extremely popular at his middle school. His mother said:

George came home the other day and told me, "You know, I'm so popular that more than half the kids at school know me." I told him that he should just say, "I'm well known," because it doesn't sound good to say you're popular. But he's really got all sorts of friends. He has several circles of friends. Some are in his first circle and some in the outside circle. And you know, adults just love him. I met his principal from camp at a party, and when he found out I was George's mother, he jumped up and said, "Oh, *you're* George's mother! What a great guy," and he went on and on.

And others:

We worried about her at first, but she is just blessed. In fact, she is so special that she was put on this earth as a blessing to show other little people what you can do. She has always had this wonderful personality. She was very shy when she was young, but then she always made people laugh. She has always gotten along well. We worried, and worried, and worried. In the sixth grade she was popular, but when she went to junior high school, she also was just immediately popular. She was a class president. So she has never really had a problem. In college she was the one who left other groups; she was the one who wouldn't write letters to kids or left them behind. She got seventy-five Christmas cards last year and just arrived home in time to find them, whereas she didn't send out any. She gets three calls a week from people from the past wanting to know where she is. So people are always desiring her.

He was always well liked. It's just that he was a mouthpiece. He's always been picked out as this kid that's got a mouth. He can verbalize things very well. He writes his own speeches and stuff. We don't help him with that kind of thing. So he fit right in with junior high and did well. There are two junior highs, and he had the advantage of going to both. For one year in sixth grade he went to a handicapped school for therapy, and he needed it all day. Later they had an integration or mainstreaming program where he would go to the junior high for half a day. He did so well he ended up going all day. Both of those junior highs feed into the high school. So there he knew more kids than most. Everyone seemed to know him.

One father described a dimension of vulnerability that has both attracted friends and protected his son: "Rob has had the outbackers, the tough guys as friends. He is friends right now with both sides. I mean, he is accepted because they feel, Hey, you're down and out, call me. Like he had his skateboard ripped off, and all he did was tell Harry, who is one of the toughest kids at school, and his skateboard was back the next day. Harry put out the word to everybody, and they hunted it down, and they almost tore the kid apart that took it."

Several parents stated that they thought their children's personalities were determined by heredity:

[Why do you think Susan is so extroverted?]

Oh, it's heredity. I think extroversion or introversion is a matter of heredity.

[Do you think you've contributed at all to that in child rearing?]

I don't know. I don't think so. However, Susan had a brother and sister who were considerably older, and so she had role models ahead. She also had to fight to get what she wanted. They're not protective of her at all. She has to struggle for everything she gets.

[How would you say Ross is reacting to things?]

Well, Ross is sort of very placid in a sense. You know, he won't say anything. Even when he was very small he was that way. When younger children would take things away from him, he wouldn't fight back. He would just let them take it, whatever it was. If it were me, I would have resisted, but he didn't. The thing is he's very quiet. But he also holds things in and holds things in, and then he explodes after a while.

[What would he do when people would insult him or call him a name like "shrimp"?]

His best friend just called him "shrimp" yesterday. He was spending the weekend. He wouldn't say anything. He just sort of takes things in good nature.

[Where do you think he gets his personality?]

Oh, his personality—he's so outgoing. His personality is just like my father's sister. And I think he gets it from her.

[Is she around him very much?]

Oh, she has been in her lifetime, but she's in her eighties.

[Are you saying that he gets it in the genes?]

Yes, he gets it in the genes.

The kids all do have different personalities.

[Where do these come from?]

It's a combination of environmental training, which is our training with them, and their heritage. I think they definitely inherited a part of their personality, and then their personality also reflects some of their learning. There's both.

In commenting on their dwarf child's outgoing nature, many families noted that another of their children, in two cases the only other sibling, was much shyer and socially insecure, and often had fewer friends than the dwarf child.

Sissy [Lee's average-sized sister] is very bright. She does very well in classes and doesn't even try that hard. And she has a lot of friends who call her to go places, but strangely, she's the one who lacks security. In fact, I think Sissy is the one who is having problems if you think of either of them as having problems. Also, she's becoming very dependent on Lee. Sissy is the shyer, quieter one. But the girls are very close. [In observing the girls, I see that Lee is very talkative, dances around, and talks continuously.]

In point of fact, many preteen dwarf children in these families are very outgoing and gregarious and have many friends. Their social success could be interpreted in several ways. Some have capitalized on their short stature, while others have attempted to normalize themselves. For example, one aspect of many young dwarfs' popularity may be the fact that they often become widely known chiefly because of their size. Both children and adults recognize them and often know their name. In a classic work on the psychological aspects of dwarfism, Money and Pollitt (1966, p. 388) stated that the dwarf's smallness confers on him "an index of recognizance—an animadversion index—so that without any effort on his part, he becomes widely known in his community and school. This notoriety places another burden of sorts on the dwarf, either as an instrument of mortification to him, on account of its origins, or as an instrument of popularity and friendship."

Money (1967) further defined the situation of "mascotism" wherein the children capitalize on their notoriety and define a "positive" role in the social structure based on their size. The mystique of dwarf children's shortness may then account partially for their popularity. For example, one mother reported: "When Sue goes downtown with Hal, people know her and they stop and say, "Hey, how are you?" Some of them know her by name and others don't, but the fact is that they know her. They never knew our other kids. You know, she sort of makes use of this, and it's true at school, too. She takes advantage of this. You can turn a handicap into an asset and find ways to use it." And in fact, many dwarf children are proud of how many people know who they are. Appendix C summarizes the psychosocial literature on dwarf children.

THE DILEMMA OF BEING DIFFERENT BUT NOT DIFFERENT

One secret of the social success of a dwarf child might be that he or she has been successfully raised by their parents, to the extent possible, to feel that he is not "different." Yet even those children who feel that they are not different, just as in fact most dwarf children, almost invariably confront major social problems when they reach their teen-age years. Then no matter how popular they formerly were or how attractive or well dressed they are, they may meet a painful and usually unconquerable barrier in the social pressure for conformity when dating begins by other children in their age group. Their predictable exclusion may be a dramatic declaration that there *is* a difference and a severe one. Both children and parents then must deal with some of the cruelest ambiguities of the dwarf's situation.

Adult dwarfs have poignantly reported (Ablon, 1984) on the difficulties of their teen-age and young adult years:

The peculiar social problems shared generally by adolescents have their own special difficulties for dwarfs. High school often is the chief social context for problems. Though most subjects still had their friends, the conformity to social standards so important to adolescents often brought more loneliness as some found themselves being left out of friendship circle activities. For example, one young man contrasted the difference in social discrimination between elementary school and high school in this way: "In grade school you get more teasing. You'll be invited to parties, even though the kids will make all sorts of comments. In high school, they won't make the comments, but you won't be invited to the parties." . . .

[S]ubjects tend to emphasize their memories of hardships [in these years] having the most to do with dating. Dating in American society is the chief social ritual which either marks success or failure in adolescence and early adulthood. This symbolic significance accorded to dating may indeed outweigh its practical preparation or predictive value for marriage. Short stature was a feature that markedly reduced both boys' and girls' dating opportunities. And, in fact, most subjects report that they did not date at all in their high school, post-high school, or college years, until they joined LPA. Some kept themselves very busy with school or sports activities consciously or unconsciously to compensate for their lack of paired-off dating activities.

Most women remembered staying home on weekends while their friends and siblings dated. Men recall that while they at least had the option to ask [average-sized] girls out, and did not have to sit and wait for invitations, they often could not get dates. Boys, however, often went out in cliques on the weekend, sometimes drinking heavily in an effort to deal with their differentness. Particularly hard for both sexes to face was that their younger siblings were dating actively at earlier ages (pp. 48–49).

Exacerbating this problem for many dwarfs was the massive denial of their dwarfism employed as a coping mechanism to deal with their profound short stature before membership in LPA (Ablon, 1984, pp. 91 ff.). Today, children who have grown up in LPA often have established close friendships with other members in their area or across the country. Even if they have not wished to be active before this time, many now realize that LPA will provide a large pool of available partners for dating or marriage. For example, most teen members are able to procure dates for the all-important school proms in a relatively easy manner by asking friends, even if they do not have a boyfriend or girlfriend. These years may be a considerably more painful period for those teens who have denied their dwarfism and have not become involved with LPA.

NOTE

1. Many adults dwarfs and dwarf children respond to teasing or bothersome questions with humorous retorts. Money (1967) in fact suggested that a child might be rehearsed in how to respond with humor. For example, an adult dwarf states she often answers questions about why she is so short by saying, "My mother left me in the dryer too long and I shrank."

Chapter 7
The Dwarf Child in the Family System

The career of a dwarf child as a family member involves the history, structure, and nature of each respective family and the personalities therein. Although every child born and growing up in a family is affected by these factors, the status of the exceptional or different child is particularly vulnerable. Power and Orto (1980) discussed a number of factors bearing on family coping patterns and response to childhood disability:

1. The age of the child and the child's ordinal placement, or order of birth;
2. Family size and structure;
3. How the affected child understands the condition;
4. The complexity of demands on the family caused by the particular illness;
5. The visibility of the defect;
6. The religious beliefs of the family;
7. The degree of financial burden and availability of community resources;
8. The stage in the family cycle when the child is born or develops a disability.

The age of the child, the child's ordinal placement, family size and structure, the visibility of the defect, and the stage in the family life cycle when the child is born or develops the disability are objective features the impact of which can perhaps be examined and analytically assessed more easily than some of the others. Such factors as how the affected child understands the situation, the complexity of demands on the family caused by the particular condition, and the degree of financial burden and availability of community resources are more complex considerations dependent on the nature of the condition and the time and emotional and economic demands the condition makes on family resources.

The religious and cultural values and beliefs of the family constitute more idiosyncratic factors involving the internal and external culture of the family unit and its significance for the specific condition of the child.

Most types of dwarfism do not involve physical disability for children either at birth or in early childhood. In fact, apart from concerns about hydrocephalus, the complications of limbs and back or other medical considerations are usually most severe in adolescence or later. Thus, logistic demands, financial burden, and necessary reaching out for community resources tend to come after the early childhood years. Families, particularly if they have been referred to LPA, have come to understand the condition and begin the journey of acceptance in the early years of their child's life. As the child grows and his/her physical char- acteristics become more obvious, parents and children adapt to the visibility of the condition.

Parents often spontaneously brought up in interviews such issues as the ordinal placement, that is, order of birth of the dwarf child in relation to his or her siblings, how the child might be affected by the number of other children in the family, and when he/she was born into the family. For example, a number of parents commented on the significance of the birth order of the dwarf child in the family. This issue is often a crucial one in terms of basic knowledge of child rearing. Said one father: "It really would have been helpful if our dwarf child wasn't our first child. That way we'd have known what some of the normal problems of children are and what the growth patterns and growth behavior should be. Then we'd have had a child we'd have known what to do with."

When the dwarf child was the first child, more emphasis may have been placed on the fact that this was not the perfect child the parents had awaited. Indeed, the one mother who was the most depressed stated that after her second child was born, an average-sized "normal" child, she was able to love her dwarf child even more because she now felt complete with the birth of a "perfect" child. Three couples commented spontaneously that parents always have higher expectations for their first child and are more critical of him or her. While parents are often more obsessively focused on the first child because *they* are learning about child rearing and children in general with this child, they will not likely spoil the child in the way they might a younger child. By the time younger children appear, parents often have lowered their expectations for perfection and relaxed their child rearing behavior.

The initial intensive focus on the first child might set the stage for a family built around continually meeting this one child's needs, with secondary attention given to the others. In contrast, when the dwarf child is a younger child, he or she is born into an ongoing family system and is more likely to be "plugged in" as just another child. Less emphasis may be placed on the child's difference. Parents also comment that the lot of the dwarf child who has older siblings is an easier one because his family is known in school by teachers and students alike, and he can be befriended and protected more easily from teasing or insults. Said one parent: "I really think that children who come last, who come after other children do better. Because if you're the first one, you're the first one in the family just pushed into school. If you're last, the other kids have already gone to the school. Also, if there are brothers and sisters, their friends are running in and out of the house. I just think that if you're the first one and all the attention is put on you, it's really much harder."

Parents were asked if they perceived any differences between the way they have raised their dwarf child and their other children. Many brought up issues of birth order in their response to this question. For example, some stated that if the dwarf child is the last child, they cannot distinguish between preferential treatment they may give because the child is smaller or because the child is the youngest.

I can see right now we're babying her because she's getting smart alecky lately. You know, she doesn't say "thank you" or "please." I really think that we're letting her get away with things because she's little. When you have your first child, you don't know much about raising children. You're much stricter. You're just looking at every little thing. When they cry, you're really worried. You want them to mind you, and you want them to do every single thing just right then. Then with the next child things get a little less and a little less. Then after a while when the child falls down you can listen to them and you can tell whether they're really hurt or whether it's a cry that says, "My pride's hurt." And then you may not even go into the room. I think we would raise her differently because she is youngest, anyhow. But I think it's also because she's a little person.

Father: There is a difference in the span of our children, and we grew with our oldest. We were young and we did all sorts of things with her, and I guess I was heavy on her. Now I just don't have the energy. I work eight or nine hours a day, and I commute two hours, and when I come home I can't fight any more. Our oldest complains that she had it so hard. We agree with her, but we were both oldest children, too. So we had the same thing.

Mother: The oldest children always bear the brunt of things. I think things would have been different if Jo wasn't the middle child.
[What is the difference?]
      Well, she had Carla to lead her. She led her into each school. She introduced her into high school. She was there and knew the ropes and introduced her to people.
Father: I think that it really made a difference that she wasn't the first one.
Mother: If Jo had been the oldest, I think we maybe would have treated all the children differently.
[Why would that be?]
Mother: We've always had the highest expectations for our children. From just the first thing on, we just let them know they were going to go to college and that's all there was to it. And we just expected the best grades. I'm wondering that maybe I wouldn't have had as high expectations for Jo, and if I'd had lower expectations for her, then I would have always had lower expectations for all of the kids.

My husband was wonderful when Noah was born. He said, "He's going to be just like the others." But you know, the fact is that there is a difference. They are not just like the others. You have to be aware of the difference, but you have to treat them just like the others. I was so strict with my first son. He's twenty-four years old, and he's a wonderful person, but I look at how strict we were with him and now we've just changed and we're so much less strict with all the children.

I think Sandy [dwarf child in another LPA family] is spoiled.

[Why do you think she's spoiled?]

Oh, because she's the youngest, and they just baby her. You know, it's very easy to baby the youngest, because if you like children, you really don't want them to grow up, so you just sort of keep babying them. Oh, it's really easy to get in that. We used to be a lot stricter. I know that poor Bob, our oldest, would have to put his nose in the corner if he didn't chew his food just right. And now Genny just does all sorts of things. We've really changed a lot.

RELATIONS BETWEEN DWARF CHILDREN AND THEIR SIBLINGS

All members of a family are affected by the behavior of and behavior toward any single one of them. The fact of the specialness of one child is bound to impact on the others to varying degrees. Therefore, differential attention toward or special treatment of any child has the potential to affect negatively relations between that child and his or her siblings. Parents were asked if in their perceptions any special attention they may have given to their dwarf child had adversely affected relationships between siblings. Most parents stated that they felt the presence of the dwarf child had not taken attention away from their other children nor bred their hostilities even though many acknowledged that medical routines had necessitated special time being given to the needs of the dwarf child. An ambiguity is apparent here because time constitutes a significant sign of attention and special importance in other children's eyes.

[Do you think the other kids felt that Linda was favored and that they were in any way neglected?]

Absolutely not. The kids have not felt that way. In retrospect, in the years when Linda was five to seven when I was having to take her to Harrison Clinic for physical therapy, we didn't have the freeway then, and we had to drive there on this slow road. I had to bundle up the other kids because I couldn't leave them. It took away from their play time, but that was the only thing. In no way were the kids treated differently. They had the same tasks. Each of the kids was very different. They each excelled in something different. For instance, our oldest son was an excellent scholar and good in speech, and he did well; the younger boy excelled in sports, and Linda has always done well in her social life. In fact, we told our younger son on the weekend that you were coming, and asked him just this question. He said, "No, not at all." He said that he did remember as a child being dragged to Harrison Clinic three times a week for Linda's therapy. He also remembered that he beat up a boy twice who was older who used to kid Linda. He remembered another time at Harrison Clinic when they were giving her a test and they took her in another room and she was screaming. He started beating on the door and yelled, "Let my sister alone!" He remembered those experiences.

It's not that Lisa said anything, but sometimes things come out. Like she was asked to go down to a panel—it was on siblings of handicapped people. She got on the panel, and when they asked her some question she really just burst into tears; then she realized how maybe she had had these feelings. But we think about all those years she had to spend in hospitals while we were waiting on Robb. In those days you couldn't take children in, so she had to sit in waiting rooms. It was years of sitting in waiting rooms. But around here she was treated like the queen bee; she was the only one that had her own room, and she did have a car.

[Why?]

Well, we did that because she said she didn't have anything else; we have never given her any time or attention, so we just did that. But she actually hadn't really said that she feels any resentment, and she and Robb are very close.

Oh, there is no resentment. Both of them incorporate Marg totally into their lives because she is so much fun and they are always so proud of her. It really helped her brother to have a younger sister so popular.

Only one family reported a sibling's problem that they attributed to the special attention given to their older dwarf child. Their ten-year-old middle daughter went through a year-long period of behavioral problems. The parents acknowledged that they had no doubt given her too little attention. She was shy and had problems making friends. They felt that her acting out at school through lying and petty stealing gained for her the attention she had missed. In this case the parents also stated that she was called on to do too many things. She had to help her older dwarf sister to do tasks that she could not do alone, and also help her younger brother. "We expected too much of her. Sometimes she would say to us, 'What am I around here, a slave?' " School counseling sessions with the child and parents helped to alleviate her problems. The subject of differential treatment and the potential for sibling resentments is discussed further in Chapter 8.

PARENTS' CONSCIOUSNESS OF THE DWARF IDENTITY

During discussions of parents' consciousness of their child's dwarf identity, a number of parents explicitly and implicitly expressed both their ambivalence toward their child's condition and its implications for the child's identity and behavior, and the ambiguity of the status of dwarf—being very different, yet not different. Some stated they rarely were aware of their child's difference. For others the awareness was brought about by specific situations. Some stated that they are constantly aware of their child's dwarfism.

Oh, we go for many weeks or months just thinking of Sue as the person she really is, not Sue, the dwarf. [Sadly, suggesting it was reflecting on her own capabilities] I really did have a much harder time than he did. It's only recently that I've really been able to accept Sue's problem—that she is a dwarf, and this is the way it's going to be. You know, we do go for a time when we forget. Just yesterday I was lying in bed, and I looked at her picture on the wall, and I caught myself up short, and I said, "Hey, you really haven't thought about Sue, the dwarf—what she's thinking, what her own particular problems are as a dwarf." I started thinking that I really have got to tune in to her and her needs, rather than just sort of think of Sue, my daughter, as one of the kids.

[Is it something you would rarely think about or think about all the time?]
    No, I guess it is not something I think about. I would only think about it when there was just a physical problem or something he can't do. But then again, I guess that's every day.

We don't think about that at all. We are just not that aware of it; we think of her like all the other kids. [Pausing] Well, in subtle ways we *do* think about it. We will go some place, and then all of a sudden someone looks at her or they say something, and when that happens, we are aware of it.

Oh, we go for times when I don't even think about it, because that's just how he is. But last year I took the boys into some shopping center, and Guy went in with this friend of his. I was sitting in the car waiting for them, and they came out and all of a sudden I see these two boys walking out the door, and here's this big husky boy, his friend, and here's Guy, I see this little bitty thing. And all of a sudden I thought, "My God, that's my son, that's this little bitty thing." Then I started thinking about how he must look to other people, and it really was very funny. It brought it to my awareness how he is compared to his friends who are regular size.

One couple stated their continual awareness of their son's difference:

[Are you conscious very much of Rod's short stature?]
Both: Oh, yes.
Father: Yes, we're constantly conscious of it. Every day, all the time. The fact is that there are so many things he can't do. Just to go to reach for something, he can't do it. He can't walk certain places. You always have to be conscious of it.
[Some parents say they're not conscious of it that much.]
Father: Oh, no. We're always conscious of it.
Mother: Well, it's just that if he were in a regular routine with just a certain number of things to do during the day, maybe we wouldn't be so conscious, but he has to do so many things. He has to be in different places, and he has to walk here and there. I was concerned about his walking, because today he had to go to some swim thing, and I didn't want him to walk that length and then have to do other things and have a long day.

In contrast, another couple stated they are never aware of the difference:

[How much are you aware of her dwarfism?]
Mother: Not really; not at all; we really don't think about it. We just think of her as our daughter.
[Do you think she's aware of it much of the time?]
Father: She's aware of it, but she lives with it and it's something she seems to work out. You know, we *like* her, and she likes herself; she thinks she's pretty good. She feels

good about herself, and we feel good about her because we like her. She's a caring, warm, sensitive person. She's bright, and she's fine to have around, and she thinks of lots of things to do.

The complexities of awareness are clear in this couple's comments:

Mother: Adair is a particularly good skier, because her center of gravity is so low. It is surprising to many people to see her come down the slopes. They think she's a small child. They don't realize how old she is. The only problem is getting on the ski lift. She's not heavy enough to push down something. She has to ask the attendant for help.
[Does that bother her?]
Father: I don't know. She never says anything.
Mother: Yes, I think it bothered her at first. But we would get on, too.
Father: Yes, *you* think it bothered her, because it bothered *you*. You were afraid of her being there.
Mother: Yes, that's probably true. On the other hand, Adair never really talks about anything that bothers her, so this is something we don't know.

Parents often feel, on the one hand, that they do not treat their dwarf child differently from the rest of their children and are not ever-cognizant of their differences in relation to the other children, and on the other hand, they know that they do have to treat their dwarf child differently at times because of their dwarfism. This ambivalence was expressed directly through statements and indirectly in their accounts of family activities and behavior.

Mother: Oh we're hardly ever aware of it. You know, it's not something that we think about that much.
Father: [quickly] Oh no. We just treat her like anyone else. Of course, in the first year she was not all that different from anyone else. But it will probably change. I'd say 90 percent of the time I never really think of her as being a dwarf. We just think of her as one of the other kids. We kid her, and we say to her, "You're a dwarf, you're little." We figure that we have to prepare her so that when she goes to school and has these kinds of things said to her, she's going to be ready for it. She is not going to be thin-skinned or hurt by it. I wish you were here last night. Sue was sitting reading to her. She read her *Snow White and the Seven Dwarfs*, and she said, "You know, here's what you are, Pam. You're a dwarf. See these little persons?" This is the kind of thing we try to impress on her. But we just treat her like everyone else. It's not something we think about.

[Do you find yourself as strict with Kevin as with your other children?]
Oh yes. I don't think there's a difference, but you know, when you stop to think about it maybe we have favored him subconsciously, and let him get by with a few things. If I stop to think about it in the last year, maybe for a seven-year-old, he's getting by with a few things. But it's not a conscious thing that we would think about. You know, when we look at his other friends who come here, I don't see any difference.

[Do you feel that you raised Helen any differently than your other children?]

Mother: [Immediately] No. I really tried to raise her with as little difference as possible so that she wouldn't feel she was different.

Father: Oh, you're overprotective with all of the kids.

Mother: You're right. Today, for instance, I worried about her driving to Macy's alone at night. I guess I don't like to see a girl drive alone at night, but I particularly worry about her. I thought, would I have this fear with Marge, my older daughter? No, I would not have this fear.

OVERPROTECTIVENESS

Although there is not a common ideology followed among LPA parents concerning child rearing, overprotectiveness is talked about in Parents' Group discussion meetings as one of the worst behaviors in relation to preparing dwarf children to face the world. Overprotectiveness is a pitfall most parents see themselves falling prey to at one time or other. Overprotectiveness extends to both not allowing the children to do things they should be able to do and also shielding them from comments about their condition. Parents often talk about their own or their spouse's overprotective attitudes or comment on the over-protectiveness of others:

You know, there are some young couples in LPA that really baby their children. They just worry about every little thing. They'll come in and tell you how angry they are that somebody said something in the grocery store and they bawled them out or they felt like really telling them off. They let everything bother them, and that passes on to the child. That child needs everything they can get. They've got to be tough. They've got to be able to take things. If these people are thin-skinned and they get that upset, you know the child's watching that and they're going to pass that thin skin to the child. I don't believe in that. You have to be more casual about it; you have to accept things. Just say, "Well OK, this kid's a dwarf, he's small, and then we'll go on from there and make the best of it."

I think that parents hold their kids back.

[What do you mean?]

Overprotective. I really think that a lot of parents of LPs hold their kids back. If they could see all the things that Melinda does, they can see that they don't have to hold them back—that their kids can do these things, too. You know when a person this big [holding his hand down to about the size of his daughter] can do the same things that a person this big [holding his hand up] does it's going to make them feel good. They're going to feel like they can fly.

At a recent LPA Parents' Group meeting, Mrs. Lindstrom came in and she said she was having problems because her child would hear people saying, "She's a dwarf," or "She's a midget." Mr. Allen said, "You're going to have to prepare her for that. It's not going to be bad. As she goes through life, she's going to hear that. So you're going to have to prepare her for it. Because she *is* a dwarf.

[Eyeing people up and down as they came in the door] That's the value of coming here [LPA meeting]; so you can see that you're not alone."

THE DWARF CHILD AND "HANDICAPPED" STATUS

One of the dilemmas posed by the marginal position of dwarfism is apparent in varied attitudes toward handicapped status. The same ambiguity and ambivalence that characterize the general life situation of dwarfs is highlighted in the issue of handicapped status. Adult dwarfs typically do not think of themselves as handicapped unless they have pronounced limitations on their activities. Most dwarfs pride themselves on their independence and also on their activities. Admitting to a handicapped status would give them two stigmatized labels instead of one (Ablon, 1984; Folstein, et al., 1981). Although almost all dwarf children of families in this study have at one time or another attended special preschools or classes, neither they nor their parents ordinarily think of them as actually within a handicapped category. An expedient attitude is evidenced toward the status and the benefits it may bring. Parents and children typically would agree to the child's attending a special school, gym, or driving class for handicapped people that is helpful at a particular time or for a particular purpose and would not feel stigmatized by this. Parents do not consider their child to be handicapped in any traditional sense of the word, even though the child may have some physical limitations. For example, said one father: "Lisa has no vision of herself as handicapped. But we would have no problem using the term handicapped if we need to get her anything. It wouldn't bother her or us at all. However, in no sense do we think of her as handicapped."

Parents described their children's use of handicapped classes or privileges. Considerable ambiguity is apparent both in their patterns of use and the attitudes associated with these.

He gets on the subway with a special ticket. It's for senior citizens, kids under ten, and the handicapped.

[Does it bother him if he gets on the subway with his friends and they pull out a white ticket and he has a red ticket?]

No. But he refused to get in the handicapped gym class because he said, "I'm not handicapped."

[Who was in the class?]

Somebody who has arthritis, and there are people with wheelchairs. He said, "I'm not getting in the handicapped gym class. I'm not handicapped."

[Then why would he use the red ticket?]

It's cheaper, and it doesn't seem to bother him.

[Would it bother *you* to use the term handicapped for him?]

No. The fact is, he *is* handicapped in certain situations where he's just got limitations, and that's all there is to it. He can't do certain things, and that's just it. Another thing about the red card is that about 90 percent of the people use them, so it's not that rare.

[Does Robb use this handicapped status?]

Oh, yes, there are handicapped classes at the high school—though he chose not to be in the handicapped classes. They really mainstream them mostly, but it's like a home room. He sort of hangs out in the handicapped room and has his best friends there. Robb made a point in junior high of mainstreaming and running all around, and then when he got his junior high diploma, he was very angry to see that on the diploma it didn't have the name of the junior high he went to; it had the name of this handicapped school. When he complained about it, they said they needed to get the money; in other words, you have to have a headcount of how many people are there, so they just registered him through that, even though he had mainstreamed himself. So when he went to high school he really made it a point to be totally mainstreamed so they couldn't count him as handicapped.

[Do you use the term?]

Oh yes, we wouldn't hesitate; he knows he is handicapped. He would not hesitate to use it. But there's a big problem because he is *not* in the handicapped program. We have all these problems getting him to school. Yet that bus cannot pick him up because he is not in the handicapped program. Even though it goes right by here, they just can't do it.

EXPECTATIONS FOR THE FUTURE

When asked about career or life expectations for their children, fathers tended to respond more quickly than mothers. Possibly fathers had given more thought to their child's employment future, while mothers were more concerned about their social life. Some parents saw dwarfism only as a minor factor in their child's career choice. Others saw it as a major barrier to the full range of choices open to other persons and one that specifically precludes occupations requiring certain types of physical effort.

Father: I fully expect Sharon will be a professional woman. She's bright, and that's what she should do. She is only eight years old, but she expects to be a professional. Of course, I expect the boys to be also. We have high standards for them. We expect them all to achieve, and we expect them to do well, and they are highly motivated. It will be harder for her, whatever she does, but I expect her to do it.

Mother: We are keeping all the doors open for her; she may consider medicine or veterinary sciences. I wouldn't close the door on it. If *she* decides to close her options, she can do that, but I would never discourage her from anything. I have the same expectations for her as I would for any other person.

Father: We're concerned about her scholarship because she'll need a good job. Maybe she'll have more hardships in life than the other kids. Now she's making poor grades. I don't know what she's going to do. Her personality is outgoing. Ordinarily someone else could do something like being a waitress or something like that, but she can't be a waitress. For LPs that's not something they can do very well, and that's one of the problems.

[Do you have any different expectations for Greg than for your other children?]

Father: [Thoughtfully] Well, he is going to have to make his living by his head. I really wouldn't care how the kids make a living. His brother Chris could make a living however he wants by being a mechanic or whatever. Aaron could too, but Greg is going to have to do it another way.

[Do you feel you have different expectations for Ann and Ken because of their dwarfism?]
Mother: Well, that's hard to answer because, you know, we have changed so much ourselves because of what has happened to them. We are really different people than we would be, and have different expectations than if we didn't have all these health problems in our family.

Most parents stated that they did not care whether their child married an average-sized person or another dwarf. However, several expressed considerable concern about their child having children who might also be dwarfs.

[If you had your choice, would you prefer her to marry a little person or an average-sized person?]
I really don't care. It absolutely does not make any difference to me. I don't care who she marries. But what I do care about is grandchildren; that really worries me. I do not want her to have children. I just think that with the physical complications, with her back problems and the other things that she has, she shouldn't have children. It's really hard for achondroplastics to have children.[1] And that I feel strongly about [vehemently].

Father: Well, one thing that worries me is having children. I just wonder about these LPA couples having children—bringing another dwarf into the world. They have these problems—structural problems, or other problems, and then it intensifies them to bring another child in, and I just wonder if there isn't a real moral problem.
Mother: Well, I really think that is her decision. That is her problem to make a decision.
Father: I guess it is, but it is something I would really wonder about.

I really think that he would do best with an LP. She'd be shorter than he is, they'd look good together, and they would have shared a lot of experiences, and I think it would work out better. But if you want to look at it another way, if he did marry an LP, if she were achondroplastic, there would be a good chance they'd have an achondroplastic child. And with his problems, he cannot carry an achondroplastic baby; he would really have a problem with a dwarf child. His type of dwarfism will not be passed on by him, but their chances of achondroplasia would be very great. I just think that it would be a mess physically. [Pause, thinking] I guess I really think that probably the best thing would be if he could have a very short, average-sized girl.

DWARFISM AS IT HAS AFFECTED FAMILY LIFE

The six families in the subsample were asked if they felt their family and family life would be different if their child were average sized. As an open-ended question, it elicited a wide range of answers that contributed commentaries on attitudes toward family life and activities, and sports in particular. Spouses in five cases responded in unison. Three couples said yes, their life would be quite different; two said no; and in one case the spouses disagreed. Three couples emphasized attitudinal differences caused by the presence of a different child.

These couples stated that they felt their experiences had made them more sensitive persons. The following are two statements from fathers:

Giving a lot of thought to her has made us more sensitive to the needs of handicapped people and toward a lot of things. I think it has made us more sensitive and caring toward people.

[Thoughtfully] You know, I think *I'm* different. I guess in some ways better and in some ways worse. I think I'm more sensitive toward people and more understanding because of that.

Those who said their life would be different all stated that they would be doing more outdoor sports or action-oriented activities—biking, hiking, or camping—which they couldn't do as family activities because of the physical limitations of the dwarf child. One couple in particular speculated that their life would be very different:

Mother: Our life could have been very different. I mean, we would have been more athletic, and we could have lived in a different place. Before and right after Hal was born we used to talk about the plans we had—we're both very athletic, and we had expected that we would do a lot of camping and hiking. Of course, we still do camping, but we expected to be a much more athletic family—and we are not. So we really are different than we would be. And there's another thing, you know, with our son—he can't do a lot of hard work. Ordinarily, if he were not a dwarf, he would probably be very big. If you look at Ross's brother's children, they are all over six foot, and they are all very massive. If Hal wasn't a dwarf, he would probably be big and strong, and there would be the chance we would be out living in the country.

[Do you mean in a rural area?]

Oh, yes. It's something we had thought about; but he would have had to have been able to help. As it is, he can't do anything.

Father: There is not a way that he could help on a farm.

Within each family the dwarf child is valued, treasured, and planned for in keeping with both his/her individual characteristics and the family good in mind. While some families continued to struggle with the fact and conditions of their child's dwarfism, most families had absorbed the novelty of their situation and had succeeded in developing realistic and successful patterns of adaptation to their child's dwarfism.

NOTE

1. Achondroplasia is caused by a genetic mutation and may then continue to be an inherited condition. In a situation in which one parent is achondroplastic, there is a 50 percent chance of an achondroplastic birth. If both parents are achondroplastic, there is a 75 percent probability of achondroplasia in any birth. Delivery is always by Caesarean section (Centerwall and Centerwall, 1986).

Chapter 8
Little People of America

Little People of America today has a national membership of about 4,000 persons, composed of some 2,000 dwarfs and their families who represent a diversity of socioeconomic categories, educational backgrounds, and occupations. Little People of America sponsors many types of activities and through these serves a great variety of functions for its members. Meetings are held on local, regional, and national levels. Weinberg (1968) historically and, more recently, Ablon (1984) have provided descriptions of the organization, its goals, and functions. Only in recent years has this group become known to the general public or even to professionals, who increasingly have come to use it as a very valuable referral resource. Considerable publicity about the organization is currently generated primarily by the media through interviews of individual members or by coverage of regional and national meetings. This publicity conveys a positive and energetic image of the organization and the potentials of life for LPA members today.

HISTORY AND ORGANIZATION

Little People of America, Inc., was founded in 1957 by a Hollywood actor and entertainer, Billy Barty, when he gathered together twenty-one dwarfs in Reno, Nevada. In 1960 a second convention was held in Las Vegas, where the attendance rose to more than one hundred persons. The group began meeting yearly and was incorporated in 1961 as Little People of America, Inc. The phrase "little people" was chosen by the early members at the first 1957 meeting as the most neutral vehicle for expressing the requisite short stature shared by LPA members, who can be no taller than four feet ten inches, according to membership requirements.

The goals of LPA are stated in the bylaws: "The purpose of LPA is to assist its members in adjusting to the social and physical problems of life caused by their small stature through mutual assistance and the personal examples by each of its members." The bylaws further note that LPA was organized by a concern with "the need for people of small stature to become useful members of society through education, employment, and social adjustment, and to focus public attention to the fact that the magnitude of any physical limitation is a function of attitude of both the small and average-size person" (Little People of America, S–1).

Little People of America is governed by an executive committee elected by the general membership. There are many standing committees with such varied services as assisting in the adoptions of dwarf children by members, awarding of fellowships for academic and vocational training to eligible members, coordinating relations with individuals and groups in other countries, planning of special events for different age groups, arrangements for public relations, and a host of other services.

There are twelve geographic districts of LPA covering the continental United States, Alaska, and Hawaii. Some forty-five chapters exist within these districts.[1] A local chapter may include members residing in an area of several hundred square miles. In a large district with members geographically dispersed, meetings often are held only several times a year, usually in the form of social events. In more heavily populated areas where many members live near one another, regular monthly chapter meetings may be the rule with varied social events supplementing these.

The local chapters wherein this research was based dates back to the 1961 national meeting in Las Vegas. Eight adult dwarfs from this area attended that meeting and were inspired to begin a group that would meet regularly in their home area. The first local meeting was held in 1962 with nineteen persons attending. This chapter is a large and vigorous one, covering a nine-county area with more than 200 members; one half are dwarfs. The group holds regular monthly business meetings, supplemented by an annual formal banquet, a Christmas party, and special summer picnics. The chapter sponsors a very active Parents' Group. This chapter has maintained a considerable stability of core membership of about fifteen people over time—an enthusiastic population who attend almost all functions sponsored by the chapter and the Parents' Group. The chapter is unique in the number of teens and young adults who are regular participants in group activities. Regular monthly meetings average twenty to thirty-five persons.[2]

The format and nature of regular chapter LPA activities differ in significant ways from those of many other peer or mutual-aid groups in which members share a specific health-related problematic condition. Perhaps one of the most significant differences is that in local LPA adult gatherings there are few direct discussions of the reality or consequences of the short stature shared by members, and there is no formal or ritualized relating of members' painful personal experiences connected with the condition. Regular LPA meetings are structured business meetings with a social hour following. Picnics or holiday events likewise are forthright social occasions. The activities are a coming together of persons of differing statuses and occupations who share a highly significant physical condition. They then return to their own divergent worlds, worlds common only in that they are constituted by average-sized persons.

THE LOCAL LPA PARENTS' GROUP

A significant component of LPA nationally and locally are Parents' Groups. There are approximately 650 families within the national LPA membership who have a dwarf child or teen-ager (Little People of America, personal communication, 1987). The Parents' Group membership typically has been constituted of average-sized parents of dwarf children. In recent years many short-statured parents have joined these groups, and because of this fact the original name, which had been Parents' Auxiliary, was formally changed to Parents' Group in 1984.

Most districts, even those including large cities, lack a sufficient critical mass of Parents' Group families. In these districts Parents' Groups rarely meet more than three or four times a year, or they will join with adult members at regular meetings. In some districts families travel to other cities for meetings. For example, families in Tucson and Phoenix, areas one hundred miles apart, come together for meetings, and families in the Seattle and Tacoma, Washington, areas meet together.

The Parents' Group described here draws members from a nine-county metropolitan area. This group began in 1968 after the present coordinator, an LPA adult member, moved to the area following her marriage to a local member. At that time a few average-sized parents and their dwarf children met with the regular adult LPA chapter each month. The coordinator felt there was a need for a separate group for families that would meet regularly for social interaction among average-sized parents, their dwarf children, and adult LPA members, and she soon began such a group.

The coordinator calls the early years of the development of the group, from 1968 to 1973, a period of "building a reputation of reliability and dependability with medical centers and local hospitals." By 1973 the attendance of clinical specialists at regional and national LPA meetings held in the area helped in winning this trust, and the organization's credibility among local medical resources was established. Referrals by physicians and allied health professionals have been regular since that time. Ninety-five families have been involved with the Parents' Group since its inception in 1968. Currently, forty-six families attend meetings or are in contact with the coordinator.

Regular functions of the Parents' Group typically are held five times a year on Saturday or Sunday afternoons and are often built around a holiday theme. Events rotate over the nine-county area to equalize families' driving distances.

While some groups of parents elsewhere in the country meet without their children, the coordinator of this group strongly stresses the importance of children mingling with other children, both dwarf and average-sized siblings, and adults. Attendance at events ranges from thirty to sixty persons (adults and children), with the largest gatherings occurring at the annual Christmas parties and summer picnics. In keeping with the coordinator's initial design, mingling in the Parents' Group events are average- and short-statured parents with their dwarf and average-sized children—and adult dwarfs who are members of the local LPA chapter. There typically are twelve to fifteen children, with child members predominating and many fewer teens. Many young adults who have been members of this chapter from their childhood years also attend.

The host families for group events provide snacks, drinks, and dessert, and there typically is a sumptuous potluck meal. This is followed by a short business meeting at which newcomers and guests are introduced and welcomed, and announcements of upcoming events are made. At Christmas Santa Claus distributes gifts to the children, and at Easter an Easter Bunny cavorts with young participants. However, the most important activity is the informal mixing and conversation. Newer parents typically discuss their child's practical, medical, or social problems with more experienced parents and adult dwarfs and, often with some difficulty, may state their fears and apprehensions about their child's health and social future. They are given advice and encouragement by those who have coped with similar situations. The coordinator typically moves about during social events facilitating interaction by bringing together families that share similar problems but have not yet met.

A number of younger couples are now very active in planning and outreach activities, and they serve as key contacts for anxious parents with new babies or those with recent diagnoses for their children.

One of the most telling signs of the success of the Parents' Group is the extremely active group of young adults who frequent every event. Most of these young people first came to LPA as children and attended meetings with their parents through their teen-age years. They now are self-confident, highly active young individuals who are in college or working. The active participation of this group is a particularly significant phenomenon, because this age-group cohort nationally represents the first one growing into adulthood who have had LPA as a major social reference group throughout their childhood and teen-age years. Thus, they represent the first dwarf adults who have had LPA as a significant element in their early psychosocial development.

DISCUSSION GROUPS

Regular evening discussion groups that address the practical problems of parents in a more focused manner were introduced in this Parents' Group in 1977. Mr. and Mrs. Baird, average-sized parents, appeared at a regular chapter meeting and stated that as average-sized parents they felt ill equipped in aspects of rearing their dwarf daughter. They proposed a discussion group for parents and adult LPA members with children under eighteen to be excluded. The first meeting was held at their home; thirty-five parents and adult dwarfs attended. Mr. Baird earnestly stated his concern: "Claire and I are trying to be the best parents we can for our daughter, but in terms of our life experiences, we don't feel we have as much of a basis to do so as we do for our other children. What we want to do is ask some of you little people to share some of your life experiences; to tell us what were the really good things your parents did for you and what were the things you really didn't like, or that didn't help." Mrs. Baird said: "Our daughter will be ready to begin school next year. We don't know whether to put her in a public or private school. What do you think?"

An intense discussion of problems experienced in both public and private schools ensued. The consensus of adult dwarfs and other parents was that the logistical, social, and psychological problems confronted by dwarf children are the same in both. Although most schools help with physical problems, a major concern of parents was how to reach solutions for social and psychological problems with administrators and teachers.

Also considered at that initial meeting was the problem shared by dwarfs of all ages, that of being stared at and commented on by children and adults in public places. This issue arises for discussion repeatedly, regardless of the specific topic set for these evening meetings. Other discussions have dealt with a wide variety of topics, such as the following: relationships between dwarf children and their average-sized siblings and peers; how dwarf children can protect themselves from harassment; if and when you should encourage a child to fight back; how to answer your dwarf child's questions about his/her size; how to respond when dwarf children blame dwarf parents for bringing them into the world; how dwarf teenagers can survive the difficult teen years; and how to make informed decisions about surgery and other medical procedures.

As an example of issues dealt with in child rearing, one discussion group began with a parent posing this question in relation to his son: "Friends have told us that the most handicapping thing to our son may be our attitude. How can we let this child grow up as a handicapped child without his knowing that we think he is handicapped, or without being handicapped by our thinking that he is handicapped?"

Discussions are characterized by a sharing of different viewpoints, all of which represent a realistic recognition of the child's identity as a dwarf and the legitimization of this as an acceptable identity even though different from his/her peers. Parents who have attended the discussion sessions state they have found them very helpful, many noting their appreciation of adult LPA members' candid sharing of experiences and vulnerabilities.

The author's observations of discussions at Parents' Group meetings at national conventions over a ten-year period suggest that the level of sophistication of information exchange maintained by this local Parents' Group is exceptionally high. New parents in this local group are quickly briefed about the same subjects that recur with regularity at national meetings, and parents then have benefit of much more intensive and far-ranging discussions than are available for persons who only are able to meet several times a year. Because parents can quickly absorb a relatively large amount of general information on the local level, it is possible to plan discussion groups that focus on the wide variety of specialized topics noted above.

Much of the success of the local Parents' Group must be attributed to efforts of the coordinator. The personal life experiences of this coordinator, a warm and gregarious person, have been enriched further by graduate teacher training and considerable teaching experience in rural and urban elementary schools. She is remarkably aggressive in bringing new families in and urging old ones to return to meetings. She and her husband have extended themselves in outreach activities during vacation trips to visit families in rural areas of their state who are isolated from organized LPA functions. Perhaps more important are her telephone and house calls to new, frightened parents to discuss with them the implications of their child's dwarfism. The significance of the persistence and enthusiasm of the coordinator cannot be overestimated in understanding the success of this group or in the planning of other groups.

HOW FAMILIES FOUND LPA

I have reported elsewhere (1984) on the remarkably varied modes in which adult dwarfs came to learn about LPA. Many of these involved serendipitous encounters with average-sized or dwarf strangers who told them gratuitously about the organization. Some persons heard of LPA through family members or through the media. Rarely were persons referred by professionals, such as physicians or social workers. The same situation holds true for the more senior Parents' Group families. Those who joined the LPA Parents' Group more than ten years ago often first heard of the organization quite fortuitously. In recent years early referrals by physicians are standard, and the coordinator of the local Parents' Group gets two to three calls a month about newborn dwarf infants.

The six families in the subsample learned of LPA in a variety of ways. For example, in three of the six cases physicians or social workers told them about the organization and obtained the name of the Parents' Group coordinator for them. In one case a father with his one-year-old achondroplastic son was approached in a barber shop by an adult LPA member who told him about the organization and its activities. In another case the referral was made by a physical therapist when the child was two. And in another case the parents encountered some adult dwarfs by happenstance when their child was seven years old:

We were walking on the beach, and we saw four little people. I decided I'd follow them. I had to talk to them. I followed them for a long way, and then I went up to one of the women and said, "Excuse me, but I think my son is a little person"—I don't know what word I used, maybe "dwarf"—"like you are. Could you tell me something about what your life is like?" The woman told us about Little People of America. I had read about LPA in *Life* magazine before, but I didn't know how to contact them. When we got back, we wrote to Susan, and she had a mother call us in a few days.

Other subjects described a multiplicity of modes of discovering LPA.

We were used to people coming up and talking to us. They'd come up and say, "Oh, isn't she cute! How old is she?" And we'd say three years, and people would be so shocked because they thought she was about eight months. We were in the Chicago airport, and it turned out that Dr. Grey came up to us, and he looked at her and said, "You know, I see many children like your daughter." And we said, "We're moving to Cleveland." And he said, "Well, maybe sometime I'll see you," and he left. We didn't know anything about him. So then we moved there, and about a year later our other daughter fell and broke her leg, and we took her to an orthopedist. While we were there, we said, "We have a daughter who is an achondroplastic dwarf, and she seems to have a problem with her neck." And so he said, "Maybe you should take her to a doctor here who is very good with that," and we made an appointment for her. We were sitting in the waiting room, and I said, "I wonder if it might be that doctor we saw in the airport." We walked in, and there he was. We got to know him very well, and he told us about LPA, and he said he would tell us when there was a meeting. He called the next month and said there was going to be a large meeting coming up, and I went over at lunch time to see what was happening, and I never did get back to work that day. Then the next day I took my wife, and we stayed there three days, and from then on we had a very regular group in Cleveland that met for all different kinds of functions. We were spoiled by that.

Well, actually we met the Garcia family on the beach one day. It was totally by accident. We'd been at the beach, and I was looking for my son, Jimmy, and I saw this profile and I thought it was Jimmy, and then I realized that it had long hair and that it wasn't Jimmy. It was the Garcia's daughter. She is also achondroplastic. Then they saw us and we saw them, and they started talking to us about LPA.

Mr. Evans saw Ed driving a car and saw that he was a dwarf. So he chased him in the car, and when Ed stopped at a light, Mr. Evans jumped out of his car and started beating on the window. Ed didn't know why he would be chasing him. Mr. Evans said, "I have an eight-month-old dwarf son, and I think he's like you, and I'd like to talk to you." Ed pulled over and they talked. He later came to the Evans' house for dinner, and he told them about LPA.

FIRST ENCOUNTERS

Two primary emotions are apparent in parents' descriptions of their first meetings with adult LPA members and their attendance at LPA events. First is a *resistance* to seeing the actual image of what their dwarf child will look like as they mature and, second, *relief* at the normalization and demystification of the dwarf identity. These emotions are often intertwined in parents' responses and in their accounts of these first experiences. Although parents were helped in the process of seeing that their child could lead a normal life, the cognitive process of accepting the reality of their child's dwarfism and the implications of this permanent physical difference were very disturbing.

We wrote a note to the LPA members we had met on vacation, and they had a mother call us. She invited us to a meeting at her house the next week. She told us there would be a lot of people there, and there would be little people and a Parents' Group meeting. This was in 1975. We couldn't bring ourselves to go. I don't know. Maybe we couldn't stand to look at that ourselves, but we didn't want our daughter to look at that. Maybe we didn't want her to see what she was going to look like. We didn't want her to know that she was never going to be tall, that she was always going to be that short. So we didn't go. We did go to the next meeting, which was a couple of months afterwards. That meeting was just marvelous. That was the turning point. Because at that meeting we began talking to a number of dwarfs, and that's when we found out that it was going to be OK; that dwarfs lived like other people. They married; they drove cars; they held jobs; they took vacations; they could be like other people. So it wasn't going to be this terrible kind of thing.

Paul said, "Why don't you come over to our house after the meeting. We're going to have dessert in the evening." We went, and I remember sitting on the couch and talking. They had all their furniture cut down. Well, we had the best time. When we were ready to go and we stood up, that's when it hit me. Because when we were sitting, everyone was the same. When we stood up, these people were down below my waist. Our heads were spinning and our stomachs were churning and we went home. We ended up being involved, going to other meetings that they had because we felt it was important for Joe to have that exposure at that time, if he was indeed a dwarf, which is a permanent condition. These people were real people in different professions, and a lot of members were a big help during that time. But we used to have to take Pepto Bismol when we got home, because even though we'd have a good time, it was the reality of it all. And I think that's what's good. I think that's good for parents, to be hit with the reality. You find you're enjoying it, but when you go home, you suffer the effects of that reality— that my child is not going to grow. He's really going to stay small.

Father: They were going to hold a medical clinic in the afternoon at the LPA regional meeting. Dr. Smith told me over the phone to come with the X-rays in the afternoon. That was Saturday. The baby was born the previous Monday night, and Marion was still in the hospital. So people were expecting me. While she was still in the hospital, I go to Rochester and I'm sitting at the Airport Hilton in the hall in front of the meeting room, clutching the X-rays. I didn't get that much help from Smith. Actually, she had already been diagnosed. He just looked at the X-rays and said that she was achondroplastic. But there was a great asset in my being there. What I think struck me first were the combinations; that there were dwarfs married to average-sized people, there were dwarfs with dwarfs, and there were dwarfs with average-sized kids, and there were average-sized parents with dwarf kids. All these combinations were boggling my mind. But I think what really hit me was that life was going on. Here were people who were making a life for themselves. They worked and they lived and they married. They had children. They functioned. Nobody was saying, "Woe is me, why did this happen to me." Nobody looked morose. That was really important.

Mother: I'm not sure if I would have reacted that way, but it was a very positive experience for him.

Father: I was welcomed with open arms.

You go to some meetings and you come back, and you're just sick with the thought of it.

[What is it that bothers you?]

Well, it's the reality. It's the reality that this is your child's condition—the whole idea of the condition hits you. In general, when they're going to school or whatever, you forget about it, unless they're in the hospital with something particular. You could just sort of forget that you have this problem. But then when you go back to LPA, you're aware of it. It brings it into your awareness.

You know, the most impressive thing about the convention was seeing all these people. On one hand, you're very apprehensive to see all these people and all kinds of deformities. It's very surprising to see these things. Cliff's achondroplastic, and he's got this kind of form, but a lot of the rest have other kinds of conditions. But whatever they have, they are able to have jobs and do all these things. On the one hand, while you're apprehensive, on the other, it's very reassuring to know these things. Once you get over the visual shock, it's all right.

Two mothers reported very negative initial responses to this reality.

We went to the first meeting, and Laura took us around to the nursery, and she said, "Now, here are the kids. Aren't they darling? Aren't they cute?" I looked in and I saw those children, and I didn't think that they were cute at all. I didn't even want to look at them.

[What was it about that bothered you so much?]

Well, they had these short arms and legs, and stubby fingers and toes. I didn't want to see that. Now, maybe I've gotten used to it or whatever, but I don't think about it. I just don't think about it like that at all now. But I remember that very vividly.

I walked in to my first LPA meeting [waving her hand around and down], and there were thousands of little people all around. And we watched them.

And then it was worse when we got up to leave and they were all this short. We came home, and that was the last straw. The next day I called my cousin, and I said, "This is it. I have to give Josh away. I'm going to put him up for adoption. I can't deal with him. I can't deal with having a dwarf. He needs a family that can deal with him and I can't do it." Of course, I didn't give him up for adoption, and it got better after that.

Both mothers commented that although they vividly remember these initial impressions, their perceptions rapidly changed to an acceptance of the physical differences that they saw, and they now perceive today's children in the nursery room of LPA meetings to be darling little children and most adult dwarfs to be attractive individuals. The initial reactions experienced by these parents are both *generic*, typical of response to an unexpected physical difference, and also *specific* to the situation of parents of physically different children who are forced to confront the vivid reality of their own child's difference. Featherstone (1980) commented on this type of situation of parents seeing persons who share the physically different condition of their child.

Perhaps the worst part of an encounter like this is the parent's emotional response to the children. He finds himself recoiling from them; noticing this reaction, he wonders whether he could care for his own child if she or he became like these others.

Most of us know that some of the love we feel for our children is selfish. We love them in part because they enhance and ornament our lives. We wonder whether we will be able to love a child who deviates from all our dreams (pp. 20–21).

Said one father about the long-term value of the initial shocking perceptual experience that may occur at LPA conventions:

You know what really helped? When you come to convention you look at these adult achondroplastic little dwarfs, and you can see in adult women what your daughter is going to look like. You walk around with a heavy heart for four or five days, and then you work through this, because then you look at the other things about them.

[What other things?]

Like jobs and families. Then you see it's not going to be such a bad thing, because they also have these full rich lives. What's important is that in four or five days you work through what could have taken you years if you hadn't come to this convention and seen these people.

One set of parents described a situation in which they were approached by an adult member with a peculiar question for them.

Mother: Roger came up and asked us if we would sell her. It had a neat effect on John because his dander went up, and it solidified his thoughts about Kelly. He was feeling better than I was and coping much better at that time.

Father: I think that was a mechanism, because what essentially he was saying was, "She's a dwarf, but she's a person that's of value. We want you to know that she's a valuable human being. And is she of value to you?" But on the other hand, maybe he was asking me if I would put her up for adoption. I don't know. But he did tell me a twelve-year-old child was recently put up for adoption. I really got mad. I said something like, "We wouldn't think of selling her." It did serve a function to sort of pull me together and make me think a lot. We had a lovely valuable daughter at home.

PARTICIPATION IN PARENTS' GROUP ACTIVITIES

There appears to be a typical pattern of attendance of families at LPA events through the family's and the dwarf child's career. Parents often anxiously rush to meetings following the birth of their child for answers to basic questions and reassurance about their child's future. They continue attending meetings regularly for information and medical advice for several years, especially if their child is a type of dwarf other than achondroplastic, which typically has relatively few early medical problems. Families particularly seek advice for issues concerning surgery or other special procedures. Their attendance may then taper off until kindergarten and beginning school years, when they must deal with the logistic and social problems their child encounters in the new school situation.

During these early years, some parents participate more for their own psychological needs than for the needs of their child. By the time the child is in the second or third grade, parents are not only more secure and in charge of their situation, but also typically now have one or several other children to think about. They may retreat from regular attendance at meetings but will continue to attend annual Christmas parties and possibly another occasional event near their home. Their chief contacts with LPA might be telephone calls to the coordinator or other members about particular problems. LPA is considered to be a standing resource for issues that emerge when their child enters new stages or situations, or for any special problems or crises they may encounter.

As children become settled in elementary school and gain some measure of conformity with their average-sized peers, the children may then assert themselves and insist that they do not want to attend functions based on their difference from their everyday social companions. At that time it is difficult for them to establish and maintain friendships with other dwarf children seen only at LPA functions. The locus of social reference is in daily relationships at school and in the neighborhood. Dwarf children's reluctance to attend LPA functions may wax and wane from about the ages of eight to fifteen years. This often depends on their social success at school and on the nature of the available population of their age group in the local LPA chapter.

For example, one mother described the situation of her fourteen-year-old son, who told me at a convention that he did not want to go to LPA teen events: "You know when kids get to this age, they really have their own friendship circle. They're shy, and they don't go out to other people. It has to do with adolescence. They have their own friends at home, and it takes a while to start talking to other kids after they come here."

In the statement of another mother, the ambiguities of successful social experiences in LPA are apparent: "The boys are particularly good at making friends. They have made friends everywhere they've gone, and it seems like very quickly they make some very special friends. Several of them are very tall boys, and they are really fine. Our sons love the LPA meetings, too, but it's hard to go back. I guess I think too much LPA is not good because of this."

Children tend to resume attendance in the mid to late teen-age years when their school peers are dating and they most likely are not. They then might wish to attend teen functions. One adult dwarf commented on this subject:

"How many parents say, We don't need LPA because our child has friends, and his teachers love him. Well my teachers loved me, too, but I still needed LPA. It's a waiting game."

NATIONAL CONVENTION

The major event sponsored by LPA is the national convention, a week-long marathon of day and night remarkable activity. Here the varied functions of LPA and the energetic character of the organization are most in evidence. The annual convention is held in the summer and lasts approximately seven days beginning on the weekend. There are preconvention social activities on Saturday and meetings of the Medical Advisory Board and Parents' Groups and other special events on Sunday. The week formally begins Monday morning and closes the following Friday. There is a plenary session most mornings, during which time business is conducted. On some days workshops are held on such varied topics as employment, insurance, social skills, and special discussions sponsored by the Parents' Group. Afternoons are full with sports events, sightseeing, and shopping tours as featured activities. Meals are taken together in a dining area, and announcements may be made at this time and special programs presented. Varied social events are held each evening. On one night there is a fashion show exhibiting the latest average-sized fashions adapted by members for short-statured persons. On another night a talent show of two or three hours features singing, dancing, acting out skits, and playing musical instruments. On Thursday evening a formal banquet climaxes the week's activities and events, featuring an elegant meal and a program that reports on the activities and accomplishments of the week. A particularly important aspect of the convention is nightly dancing. Each night a band provides music for dancing from 10:00 P.M. until 2:00 A.M. For a more detailed discussion of the national convention, see Ablon, 1984.

An extremely important component of the convention week is the presence of the members of the Medical Advisory Board, distinguished specialists from Johns Hopkins Hospital and other institutions across the country with particular interests in problems of medical genetics, human growth, and related areas. These physicians offer free examinations and consultations for members in a designated area of the hotel site and give presentations and hold workshops on various specialized topics. Also available are the services of a social worker on the staff of Johns Hopkins Hospital, a member of the Medical Advisory Board, who as one of her special interests, focuses on individual and family problems relating to short stature. The members of the Medical Advisory Board sometimes ask LPA members to engage in research projects they are carrying out—for example, to allow body measurements to be taken, to give blood samples, or to answer questionnaires. Indeed, many recent publications on dwarfs have resulted from the recruitment and positive participation of LPA members at annual conventions.

In 1987 for the first time a one-day short-stature symposium was included in the convention-week activities. The symposium featured panels of specialists in dwarfism and related areas and workshops led by professionals and dwarf members who shared their own experiences. The model for this educational event was designed and instituted at the Johns Hopkins Medical Institutions in Baltimore in 1972, and short-stature symposiums have been held by Hopkins almost yearly. Regional LPA meetings in various parts of the country have also sponsored symposiums.

During the convention week, a new social world, which is composed primarily of persons of short stature, is created. Members share this world in a space of their own, relatively away from the average-sized world. The organization frequently takes over most of the rooms in a medium-sized hotel. Most significantly, members are freed from the daily cultural ambiance in which they live, which dictates an omnipresent disparity in how they are treated in much of what they do. Away from this ambiance, they are able to experience the same social rituals and interactions in the same way as do other persons in their society. This indeed is the only week of the year when dwarfs may relate almost totally without disparity of size being a dimension to consider in their interactions. Freedom is born in the escape from the stares of society.

Recognition of individual members at the fashion show, talent show, banquet, and other events is an important aspect of the convention. Most events function to highlight members' accomplishments: their sports abilities, sewing skills, entertainment talents, or musical abilities, all of which may not be recognized or acknowledged in the average-sized world because of the size discrepancy and its social implications. Indeed, the opportunity to see other dwarfs so recognized serves a particularly important modeling function for dwarf children for whom the everyday acknowledgement of their dwarfism may be curiosity or ridicule. At the convention they have the opportunity to see adult dwarfs who are engineers, teachers, secretaries, or bookkeepers, dwarfs who are successful professionally and who boast homes, families, and the other normative accomplishments of American life. They see dwarf children and teens who successfully play baseball, swim, sing, dance, and act. The convention is a heady cognitive experience for children and adults alike.

Young people often establish strong friendship bonds with agemates at conventions in their preteen years and, in the teens, dating relationships also. Relationships are maintained across geographic distances through letter writing, telephone calls, and visits back and forth. Most parents realize the enormous significance of these relationships for their children's self-esteem and feelings of social success. For example, one mother said: "Our [sixteen-year-old] son has friends from all over the country that he's made at convention. He talks to them all the time on the phone. Our phone bills are astronomical, but we feel that it's worth every penny in terms of his good feelings about himself."

A perennial concern is the amount of freedom children and teen-agers should be given during conventions when there is great peer pressure to run from activity to activity and stay up until the early morning hours or even all night. A dilemma is that both children and parents take into consideration the brevity and importance of the precious hours of the convention week for young participants.

PARENTS' DISCUSSION GROUPS AT CONVENTIONS

National conventions offer the chief forums for parents to meet other parents from around the country who share similar problems and apprehensions about their children. The Parents' Group activities at national conventions have evolved in their format in keeping with the type of activities that parents requested. One member stated that at the time of conventions in the early 1970s, whenever workshops on specific topics were planned, parents said that they just wanted fun and not serious things. They did not want to share experiences. However, by the time of the first convention attended by the researcher in 1977, Parents' Groups were serious problem-sharing and problem-solving sessions. Sessions primarily are discussions; however, speaker sessions featuring medical specialists are often held.

Recent conventions have had Parents' Group meetings daily, varying in time from mornings to late afternoons. Several years ago, a very successful impromptu discussion session with fifteen to twenty participants was held from 11:00 p.m. to 12:00 midnight outside the dancing area after it was observed that so many parents were still present watching the dancing. In most sessions the majority present are mothers, but there is an increasing number of fathers who attend each year.

The personal relationships and networks developed among parents who live in various parts of the country are a particularly important dimension of the helping process of LPA. Said one mother to me at a national convention, "You know, more counseling goes on in the halls and bars than at the parents' meetings!" These conversations may also be continued by mail over the years and are of particular importance to parents whose children share unusual or less common conditions. These parents often have no one to talk to in their local area.

Because there is now such a large number of parents and their children represent many age groups, sessions are often divided into those for parents of preschoolers, school-age children, preteens, and teens. Discussions are usually led by some of the more experienced parents. There often are a number of dwarf parents present who share their experiences of growing up as profoundly short persons.

At Parents' Group meetings at conventions, an array of problems are discussed, from those dealing with the best language to use in relation to dwarf children to technical problems attending surgery. A brief profile of common issues considered and parents' advice on these issues are presented here. The use of "dwarf" and other related terms is often discussed. Issues of discrepancy in language that arise because of size are considered. For example, the dwarf child might be the oldest, but not the biggest child in their family. Younger children may be encouraged to refer to these siblings as "older" rather than "bigger." Parents may speak of the dwarf child as "getting older" rather than "growing up."

The importance of open communication within the family is emphasized. For example, one mother said that she tells her dwarf daughter that even though she has raised two other children, she has not been the parent of a dwarf teenager before and that her daughter must help her to know what she needs to know to do a good job.

Relations between dwarf children and average-sized siblings are a frequent topic of discussion. Parents may have to spend disproportionate amounts of time with their dwarf child because of medical problems, thus shortchanging average-sized siblings. Said one mother: "We spent so much time with doctors that the next younger child ended up with babysitters all the time. If I knew then what I know now, I would have planned for that and tried to make other arrangements, but I was not aware of it at the time."

In fact, resentments held by average-sized siblings because of larger amounts of time and attention given to the dwarf child may often appear when the children are older, in the late teen-age years or early adulthood. One adult dwarf said that her sister, who is in her fifties, is only now talking about the resentments that she has held in all these years.

A subject that is repeatedly talked about is whether staying in one locale throughout the dwarf child's developing years is better for him/her than movement through ever-changing social environments. Some parents feel that it is easier if the child has the same peer group or circle of friends from kindergarten through the high-school years. The child then is not barraged by continually new groups of children (and adults) reacting to their size; thus, he/she develops a better sense of security and identity. In contrast to this point of view, some parents feel that if little people stay in one place, everyone gets to know them and approaches *them*, so they do not have to "push." They then become passive. In keeping with this perspective, it is argued that children gain more coping skills if they do move around. However, of utmost importance is that their families can provide them with a great deal of security and stability. Most parents would agree that certain periods are the worst for socially uprooting dwarf children and this should be taken into consideration when planning for relocation.

Keeping open communication with the school is emphasized. For example, one mother stated that she volunteers one day a week at her dwarf child's school so she can know what is going on and keep in contact with her child's teachers.

Issues dealing with how to let dwarf children be independent and not overprotected are frequently brought up. How does one evaluate the realistic implications of physical differences? What are the actual physical limitations of a dwarf child? These should be considered in relation to giving permission or encouragement for specific activities, such as sports, typing, or playing the piano.

How does one distinguish typical responses of the adolescent or teen-age years, such as grumpiness or withdrawal, from those specifically related to children's short stature? A recurring theme throughout discussions is that all adolescents experience "normal" problems in the crucial teen-age years. Normal problems should not be obscured by issues related to size and problems of self-image that are connected with physical differences.

Potential problems of teens finding and maintaining jobs are discussed. Many first jobs that teens have are babysitting jobs. One question asked is, "How can you get neighbors to accept your child as a babysitter even though he or she may be smaller than the kids they're sitting with?" One mother answered that in this situation her dwarf daughter clearly demonstrates her authority, illustrating that the issue is one of control, not size. As dwarf teens go out into the world looking for work, the normal problems all teens have in job hunting are even more problematic for them. One mother said, "They have to find a hiring person who's a risk taker."

A common topic of discussion is the quality and quantity of their children's social lives. Although there are a few dramatic examples of children who appear to be ostracized by their peers, most parents report their children have many friends and are socially very active. In fact, some parents express concern about children's sometimes seemingly frenetic social activities. For example, at one meeting many parents said their children were very well known in their communities and had a remarkable number of friends. One woman said her daughter was in five cliques. Some parents wondered if these children were normally "social minded" or did their dwarfism cause them to seek out or form an inordinate number of relationships because of a need to be accepted? In this situation the "mascot syndrome" effect may also play a role in their children's popularity.

Problems in dating are perennial for dwarf teen-agers. Some parents think the situation is easier for girls who can just "sit back," while boys have to ask for dates. Others think that the male is more fortunate because he at least can be more aggressive, even though today there is more cultural permission for girls to be the aggressors in relationships and dating.

The exchange of information also includes data on such subjects as which dress and hair styles may look better on little people. Problems with clothes and hair styles are often major considerations for children. Children's push for conformity with their peers may vie with the fact that some fashions may be more flattering for dwarf children. Specifics are often dictated by the type of dwarfism and individual body build.

A tribute to the earnestness of parents' seeking to help their children was made at the close of a convention week of daily large discussion meetings by an adult dwarf who said, "I want to tell all of you that my wife and I got to know our own parents better from hearing you talk in these meetings."

Medical sessions presented by physicians deal with the genetics of dwarfism and with problems common to varied types of dwarfism. Hereditary factors in dwarfism are sometimes discussed, and dominant and recessive patterns are described. Medical problems are also explicated: some types of dwarfs are prone to ear problems; ear infections frequently follow colds. Many dwarf children benefit from tubes inserted in their eardrums, however, these children need special ear stoppers for swimming, which is excellent exercise for achondroplastics and one of the recommended sports. One mother said that at her first convention she heard other LPA parents talking about ear aches and immediately took her daughter to a specialist. In her daughter's case there had already been some scarring, but there was little permanent damage to the ear drum. She was very happy that she was made aware of this possibility and had gone immediately for medical attention.

Little people with bone dysplasias are also more prone to arthritis than are average-sized persons. Complicating health problems of the skeletal system is that many achondroplastic adults have a tendency to be overweight. Although dwarfs should eat less than average-sized persons, they ordinarily are served the same-sized portions and thus develop habits of eating more than their bodies need. Mothers often comment on the structural problems obesity contributes to and their attempts to avoid obesity in their children:

People do make comments about her body. For instance, a boy at school commented how her rear stuck out; and then at the swimming pool last summer a girl kept going up and yelling comments at her about why her rear stuck out, and saying, "Why do you have such a fat bottom?" I'm very concerned about her weight. When she comes back from convention, Kelly always asks me, "Why do all these dwarfs have such fat bottoms?" So I've had her on a considerable diet because I think that's the best way of keeping her looking good and also to keep as much pressure as possible off her spine.

Certain forms of exercise, such as swimming, are well suited to varied types of dwarfism, while other forms of exercise, such as jogging or riding skateboards, are potentially very dangerous.

Separate sessions for women and men are held to discuss the physiology of reproduction and the ways that little people may similarly or differently experience sexual activities and procreation as compared to persons in the average-sized population. Special issues dealing with birth control are considered. Most dwarf women are able to reproduce, although delivery is almost universally through Caesarean section. Medical advisers are available at conventions to discuss a range of such issues with groups and individuals.

THE FUNCTIONS OF LPA FOR PARENTS AND CHILDREN

The statements of parents clearly reflect at least three differing functions that participation in LPA serves for them. Some expressed one, two, or three benefits for themselves and their children. Their perceptions of these benefits often changed through the period of interviewing with most differentiating the advantages of LPA for themselves and for their children, respectively.

The Cognitive Function

The major function may be considered cognitive: the opportunity for viewing role modeling on a number of levels. The potent impact of the modeling process for both parents and their children was richly documented in interviews. This modeling provides dwarf role models who have clearly normalized their lives. Most parents had seen few or no dwarfs before the birth of their own child; thus they had no knowledge of how dwarfs fared in life or what their abilities would be. Parents were susceptible to fears and apprehensions that they later recognized to be exaggerated. The opportunity to view and interact with adult dwarfs who are successful wage earners, parents, and happy and attractive people relieved many parents' anxieties about their child's futures. Witnessing the successful functioning of short-statured adults and teen-agers, and of other children of their own child's age (some of whom may actually have more significant physical problems than their child), enables these parents to envision a successful and happy life for their child. The following statements illustrate the importance of role modeling:

It gave us the chance to meet other dwarfs; to see little people in small bodies who have been able to deal with life and to actualize themselves; to know that there are people who have lives and histories that are just packaged a little differently but who have been able to live and have jobs and do things. Also, we have seen people so much worse off, and that's important, too.

Oh, LPA did much more for us than it did for her. When we first came in, we didn't know what to expect for our daughter. Would she have to go to a circus? What would there be for her? The way she really benefited was that after we got into LPA and saw other dwarfs we relaxed and stopped putting so much pressure on her, and she could get along better because of our relaxing.

Without LPA I think that we wouldn't have understood as much and we wouldn't have been able to give him what we have given him. When he was born, I had never seen a little person, and I didn't know what his future was, and I didn't know what the possibilities in life were for him. Through LPA we learned that he had *all* the possibilities in life, and we were told that if we taught him that he could do anything that he wanted to do, he could. So we all benefited from this. Maybe if we hadn't learned that, that we had to give him a positive self-image, if we hadn't learned that and learned to feel this positively ourselves, then he wouldn't have been like this.

It wasn't that we needed other parents to talk to to learn about child rearing, because we knew that. There is not that much difference between her and any other kid up to five years old. But what we needed was to see some adult little people and to see that life is going to be OK for her.

Father: It was the models. I think it was like taking a sedative. Seeing these little people was like saying, "Boy, there's some relief in sight."
Mother: I don't have to worry. I don't have to get anxious about the future.
Father: There's a way out.

Mother: When we came in with our baby, we both had tears in the eyes, and then my husband sat and talked to Mr. Harris [a high-placed professional], and he told us that our son would not be some miserable failure. That was the greatest thing for us.

Both: Looking at adult little people was the most important thing.

Father: To see that they are people who can have jobs, and they can laugh and have families and have a good time. You also see people that are a lot worse off than you are. I guess it's really terrible to say it, but it just makes you feel better to see that there are people whose children have worse conditions than yours does.

Mother: Maybe people look at us and think that they are happy because our child has a worse condition than they do.

Father: That makes you feel better, too.

The modeling function for dwarf children may be more complex. Many adult dwarf members acknowledge that they had denied their dwarfism for most of their lives before coming to LPA (Ablon, 1984). For children who are just beginning to experience the responses of their peers to their differentness, seeing and playing with other children who have physical characteristics and appearances similar to their own is a significant cognitive experience. They are forced at an early age to see themselves in the persons of other dwarf children. In the course of this experience, they journey through a complex process of self-perception and positive acceptance; they internalize the message that "I'm OK." As they grow older and are able to articulate their own concerns about their future, the opportunity to see attractive, well-dressed, and happy short-statured teens with active social lives, and adults employed in various occupations reinforces their positive self-image. It allays some of the fears and apprehensions that result from daily experiences with average-sized peers who often direct cruel verbal and physical messages toward them regarding their difference. Said one father of his son's early experiences in LPA activities: "Those casual gatherings have given Greg a good feeling about himself. His early exposure to LPA has made possible his outgoing personality and his good view of life, enough to assure his interactions on a daily basis." Another said: "I really think the biggest thing is for Laura to see herself in other little people." And another: "When that bunch of guys [teen members] came for the skiing trip, that was the neatest bunch of guys you'd ever see. They really looked healthy, strong—they looked 'macho.' They really looked good. Our son loved it."

Parents also benefit from the opportunity to see other more experienced parents who have learned to accept and comfortably manage their children's problems and the array of possible consequences for their families. Since dwarfism is a rare condition, the random chances of parents meeting other parents who have dwarf children are extremely slim. The importance of meeting other parents in one's own seemingly unique "boat" is enormous. Peer-support groups will be discussed further in Chapter 10.

The Educative Function

The educative function of LPA is the most apparent and straightforward one to the observer. The majority of parents stressed the value of specialized information they have gained from other parents and from physicians who visit regional, national, and more infrequently, local Parents' Groups:

I had the opportunity to ask questions I would never ask anywhere else, like how can she fasten her clothes? How can she wipe herself? And I found out all these things without being embarrassed about it.

The technical aspect is the easiest thing. The doctors can tell you all about that. What makes it so difficult is what you do every day and how you raise the child. And no one can tell you that except right here at this meeting.

We've learned a lot. Just yesterday, my son said he wanted to be a doctor, and I kept saying, "With your fingers, you couldn't be a surgeon, you couldn't operate." And then here I heard these people say that their kids play the piano and do typewriting. I don't know why I discourage my son. I guess I am learning from the meetings, too.

Father: The doctor was talking about different things. We were learning about ears. What's really important is you learn the physical kinds of problems that come with this condition. We'd never heard of tubes in the ears. We never heard of that, and we didn't know what it would mean or how bad it was going to be, or what were the consequences. But then after we heard all about it, when our doctor said to us that she needs tubes put in, we didn't think anything of it. So what? Because we had learned about it.

Mother: There was so much to learn at that time. Well, it's for her now. But in the past it answered our questions and allowed us to think that this isn't a terrible thing; it's not a bad thing at all. We could relax. She had this kink in her back, and we went to this orthopedist at Blue Center, and he told us that she'd have to be in this horrible brace. Then Roger [adult dwarf] said, "Oh, don't worry about it. Many achondroplastics have that. She'll grow out of it. Forget the brace." We didn't know. We were listening to the doctor. We had to strap her in and she was so uncomfortable, and she cried a lot. So we did forget the brace, and sure enough, the kink went away.

I think we had a tendency to overcompensate. LPA helped us in that, to keep us from overcompensating. And it also helped us not to undercompensate, to know there are certain things we have to do and certain things we don't have to do.

I think the importance of this group is not for the kids, but for the parents to learn and to put themselves in order. We are trying to put our heads in order right now. The best thing for a child is if he knows his parents think he is capable and he is all right and can do things. Then that child is going to be capable.

The Community Function

LPA also constitutes a community with very specialized security-providing functions for members. For some, it has brought "peace of mind." Said one parent, "Just knowing that LPA is there has given security to our lives." And another said, "You realize you are not alone." Parents also expect that LPA will provide a pool of eligibles for their children to date and marry. I have discussed elsewhere the significant mental-health functions that attach to the opportunity of meeting other little persons for the intimacies of deep friendship, dating, and marriage (Ablon, 1984).

NOTES

1. For a listing of LPA districts and chapters, see Appendix E.

2. There are a variety of membership categories in LPA: child, infancy through twelve years; teen, thirteen through seventeen years; young adult, eighteen through twenty-three years; regular, twenty-four years and over; auxiliary, average-sized relatives of little people; and supporting, doctors, professionals, and other close friends of LPA.

Family portrait with achondroplastic son, five years old.
Daniel Margulies. Reprinted with permission.

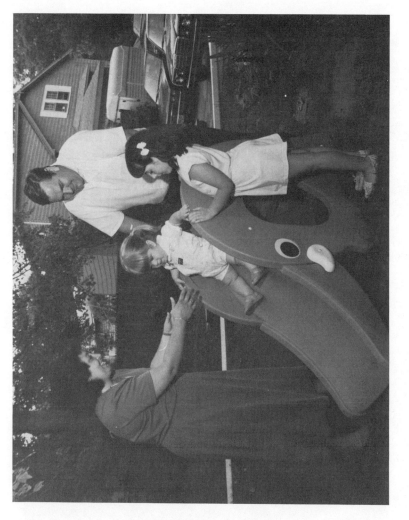

Family portrait with achondroplastic daughter, three years old.
Daniel Margulies. Reprinted with permission

Family portrait with diastrophic daughter, two and a half years old.
Daniel Margulies. Reprinted with permission.

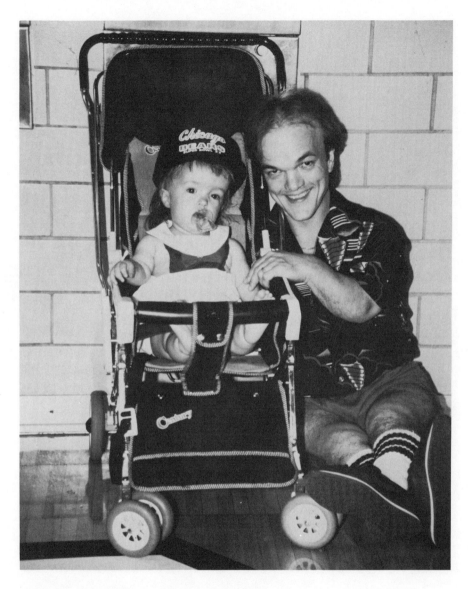

Achondroplastic father and daughter, eighteen months old.
Daniel Margulies. Reprinted with permission.

On scooter, eight-year-old achondroplastic.
Daniel Margulies. Reprinted with permission.

Bicycle check, cartilage-hair hypoplasia, fourteen years old. Daniel Margulies. Reprinted with permission.

Flying with dad, achondroplastic teen-ager.
Daniel Margulies. Reprinted with permission.

Shooting from free-throw line, achondroplastic young adult.
Daniel Margulies. Reprinted with permission.

Violin recital, achondroplastic teen-ager.
Daniel Margulies. Reprinted with permission.

Well-accomplished boy scout, achondroplastic teen-ager.
Daniel Margulies. Reprinted with permission.

Communications major shooting video, achondroplastic young adult.
Daniel Margulies. Reprinted with permission.

Married couple modeling their wedding clothes, achondroplastic young adults.
Daniel Margulies. Reprinted with permission.

Downhill skier, pseudoachondroplastic young adult.
Daniel Margulies. Reprinted with permission.

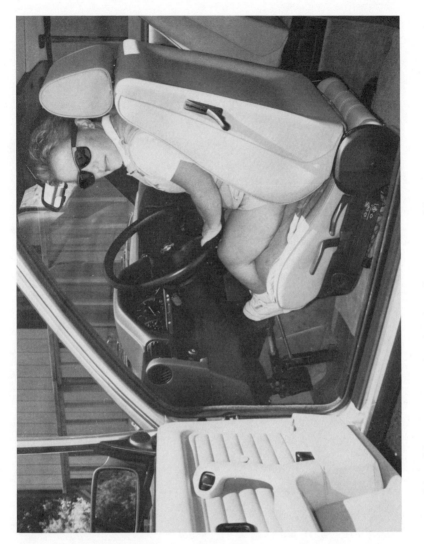

Automobile pedal extensions, cartilage-hair hypoplasia, young adult.
Daniel Margulies. Reprinted with permission.

Reservation booking agent, achondroplastic young adult.
Daniel Margulies. Reprinted with permission.

Chapter 9
Case Studies

Families adapt to the birth and presence of a dwarf child in varying manners in keeping with the multiplicity of differences in personality characteristics of family members; their culture, values, and attitudes; circumstances of family life; the characteristics and physical needs of the dwarf child; and many other factors. The following case studies are presented to illustrate some of this variation and how these factors come together. Details of family life have been changed to prevent immediate recognition of families, but not so radically as to alter the basic patterns of family adaptation that have occurred.

THE LAWRENCES

The Lawrence family live in an upper-middle-class suburb of a West Coast metropolitan area. Their handsome older brick home is on a winding, hilly road. The several cars parked, entering, or leaving their driveway reflect the busy comings and goings of an active and energetic family. Their home is full of fine old antiques that give a hint of the European parents of Bob and Nancy Lawrence and of the motivation that has guided them in pursuing a comfortable life style for themselves and their children. At the time of the first interview the Lawrences had been married twenty-one years. Bob was in his mid forties, and Nancy was a few years younger.

During the researcher's many visits to their home over almost a decade, Bob typically sat in a large red leather chair and Nancy moved around bringing refreshments or attending to their guests or questions or necessities surrounding their four children. The informality and warmth of this gracious couple is also apparent in their children—Hal, a handsome son in his early twenties; two equally handsome daughters in their late teens, Sue and Megan; and their attractive blond achondroplastic daughter, Pam, five years old at the time of the first interview.

Bob Lawrence, a highly successful businessman, is a self-made man. His energetic problem-solving attitude and his wife's practical warmth have clearly set the tone for a practical, productive "get with it" attitude toward their child's dwarfism. Bob succinctly states his philosophy: "My father stepped off the boat without ten cents in his pocket. He couldn't speak the language, and he wasn't educated, but he worked out a good life for himself. This country promises you opportunity, and you ought to be able to make it. People today have every opportunity. I believe you can do anything you set your mind to. You take a challenge, and you run with it."

Pam is seven years younger than Megan. Nancy was thirty-six when Pam was born. Her pregnancy with Pam was a totally normal one, and the birth went well. There was no hint that anything unusual was to occur. In contrast to the normalcy of this pregnancy and birth, the Lawrences' hospital experience was among the most negative. Bob recalled that situation:

Here everything looked all right, and the chief nurse told the doctor thirty minutes before we were leaving that she thought something was wrong with the baby; the proportions weren't right. So they sent her up to X-ray. Here I came to get Nancy and take her home, and I say, "Where's the baby?" And she says, "I don't know; they're taking X-rays." The doctor comes back and says, "Well, we think maybe your baby has achondroplasia, but we don't know." I say, "What's achondroplasia?" "It's dwarfism, but we won't know for a year," and he has his arms out and hands us the baby. [Pause] We walk out, and Nancy's hands are shaking. Here they tell us we may have a dwarf, we don't know what it means, nothing.

We weren't going to wait a year. We couldn't get much out of the hospital. We went to a private doctor, and that doctor said, "I don't know anything about dwarfism, but there is a doctor, a radiologist at Children's Hospital who would know." We got the X-rays with great trouble, and the doctor looked at them, and he said he was 99 percent sure that our child was an achondroplastic dwarf. Who knew what that would mean? We were really in a state of shock totally. This was the real problem—what would our life be like? What should we do? There we were, just cast loose. We went to the medical library at Bailey Center; we went to the county library, and we went to libraries all over, and all we could find would be one paragraph on dwarfism. I read everything, and after I read that we knew more than any doctors did. We thought this was very shoddy. Talk about trauma! What do you do with such a thing?

The Lawrences left this experience with a no-nonsense direct approach to find answers as quickly as possible to their many questions about the physical and social dimensions of their daughter's dwarfism. Within several weeks they had a solid diagnosis of achondroplasia from their local Children's Hospital. However, their personal acceptance had yet to come. Bob and Nancy frequently emphasize the importance of good communication within a family. They agree that their ability to talk to each other candidly about their apprehensions was of great value at the time of Pam's birth. Said Bob: "It was really helpful that we talked a lot right after Pam was born. We were upset, and we would talk and talk and talk. We've always rapped. Even now sometimes we talk until 2:00 or 3:00 in the morning. We talk about everything—philosophy, religion. I believe in getting it all out. I believe in talking out everything. If you feel something is good or bad, say it. We taught our kids that, and that's the way we all operate."

Although Nancy and Bob's parents were at first shocked and even denying of their granddaughter's condition, they soon became accepting.

Nancy had a number of friends who were particularly helpful. One called the Easter Seal Society and got the name of LPA from that agency. Their first contact with LPA was instrumental in their positive adaptation to Pam's birth.

Nancy: We did experience shock at first for about two weeks. But we pulled out of it right after Harold and Madge came over.

Bob: We got their number on Friday afternoon when Pam was two weeks old. On Saturday morning we called them. They said, "Are you busy tonight? If not, we'll come over." They rang the doorbell, and we looked at them and, you know, we'd never seen any dwarfs before. I cannot remember ever seeing another dwarf. I didn't know whether to laugh or cry when I saw them. We looked at them and thought, "Is this what our daughter is going to look like?" You know, when you look at a baby, she doesn't look that different. But this is what she's going to look like. We really had to come to terms with it—that our child was a dwarf. This is how she's going to be. But she'll be able to dress and work and live like other people. The only difference will be her size. In the course of that evening—it was just wonderful— we finally exhaled for the first time in two weeks. We saw that it wasn't a terrible thing. It wasn't a bad thing at all. Here were functioning, normal people who had jobs and families. It was as if we'd been in the darkness for two weeks, and all of a sudden they came in and we walked out into the light.

[Why do you think you were able to make such a rapid adaptation?]

Bob: I just don't look back. You make a decision, and just go with it. I just wanted to find out the answers. Here we were thrown a challenge, and I just wanted to find the answers to it. When Harold and Madge walked out the door that first time, all of our problems were over. That was it.

When Pam was five months old, the LPA annual convention was held in another part of their state, and Bob and Nancy attended. They were surprised and impressed by the many types of little people they saw and met. They found this "physical" exposure very helpful.

The Lawrences made a thoughtful search for the right pediatrician for Pam: "We knew a pediatrician whose kids had gone to school with our older kids. We asked him to take Pam. He's not an alarmist, yet he's quite sensitive to potential problems."

Pam had few children to play with in her neighborhood, but her babysitter had two children of her own in the house, and there often were also several other children there. Pam had uneventful experiences in nursery and preschool.

She is large for an achondroplastic child and early on was able to keep up with other children in games that involved running. She has experienced relatively few problems with teasing. At the time of their first interview, Nancy recounted this incident: "A few weeks ago, Pam came home and said that a boy had called her 'short pants'. So she said, 'Mama, don't sew up my pants so short now'. [Laughing] I always have to sew up her pants, and she's blaming my sewing of her pants for being short and his calling her 'short pants.' She really hasn't experienced anything bad yet."

The Lawrences made deliberate plans for Pam's first school experience. They were able to get permission for Pam to cross school districts so that she could have a kindergarten teacher that two of their other children had had in their own school years before. Nancy and Bob felt this teacher was outstanding and prepared children exceptionally well for their educational experience. Thus, they drove her to that school for the first year, and after that Pam attended a nearby elementary school.

At the time of the first interview, I asked the Lawrences how much of the time they were consciously aware of her dwarfism. The ambiguities of this consciousness are apparent in their answers:

Nancy: Oh we're hardly ever aware of it. You know, it's not something that we think about that much.

Bob: [quickly] Oh, no. We just treat her like anyone else. Of course, in the first year she was not all that different from anyone else. But it will probably change. I'd say 90 percent of the time I never really think of her as being a dwarf. We just think of her as one of the other kids. We kid her and we say to her, "You're a dwarf; you're little." We figure that we have to prepare her so that when she has these kinds of things said to her at school, she's going to be ready for it. She is not going to be thin-skinned or hurt by it. I wish you were here last night. Sue was sitting reading to her. She read her *Snow White and the Seven Dwarfs*, and she said, "You know, here's what you are, Pam, you're a dwarf. See these little persons?" This is the kind of thing we try to impress on her. But we just treat her like everyone else. It's not something we think about.

Pam's only special problems at school later had to do with older children in the third and fourth grades who made remarks to her. In fact, parents from around the country speak of teasing by children older than the dwarf child to be a common happening at school.

She said someone had said something to her, but she said "I ignored it."

[Have you taught her to do that?]

Yes. We've told her to just ignore it. Actually Bob told her to tell them to "go to hell," but I don't want her to get in the habit of doing that. But she seems to ignore any remarks, and it doesn't seem to bother her.

[Do people in this area say things to her?]

Oh, some people would, but not really. You know the people here are middle class, and they've taught their children not to say anything.

As an infant and small child, Pam had few medical problems. Although she has had a number of inner-ear infections, her pediatrician has reminded them that many average-sized children have inner-ear problems, too. When Pam was ten, the Lawrences took her to an annual LPA convention, and she was examined by a noted orthopedic specialist. He told them that she is as "ideal or normal a model of achondroplasia as you can have." By planning for annual consultations at conventions and regular checkups at home, the Lawrences feel confident they will be taking every available precaution against future problems.

While Nancy and Bob have relied heavily on LPA for knowledge and advice, Pam's interest in LPA has been uneven and changes from year to year. For example, when Pam was nine years old during one of our discussions of LPA events, her responses reflected the strangeness of a social reference group that was secondary to her daily world.

[Did you enjoy the convention?)
Pam: Well, when I go to LPA things I feel sort of funny. I get nervous before.
[How do you mean "funny"?]
Pam: I feel strange there.
[Do you feel strange when you go to parties with your friends?]
Pam: No, I don't.
Nancy: Well, that's because you see them everyday.
[If you stay at an LPA event for a long time, like a convention for several days, do you feel funny?]
Pam: No. And after I've been to a picnic for a few hours I don't feel funny.

At the time of the last interview, when Pam was in the fifth grade, she was not feeling a particular need for LPA. On the other hand, Nancy admitted that she and Bob were so busy with other family activities and responsibilities for their ailing aged parents that their situation may have influenced Pam's participation in LPA. However, as Pam has entered her teen-age years she has developed increasing interest in LPA and has met girlfriends there with whom she realizes she has a lot in common.

The Lawrences are very enthusiastic about LPA and are frequent hosts to Parents' Group social events.

[What is your family getting out of LPA now?]
Nancy: Well, LPA is for Pam now. But in the past it answered our questions and allowed us to think that this isn't a terrible thing; it's not a bad thing at all. We could relax. For example, when it took her so long to walk, we were really worried, and when we said "Gee, she's not walking," Roger [adult dwarf] would say, "Oh, don't worry about it. She'll walk in a couple of years. You should figure out that every other little person with her type of dwarfism walks—why shouldn't she?" And of course she did start walking pretty soon after that. But what I really needed was to see some adult little people and see that life was going to be OK for her. I look at all these little people, and it always makes me feel better. For example, I look at Roger, and I figure he can get a job and a wife. It made me feel so good to talk to Mary

[Roger's wife], too, because one day she was talking to Pam, and she said, "You know, if somebody could give me something to make me grow, I wouldn't take it. I like being little." Here some people think it's terrible, and yet here's someone who likes being little!

[At this point, how often do you think about Pam being a little person?]

Bob: Absolutely never.

Nancy: Well, I might think about it when we're looking for clothes or when we have a specific problem.

[In practical situations, then?]

Nancy: Yes, but that's it. We really don't think about it.

[Do you think Pam thinks about it a lot?]

Nancy: I think she may think about it where there's a physical hardship. For instance, when she can't get the shoes she wants. But I don't think she thinks about it a lot either.

When asked if Pam's dwarfism had made any differences in their family life, Bob initially stated that it had made no difference, absolutely none. Then he said: "I'll take that back. When she was about five or six years old, we really had to start thinking about her and start thinking ahead. Giving a lot of thought to her has made us more sensitive to the needs of handicapped people and toward a lot of things. I think it has made us more sensitive and caring towards people."

The Lawrences were asked whether they believe they have treated Pam differently than their other children. Have the other children exhibited resentments because of more attention possibly being given to Pam?

Nancy: I don't think we treat Pam differently, but the other kids say we do. I really think part of it is that she's the youngest.

Bob: No, not at all [Pausing]. But maybe, yes.

Nancy: You've favored her.

Bob: Well, maybe I have, but you know I think that that has to do with the fact that she was the last baby, the caboose. You know, you're so tight and strict with the first child, and then with the second you loosen up a little bit, and then when the last one comes along, you really give in. I think I've just given in. She has a way to get around me. She sort of cuddles up, and I don't know whether it's because she is such a loving, cuddling, warm child, but she sure knows how to get around me. I can't tell whether I favor her or not, or if I've been more lax because she's little or because she's the youngest. Things come up; like she's asked for an allowance. None of our other kids have had an allowance. Our oldest daughter said, "Over my dead body. You're not going to give her an allowance. You never gave any of us an allowance, and you're not going to give her one."

In fact, Pam's siblings have given her a lot of attention through the years, often including her in their activities because they find charm in her active and bubbling personality. Nancy and Bob have sensed no resentments stored up between siblings. They say further that they feel the open communication in their family tends to preclude such behavior. Said Bob:

You know, in our family we're very outspoken. We're close, and the kids say what's on their minds and that's it, like Sue did. But in another family the child may go away and stew over something and get mad over it. In our family we voice our resentments and that's it. We're a very close family. The kids seem to like to stay at home. The older ones want to live here. Sometimes we worry because they seem so close and don't go out. And another thing is that the other kids are older than she is, and they have their own lives.

Bob and Nancy have cultivated this close family spirit through their carefully thought-out approach to the rearing of their children. They set clear limits while also offering their children many options for their maximum development. They have planned family-centered activities that are both fun and enriching, such as family trips to Europe or Mexico, which they took as a total family group until their oldest children were committed to college or work responsibilities and they could not leave. Sometimes Nancy and Bob laughingly say that they cannot get their older children to move away from home, try as they may. They are, however, pleased and flattered that this is the case.

The Lawrences, as was true of most other families who were interviewed, emphasize the uniqueness of each of their children. Some are dedicated scholars, and others care much more about their social lives. Pam has always been a self-confident and outgoing child. She knows and is known by many people in her community and at school. In fact, Bob and Nancy are reassured by Pam's outgoing personality.

Nancy: I think that if you're less shy and you're more extroverted that you can handle things better. And things don't bother you. You know, you have enough of a problem being small, but when you're shy, then you have an additional problem. Pam is very extroverted and she's not shy about things and she'll speak up.
Bob: I don't care what anybody has or what they look like, if they can open their mouth and they can speak intelligently like anyone else.

When Pam was a pre-teen, the Lawrences felt that things had gone very well so far with Pam's social life. "She is invited to every birthday party. She really goes to a lot of parties. It's the teenage period to come that we're concerned about." They frequently commented that the major problems might lie ahead. Occasionally, Nancy gives voice to her apprehensions.

Nancy: You know, I look at my other kids, and they focus on every little thing—if their clothes aren't just right, or if their hair isn't just this and that. I look at these kids today, and if they're that sensitive about all that, I just don't know what's going to happen to Pam.
Bob: You can't worry ahead. You just can't worry about that.

Nancy and Bob describe their general coping styles as very similar.

Bob: Well, we both have a positive approach. Like health, for instance. Pam really has not had physical problems. But we're not ones who just run to the doctor with every little thing. When the other kids had something, we'd wait a few days to see if it would go away. We'd just take her for shots, and when she goes in for these once a year or whatever, she has her check-ups. We have a positive approach, and we're not looking for bad things. We feel fortunate that we have her. We have learned a lot, mostly through LPA. This is not a bad thing that has happened to us. In fact, I don't think this is anything. We just don't see any difference at all now.

Nancy: That's right now. Things may change later, but for right now everything is going well.

The Lawrences' attitude toward everything in their family life is a positive one, and they frequently express their gratitude for Pam: "You know I guess we're grateful. Pam has been a blessing to us. She's a charming person. And she's a joy to us. I guess I feel like if somebody should have Pam that it's good that it was us. Because we can afford special things, and emotionally we can cope with it. We don't think this is a terrible thing. We never perceived it as that. We look on it as a gift. It's a challenge, and we've jumped to it."

In the experiences of the Lawrence family, one sees a strong, positively motivated and structured approach to child rearing and family life. Both Nancy and Bob are practical, no-nonsense problem solvers. They have never spent time feeling sorry for Pam, for themselves, or their family. They very early began a search for "the answers" and went on from there to raise a confident and popular child who thus far has suffered little because of her dwarfism.

THE HARKINS

Leigh and Paul Harkins and their two children live in a two-story historic stone house in a semirural suburb of a large eastern industrial city. Leigh and Paul were in their early thirties at the time of the first interview, and their son Josh, an achondroplastic dwarf, was five. Leslie, their daughter, was three. Leigh and Paul are both quiet, highly organized, and private persons. Their demeanor gives no indication of any turmoil in their family life. No casual acquaintance surveying this handsome and elegantly dressed "model" family could guess the amount of heartache and problems that Leigh and Paul have experienced around Josh's dwarfism.

Leigh, a high-school counselor, and Paul, an accountant, met several years after they both finished college in the heart of the city on whose periphery they now live. They moved out of the city and expected to start their family immediately. However, they waited four years for the arrival of Josh, their first child. They were taking tests at a fertility clinic when Josh was conceived. Leigh had a difficult pregnancy and was told to stay in bed as much as possible. In retrospect, she believes the problems in her pregnancy were an indication of the difficulties that lay ahead.

I had a hard labor—eighteen hours. The baby just didn't come. Paul was with me the whole time. Finally, I delivered, but when I asked to see the baby, they told me I was "too tired." The obstetrician told Paul they were calling in a pediatrician. That should have been a key because he had told us weeks before that he would only call in a pediatrician if there was a problem. Paul was too tired to pick up on it though. They had called Dr. Raddison in the middle of the night, and he had come over, taken X-rays, and had gone to his office and read up in books so he could come and tell us about Josh in the morning.

When I woke up, I really wanted to see the baby, and I asked the nurse where the baby was. She left, and finally the obstetrician came in and said, "Well, his arms and legs are short." I asked, "Does that mean I have a deformed child?" "Oh, no, he's not deformed. The pediatrician is looking at your baby now." Paul came in, and we waited. All we had to do was look at Dr. Raddison's face, and we knew there was trouble. But he was very nice, and he said to us. "You have an achondroplastic child. That means he will be a dwarf, and he won't grow." We were very upset.

Paul had called their family and friends right after the birth telling them they had a "fine" baby boy. The news of Josh's dwarfism slowly trickled back. Leigh would not call anyone when she came home and finally had the phone disconnected. She vividly described this period:

I rejected the baby. I wouldn't nurse him. I had made all the preparations for nursing him, but no way could I nurse this baby. I told them and they gave me pills to dry me up. I didn't want him. If I could have gotten rid of Josh I would have, but I couldn't. What could I do? Here were my family and friends. What would they think of me getting rid of this baby? I had to bring him home. My mother came and stayed for a month, and she's the one who took care of him. I didn't do anything. Nothing. After my mother left, I would get up in the morning and bathe him and feed him and then put him to bed. And then I would go back to bed myself. You know, I just slept all day. Sometimes Paul would come home in the afternoon, and I would still be sleeping. I didn't know it then, but that was a sign of a profound depression. I just slept all day. I guess I was up during the night. Josh had the colic, and we had to give him this medicine, and he cried a lot, and he wasn't an easy baby. That was all we needed.

Leigh marveled at how "wonderful" Paul had been at that time because when she was so depressed, he was so positive. Paul also remembered this time vividly:

I put on a front, and I looked better than I felt inside. You know, it was like I'd walked into a room and someone closed the door, and I was in there by myself. If I'd had someone in there to show me around, it would have been better. I wasn't happy about it. This isn't what I wanted, but I felt like I couldn't walk away from him. He was my child. When the doctor told us about the baby, he said, "You will come to love him." I felt like we would love him.

Josh's grandparents on both sides were very supportive. They had all loved the husky laughing little boy immediately and accepted his dwarfism. The Harkins' friends by and large did also. Leigh noted that some people they knew said that God gave them Josh because they were such a perfect young couple. "Oh, what bunk that is," Leigh said indignantly and talked about the "silly" attitudes that people have. However, despite the generally warm and supportive network around them, both Leigh and Paul were very depressed and withdrawn.

During the first year after Josh's birth, Leigh went to two psychiatrists.

Leigh: A few months after Josh was born, I went to a psychiatrist in Haley Springs, and he was just awful. I went three or four times, and it didn't help at all. He finally told me I could put my child in Happiness Home, which is for retarded and developmentally disabled children. He told me that he thought I am a perfectionist and that's why I wanted everything perfect.

Paul: Well, I think you do care what people think. And you feel if you do something that's not right, people are not going to like you. And since Josh is going to be imperfect, people won't like him since he's imperfect. That's how you think they feel about you.

Leigh: Well, that doctor just wasn't helping me at the time, and my mother heard of someone in Woodlark. He's quite well known. I liked him very much. I went to him a few times. He said, "This is a normal mourning process. You are mourning the loss of your normal child. And you're just going to have to get used to this." And he said the process takes usually from one to two years and there wasn't anything to do about it but to get through it and that I *would* get through it. He said "You don't need to see me." And you know, he was right. It did take me about a year. And then I pulled out of it.

The Harkinses have had several years of marital counseling and also recently took Josh to a child psychiatrist for an evaluation. When Leigh sought psychiatric help for herself in her first year, she did not tell people about it. "I guess at that time I was more hesitant about telling people I had gone to a psychiatrist. Now I wouldn't think that much about it."

The Harkinses judged themselves to be "very happy" before Josh's birth and in anticipation of having a child. When asked the effect of the birth on their relationship, they stated that the birth neither pulled them apart nor brought them together. Leigh was more emphatic: "I just felt totally alone. I just felt totally by myself."

Daily occurrences kept Josh's dwarf identity and the disparities of size and proportion between Josh and other children of his age in the forefront of Leigh's consciousness. For example, several of Leigh's friends had babies at the same time Josh was born, and she continually was reminded of his differences. Once she went to the pediatrician's office, and several mothers were talking about how tall their children were and how long their fingers were. Leigh remembered that she was "just about ready to die" by the time she got to see the doctor, and she said to him, "How could you have me sitting in a room with those people?" "In fact," says Leigh regretfully now, "instead of looking at what a handsome little tyke he was, all I did was think about the things he couldn't do or how he didn't measure up. Part of what bothered me was that I knew that my child would have these terrible stares. I knew that through his life people were going to make fun of him, and he'd have this hard time. I just didn't want to have to deal with that. That wasn't the kind of child or the kind of life I wanted."

Throughout our early conversations, Leigh's preoccupation with Josh's differences contrasted with Paul's attempts to normalize their situation. For example, Leigh stated that once the doctor said something to the effect that he thought Josh's arms might be a little bit longer than those of most achondroplastics. Leigh said she just "seized" on that, because she was very bothered by the short limbs of the dwarfs pictured in LPA publications. She found pictures of dwarfs disturbing. In contrast to this, Paul said, "I had a brochure from the Human Growth Foundation, and it had a picture of an achondroplastic little boy standing by a couch, and he was really cute. It was a very nice picture, and that's what I kept in my mind."

The Harkins's second child, Leslie, was born less than two years after Josh's birth. Leigh had a normal pregnancy with Leslie and had an easy delivery. Leigh recounted that she looked at the doctor and said "Is she normal?" "Yes," he said, "She's a normal child." Leigh and Paul were both "ecstatic." They had a perfect child and felt they were complete. When asked if she then felt any differently toward Josh, she said, "If anything, I could love him more, because now we had the perfect child we were supposed to have." Three years after Leslie's birth Leigh returned at first part time and finally full time to the school counseling position she had left before Josh's birth.

The Harkinses in an early interview stated that they received good medical treatment in these first years. When their doctors did not know how to respond to their questions or deal with a problem, they would tell them this and refer them elsewhere. Thus, they were quickly referred to a local Children's Hospital. The pediatrician who saw them there was more concerned with their state of mind than with their child's condition. She suggested they see a social worker at the hospital, and they met with him several times. The hospital also arranged for a public health nurse who came weekly for six weeks. Leigh found her visits helpful and supportive.

The remembrances and recounting of medical treatment and attitudes toward it are often fraught with ambiguities and ambivalences, as is reflected by Leigh's differential accounts of their relations with doctors. While both parents initially stated their early treatment was good, several years later when Leigh was asked if she had experienced particular emotional responses at the time of Josh's birth, she stated "Well, I was sort of mad at the way the doctors handled it. In fact, I *was* mad at the way the doctors handled it, but I was not resentful or angry at anyone else."

Shortly after Josh's birth Children's Hospital told them there were specialists in dwarfism at a regional medical center, and they traveled there to see what more they could learn to better assist their son. Josh's identity as an achondroplastic dwarf was confirmed. Paul reported that the specialist called in "about ten" doctors and spoke to them in technical terms about Josh's condition in front of Leigh and Paul. Paul couldn't remember that the specialist talked to them at all, and felt the situation was "experimental." Although the examination did not cost them anything, Leigh and Paul felt the trip was of little practical value to them.

Josh had five doctors at the time of our first interview, and he saw each at different times of the year for specialized evaluations. Josh has been watched carefully for hydrocephalus. His head was larger than normal at birth, one factor in Leigh's preoccupation with his dwarfism. In his early years his larger-than-normal head caused him to be thrown off balance easily, and he frequently stumbled and fell down.

When Josh was seven, Leigh and Paul entered what they describe as a medical nightmare of conflicting opinions about two issues: whether Josh should have a shunt inserted to drain off fluid from his cranium, and whether he should have spinal surgery. One neurologist advised them that Josh should have a shunt inserted immediately. He said that Josh already was brain damaged by hydrocephalus and that the condition must be taken care of to prevent more damage. Another neurologist felt that although a minimum amount of brain damage had occurred very early in Josh's life, the condition had stabilized and could no longer be helped by a shunt.

Deeply troubled by these conflicting opinions, Leigh took Josh and his test results across the country to an LPA national convention, expecting that they could get a final judgement there. At the convention a specialist they saw examined Josh and emphatically informed her that Josh's spine should be her first consideration, not a shunt. He felt Josh needed close follow-up and possibly surgery very soon. Leigh went on to see other doctors at that same convention from the regional growth center they had visited six years before, and they advised her that Josh did not need the shunt, and they were doubtful that he would need spinal surgery, either. They recommended a specialist in another city, and he referred her to a doctor in their area to take X-rays of Josh's spine for him to examine. This specialist definitely advised against the surgery, feeling that such surgery would be premature at Josh's age. Josh then continued to see a local orthopedist every six months, who was referred by the growth center. The Harkinses felt they spent two miserable years embroiled in tests, examinations, and dramatically conflicting opinions centering around these two health problems.

The Harkinses gave a great deal of time and energy to investigating special preschools that might be helpful for Josh. Josh, like many other achondroplastic children, did not walk until he was almost two and a half years old. Because of the Harkins's concern about this, they took him to a special program for developmentally handicapped children and later to a special program for orthopedically handicapped children. They finally found a private preschool and nursery school that they liked. Following this, he attended a public school near them that was noted for its excellence. This, in fact, was one reason for their moving to the area before they had children. Josh's years in this school have been happy ones for him, although the academic standards are very high and he has had to work very hard to keep up with his peers.

Leigh feels Josh's major problem now (at age eleven) is his poor academic performance. In her judgment he has a learning disability. In reality Josh appears to be of average intelligence, and in his school work he has performed in an average mode. Yet Leigh feels that possibly early brain damage due to hydro- cephalus has determined a ceiling on his abilities. For several years Leigh spent hours daily helping Josh with his homework and preparing for tests. Yet this did not seem to help. For Leigh Josh's moderate level of performance symbolizes his differences and his inability to measure up to the high standards of what her child should be. Said Leigh: "I know I'm a terrible perfectionist. But I just think it's *awful* that my child has these problems. Somehow I think it's me. I see myself as the dwarf—I'm the dwarf that goes out every day—that people stare at. It's like I see myself as the person that has these learning problems."

Leigh admits that she has had her own insecurities in making her way through life. She feels she has always had a poor self-image and has always worked hard attempting to do well and overcome her insecurities. Having a child who is physically and, in her view, mentally different further exacerbates her own problems.

Leigh notes that Paul doesn't seem to worry about Josh's poor achievement in school. "He doesn't care how poorly he does in school, while I just have this awful need." In fact, many of the dwarf children in the families interviewed do average work in school. Parents are generally much more concerned about their children's social lives and personalities than academic achievements. Few take their children in for testing or even seriously speculate about their intrinsic intellectual abilities.

And Leigh herself reports that the therapist they have taken Josh to thinks Josh is "just fine": "She says 'Josh is a very happy child. He does average work. He's happy with himself; he has a good self-image. I think Josh is doing fine. Obviously, his dwarfism is bothering you a lot more than it's bothering him.' " Leigh realizes that on one level Josh is doing well and is happy. His differences reflect deficiencies in her own eyes only. Leigh acknowledges that there are other children in LPA families who do not excel in school and their parents do not worry about them. While on the one hand, Leigh manages dealing with a dwarf child much better than she did during Josh's early life, on the other, the problem of difference continues in varied guises.

Paul is considerably more satisfied with Josh's achievement. Paul said in an individual interview, "I know that Leigh feels that Josh could be better aca- demically. But I'm comfortable with him emotionally; in fact, I feel very good about him. I think how he is emotionally is more important than his academics."

In fact, Josh is a happy, outgoing child with many friends. Josh has mastered the logistical problems of school. In gymnasium class he has found limitations on his activities, such as in calisthenics and in climbing gym equipment. How-ever, he is realistic about his limitations and works out activities that are possible with his teachers. In some games Josh keeps score or is a score-card runner for competitions.

Leigh and Paul differ significantly in their awareness of Josh's dwarfism. Said Leigh:

Oh, gosh, I'm aware of it continually. Josh is not aware of it. I really don't think he even thinks about it. The therapist told us that. I don't think Paul is aware of it very much either. But I'm just aware of it all the time. I guess I think that's me. I see myself as the dwarf.

[Do you think people stare at Josh a lot?]

Yes, particularly when he goes new places. Sometimes he's hesitant to go out for that reason. Like last year his class made a trip to Washington, D.C., and although he wanted to get to see all the sights, he made all sorts of excuses why he shouldn't go. But I insisted, and it turned out fine. He had a great trip.

[When people stare or say things, does he come back and tell you about it?]

No. He used to sometimes, but I think he doesn't want us to know that people stare at him.

Paul, when asked about his awareness of Josh's dwarfism, said:

Oh, I think of it from time to time. For instance, today the school had a fair, and the kids and parents went, and I was making booths and stuff. Josh was doing things that he wouldn't have to do if he were averaged-sized. Probably there would be a lot of other things that he could do if he were average-sized that he couldn't do because of his stature—things that others do. It just happens at times that it does occur to me. It's sort of like a blink that goes by, and then you think about it. But sometimes I completely forget it. I might compare it to something like if it's raining. If it's raining, I notice it, and I realize automatically there are some things I can do and other things I can't do because of the rain.

Paul felt Josh was only aware of his dwarfism when he couldn't do things he'd like to do. He noted that Leigh is more sensitive to Josh's dwarfism because she's more aware of hurt and she's more aware of being stared at. ["Do you feel you're being stared at when you're with Josh?"] "No. *I'm* not aware of being stared at. It seems to happen more when Leigh is with him. I guess I just don't *see* it, and if I *do* see it, it doesn't bother me."

Josh and his sister Leslie are very close. Leslie is the quieter of the two children and often appears to be very dependent on Josh, not an uncommon situation for siblings of dwarf children. Leigh sees much of herself in Leslie, a shy child who is also a perfectionist.

When Josh was seven, Leigh and Paul were asked if they treated the children differently. Leigh felt they had:

Leigh: Yes, we've always told Josh that he's just great and that everything he does is great. I guess I feel like Leslie is going to make it whatever happens.

[What do you mean?]

Leigh: Well, Leslie is just an average child, so she can make it, but Josh will always have problems because he's handicapped.

Paul: Yes, I guess we do favor Josh and give him more attention.

[How?]

Paul: Well, we go to LPA meetings.

[What about on a day to day basis?]

Paul: I guess we do, I'm not aware of it but I guess we do. Sometimes I think we're more strict with Josh and other times I think we're more strict with Leslie.

Four years later Paul addressed himself to the same question with more detail:

Well, I treat the children differently because they are different, not because Josh is a dwarf. If I treat him differently, it's because he's a different person.

[Do you find yourself favoring Josh?]

No.

[Do you think Leslie thinks you and your wife may give Josh more attention?]

Yes, I think she does because she's said so. Leigh does spend more time on homework with Josh, and I'm sure Leslie would like to spend more time with Leigh. But Leslie also gets to do some things that Josh can't do, and I think that bothers Leslie that Josh can't do these things.

[Do you think maybe she has guilt about it?]

No, I've never thought about it in that way. I really don't know if it's guilt, but I do know that it bothers her. [Later] You know, you've really made me think about that.

Leigh observed that perhaps her expectations for Josh are too high, "I really want him to go to college and have a profession. I have the same expectations for Leslie, but she can do them."

The Harkinses heard about LPA several months after Josh's birth from another family with a dwarf child who lived in the village center of their community. The mother repeatedly sent Leigh and Paul LPA newsletters, but they could not bring themselves to go to an event for almost a year. With some trepidation they finally attended a regional meeting that was held about a two-hour drive away.

I walked in to my first LPA meeting [waving her hand around and down], and there were thousands of little people all around. And we watched them. And then it was worse when we got up to leave and they were all this short. We came home, and that was the last straw. The next day I called my cousin, and I said, "This is it. I have to give Josh away. I'm going to put him up for adoption. I can't deal with him. I can't deal with him, and I can't do it." Of course, I didn't give him up for adoption, and it got better after that.

About six months later, Leigh and Paul attended a Christmas party in the city, and that event marked the turning point for them. Leigh was beginning to pull out of the worst of her depression. At the party she met two other couples with whom they began friendships that have endured through the years. They visit and correspond with both of these couples, who live within a two-hour drive of their home. Both families have children within several years of Josh's age. The Harkinses feel that their conversations with these and other families proved to be the chief factor in their recovery to a normal life for themselves.

Although no regular Parents' Group exists in the Harkins's area, they attend all chapter functions where they expect other Parents' Group families to be present. When they first joined LPA some ten years ago, there were fewer than three other families in their area. Now there are seven families who attend at least sporadically. The Harkinses also attend regional meetings and have attended three national conventions. Josh enjoys LPA meetings and has several close friends to whom he writes and calls.

When Josh was five years old, I asked the Harkinses what they have gotten from LPA:

Leigh: A lot [emphatically]. The main thing is getting to know other parents who have the same problem. We just felt we were the only people in the world who had this terrible problem. At that time meeting others who also did was so important.

Paul: [separate interview] Getting to know others who had the same problem that we could talk to personally. [thinking] Actually it's not that we talk that much all the time about our problems, but it's just knowing there are other people. It has helped us to be more careful about choosing what we want for Josh.

When Josh was eleven, their answers to the same question changed as the functions LPA performed for their family had changed:

Leigh: Oh, LPA has been very valuable. At first, LPA was important for us; but now I think it's important for Josh. He likes the meetings, and he'll play with whoever is there even if they're not quite his age or size. I love to meet the families, especially the young ones. Maybe we can help them. When we started going, there were so few families, but now there are all these young families with babies.

Paul: LPA is just great. I feel very fortunate that we've had LPA, and we've been able to meet so many people. Also, I feel it's fortunate that Josh has a place to go and see himself. I think that's the most important thing now.

The Harkinses expect that Josh will be able to find dating partners and a spouse through LPA. When asked whether they would prefer Josh to marry a little person or an average-sized person, both said it would make no difference to them. However, Leigh was emphatic that she thought Josh should not have children because of the physical complications that Josh and many other dwarfs have and are able to pass on to their children.

Leigh and Paul differ considerably in their opinions of the difference that having a dwarf child has made in their lives. Leigh feels that Josh's being a dwarf has made no difference, while Paul feels the opposite.

Leigh: I really can't imagine any way our family life would be different if Josh was average-sized. I think I would be just as concerned and having the same problems if I had an average-sized son with learning problems. I'm just too much of a perfectionist, and this is the problem. I just can't see that anything would be too different.

[You can't imagine yourself out hiking or something like that?]

Leigh: Paul might want to do more of that, but not me.

Paul: (separate interview) Oh, I think that our family life would be completely different. I often think about this. I think I'd do a lot more things.

[What kinds of things?]

Paul: Oh, we'd be more physically active. I'm not active with Leslie since we can't do the same things with Josh, such as biking. Josh is interested in biking, but it really just wouldn't work, so we find things we like to do that do work. But if Josh were average sized, there would be a lot of other things we could do.

Josh meanwhile continues to flower and mature happily. Possibly, the negative effects of his mother's worrying and hovering over him are offset by the very positive tone of his same-sex parent, who attempts to spend as much time with him as possible. In recent years Paul has begun to coach the little-league team on which Josh plays.

The Harkinses have a solid marriage, despite the ongoing problems that Leigh often mentions. Although both Leigh and Paul share common goals for their family, their views on many issues concerning child rearing and their modes of problem solving differ considerably. Although both consider Josh's birth to be the biggest crisis in their marital career, their attitudes toward that event and toward Josh's impact on their lives vary greatly. Leigh's lingering worries about her dwarf son may indeed plague her forever. She said: "Oh the biggest crisis we've faced was Josh's birth. It certainly was the biggest trauma for me. It was absolutely terrible. I cried for two years. I look around at parents I meet in LPA, and no one has had as bad a time as I did adjusting to it. And I *still* haven't adjusted to it." Paul, on the other hand, is content with Josh's accomplishments and progress and the general nature of their family life.

When Leigh describes the agonies in the years following Josh's birth, she emphasizes that those bad times and feelings were in the past and that she is optimistic and generally cheerful. She says that she and Paul know that there will probably be some troubles to come, but they feel the "worst" is over. However, one suspects that new issues that arise may be perceived by Leigh as problems and might well reactivate her intense anxieties about Josh's dwarfism.

Paul also remembers those bleak days, but his view of the present is also optimistic: "Undoubtedly our biggest crisis was the birth of Josh and his being a dwarf. As far as I'm concerned, it was like walking through a door into a different world. It took a long time to get back to where the family is going." ["Do you think you're back there?"] "Oh yes, I think we're there now."

THE MACKLINS

Ed and Marge Macklin and their three children live on the periphery of a large suburban area. Their house, set off from a business street, is an old two-story shingle. The many rooms are cheerfully appointed in bright colors with antiques and craft items, many of which were made by members of the Macklin family. A bustling, active aura pervades this house and yard, often full of young people working on cars, visiting, and planning ventures for pleasure or business. Ed and Marge, a handsome, energetic couple, were in their late thirties at the time of the first visit. Ed is a carpenter and had been employed by the same company for fifteen years at that time. Marge has held a number of part-time jobs and also is a talented painter. Their three very attractive children were eighteen, sixteen, and fourteen. Their two youngest, Robb and Will, are diastrophic dwarfs.

The Macklins met through a community church group. Marge comments that she had had a carefree life before marriage. "So as for training as to how to handle two handicapped children—I didn't have any. You know, people say, 'Oh you must have a background for this; you're a wonderful person and all that.' Well, no, I didn't sign up for this course. It's not the plan I would have taken."

The Macklins married "young." Marge was seventeen and Ed was twenty-one. Their first child, Lisa, was born the next year. Two years later, Robb, their first dwarf child, was born. The Macklins observe that they both have always been healthy, athletic, and "wholesome" in their habits. Marge did not take so much as an aspirin before Robb's birth. They remember that on the way to the hospital they were hit by a car. Marge's labor pains stopped but started again at the hospital. Ed meanwhile dealt with the police.

Marge recalled vividly Robb's birth and her hospital experiences of the following several days. These experiences were detailed in Chapter 3 in the account of the second mother. Marge was given direct and indirect messages that something was dreadfully wrong with her baby. She was not allowed to see him for twelve hours and, in fact, was almost shunned by her nurses in their efforts to avoid her questions. When the doctor finally saw her, he stumbled over poor descriptions of the physical differences of her child. When she at last had the opportunity to hold the baby whom *she* thought was a beautiful baby, she was told she was not to be left alone with him.

I mean everything they did and said was so negative that I thought, "What do they think; I'm going to kill him?" At least I knew that he did have arms, he did have legs, and he did have feet. Even though they were turned in and crooked. I thought he was the cutest thing. And if you'd seen a birth picture of him, you'd know he was not the cutest thing. He was one baby that was not very handsome, but I thought he was beautiful. Maybe that was blind mother's love or something, but I thought he was adorable.

Although Robb's physical differences were very apparent at birth, the Macklins were not told anything definite about their child.

Years ago little was known about diastrophic dwarfism. We were told after Robb's birth that it was a fluke, one in a million, and that nothing would happen again. And that's the tale everyone was told. There was no central clearinghouse, no computers then. A doctor came out from the East who went to hospitals all over the world, checking for records of babies born with club feet. They picked up only about 140 in the world, so we knew it was a rare disease. Now you see more. I wonder if they're coming out of the closet or doctors are diagnosing it earlier, or if there is a resurgence of the problem.

They thought maybe our families crossed somewhere. So I started doing a family study and got old records from aunts. I really had a good time. Our families came from different places at different times. There was no occurrence of this before.

My grandmother would stretch his little legs and massage him, and we'd do all these things thinking they'll grow. And we'd hang him by his knees, you know, all these things, but I didn't do too much because we were happy.

Because Ed's hospitalization insurance did not cover the many extra expenses entailed at the time of Robb's birth, a friend suggested they contact Crippled Children's Services, which did assist them with some of the expenses. When Robb was six months old, his doctor at the local children's hospital suggested they contact Shriner's Hospital, so that they would have the benefit of prominent specialists even though they were without money. The doctor thought Robb's club feet should have been corrected by then.

We did take Robb to Shriner's, and we had all the top specialists in the field. As it turned out, they had worked with a couple of other diastrophics in the past and knew what to expect. But they still had "achondroplastic" on his chart, and no one ever told us he was a dwarf.

He was the cutest little thing. He ran around, and he always had casts on, and I just came to accept the casts and the braces. I thought what doctors do is take care of the problems that you see, and we don't worry about what we can't do. And that's good. Except you do have tendencies to think, "Now what's the future or the hope?" His chart said "achondroplasia," but it didn't say "Achondroplastic dwarf." And I got the dictionary out and turned to achondroplasia, and it said something wrong with the cartilage. Well, I knew that, so that didn't carry with it dwarfism. I don't know why, but for two years they never told us he was a dwarf. I always said, "Why do you think his arms and legs are short?" All I got was "umm."

Finally, at about two years old, he was having therapy with a physical therapist. She was very sweet. She was working on him, and I asked the old question, "Why do you think his arms and legs are so short?" And she said, "Oh well, it's dwarfism," and she went on about his being a dwarf. She didn't see my reaction was just to fall backwards, because to me dwarfism or being a dwarf was the troll under the bridge in "Three Billygoats Gruff." Not my child, you know. "Dwarf" had a very negative connotation to me.

The therapist also gave them their first information about LPA, and they went to their first event that week.

The physical therapist wrote out Roger's name and his address and gave it to me, and I jotted out a letter that day. Now that was like Thursday afternoon.
Sunday morning the phone rang, and Roger said, "Oh, hello," in a deep voice. I thought he must be one of their spokesmen, because I was sure they all talk like the Hobbit

people. He said, "We got your note. We're having a picnic at Roosevelt Park, and we'd like you to come." I said, "Well, yes, we'll be there." So we came around the bend, and they were down in a knoll. I said, "They look like the teddy bears' picnic." All these little tiny people running around. We went down, we parked, and we thought, do we get out or not? This surely isn't our son; I'm sure this is the thought of every parent.

When the Macklins first found LPA, there was no Parents' Group in the area. They attended regular monthly adult LPA meetings. They took Robb and then Will, although there were few other children present. Ed noted that when the first Parents' Group, then called the Auxiliary, began, there were real needs to be met of parents with young children, parents who had their "own set of hurts." During the first three years, the Macklins attended LPA meetings regularly. After that, they attended sporadically, usually bringing their children along.

Marge and Ed have considered LPA to be an important therapeutic resource for themselves and their sons. And in fact, they have consistently argued that the expenses surrounding LPA events, such as the national convention, should be deductible from their income tax as a legitimate medical expense. Said Ed: "From this parent's point of view LPA is not just fun and games. Taking our children to LPA activities is a serious effort to develop our children socially and to help them to deal with their handicap. The money we spend to go to conventions is medical money. We use it to deal with problems."

By the time Will was born, Marge was twenty-three. At that time they had made their third move, in pursuit of job opportunities for Ed. They had joined an interdenominational Bible class and through it found that they were even closer in their communication with one another than before. Said Ed: "When you open yourself, when you're opened spiritually, you're not afraid. You know that God is in control and your life is an open book. You don't have to hide anything then. Your communications can open with another human being." Their ability to talk out and share their problems has helped the Macklins through many difficult periods in their marriage.

At the time of Will's birth Marge remembers asking the doctor in delivery whether she had a boy or girl and if there were orthopedic problems.

Poor guy. I heard him stumble around. He said, "Oh, his feet turn in." I said, "Praise the Lord. He's the same as my other." And I really didn't feel upset. I had planned on it being a girl and healthy, but I wasn't disappointed. It almost would have been more trying had he said, "He appears to be OK. Now we have to wait to see what all the tests say!"

Where most people would say, "Oh, well, that will never happen to me," we always say "Hey, it's going to happen to us. If it's going to happen, it will happen to us." They called in an orthopedist, and he treated Will for two months, and I kept telling him that he was the same as Robb because it was obvious. I mean, he had all the same earmarks. And the guy kept saying, "No, no, he's not diastrophic." And I said, "Well, yes, he is." Then we moved over to Shriner's again. Robb had had his first foot surgery at ten months at Shriner's, and Will was six months when he went in for surgery on his feet. Still, his feet have never been as corrected as Robb's.

Medical Experiences

The experiences of Ed and Marge with the medical establishment have been complicated and varied. Many of their experiences are chronicled through scrapbooks with pictures of the boys in their hospital beds. Robb and Will have had more than thirty surgical procedures beginning with work on the Achilles tendon as infants to later foot, hand, leg, and hip surgeries. These procedures have spanned almost twenty years and many hospitals, health plans, and specialized Shriner's orthopedic services. Both boys have spent months in hospitals and missed semesters of school attendance because of surgeries. One year both boys were in the hospital for four weeks from Thanksgiving until after Christmas, strapped on gurneys for twenty-three hours a day. Years and seasons could be remembered by hospitalizations and surgeries. Summarized Ed: "These children have had over thirty major operations and hundreds and hundreds of clinical tests, and we go in for regular hospital checkups, and just hundreds of those. I can't even count those things. Broken bones don't count. Colds and coughs and flu and pneumonia and all that doesn't count. So just to give a picture, you can't possibly discuss a thousand hospital visits. It's just irrational."

The Macklins have also visited two major medical centers for problems of dwarfism. In general, their experiences have not been positive ones. Ed and Marge seem to be able to remember and distinguish carefully each experience. They met a prominent specialist from a major growth center at a national LPA convention when the boys were young. He invited them to come as a family for testing to evaluate their children and to attempt to understand better the parental union that gives rise to the recessive condition of diastrophic dwarfism. The whole family was given numerous tests over a week period. Said Marge, "Saliva, skin tests, skin biopsies, fingerprint tests, toe print tests. I mean everything. We were just dissected." The Macklins were given copies of all their test results and were told that *they* were eminent experts on diastrophic dwarfism. They felt that the many doctors who examined them had utilized their sons' conditions to confirm successful procedures or identify bad examples of timing and types of surgeries.

When the boys were in their early teen years, Ed and Marge took them to a second prominent growth center where their sons were X-rayed and photographed "from head to foot." In this case the only benefit (and one that they had demanded) was that they were able to keep a full set of X-rays for each child.

The ambivalence of the Macklins toward their sons' medical care is very typical of that of parents interviewed. However, because the Macklins have two dwarf children and have had many diagnostic and surgical experiences, their feelings are intensified. On the one hand, they have felt compelled to search out every avenue of medical expertise that could possibly assist their sons' complex and physically limiting limb complications. In the course of this seeking they feel they have encountered the best medical care available and many doctors whom they have liked and respected. On the other hand, they feel they have been used by the system. Their accounts reflect their perceptions that their sons have often been unnecessarily exposed to duplications of tests and procedures for the aggrandizement of individual doctors and for the storing of more and more data not actually needed for the diagnosis or treatment of their individual children. They feel strongly that doctors should share more information on all levels, thus avoiding duplication of troublesome tests and procedures.

Social Life

Robb has been gregarious and outgoing from early childhood. He has always been surrounded by friends in whatever neighborhoods the Macklins lived throughout the many geographical moves of their marriage. Marge notes that they always made their yard a "refuge" for the neighborhood children so that she would know where her children were. "And not because of the handicap necessarily. A lot goes on in backyards and houses; so it was better that the children be here!"

Although there tends to be a common perception expressed in LPA Parents' Group discussions that children benefit from living in one area through their growing-up years so that they are known and not continually new oddities in changing neighborhoods and schools, the Macklins take issue with this point of view. They feel that the necessity of meeting new people and learning about new places has contributed toward the confidence and positive self-images exhibited by all of their children. "We decided moving would be an adventure, and they always got excited about it." This point of view was exhibited in Ed's comments about dining out:

I changed my attitude about going out to eat. We really were on a tight budget there for a while when we were first married. I went ten years without a vacation. To go out to eat and spend that extra couple of bucks was just not in our budget. We just could not afford to go out. And yet, all of a sudden, we started seeing the value of the kids being exposed to going out and building their self-esteem, so I had a new attitude altogether about eating out. We weren't going out to eat just to eat. I was willing to dig deeper for spending money if I approached it as this definitely was therapy. The public exposure was therapy for us and the kids. It helped us adjust to the whole attitude of being confident in a public exposure. Even on that basis alone, I think that we should be able to have the IRS take this as a deduction or, better yet, a tax credit. We were never allowed to call public exposure treatment, although some kinds of handicapped children do get forms of treatment like this now. Of course, I never deducted it.

In fact, the stares have seemed to bother Ed and Marge more than the boys, who have made very positive adjustments to their physical difference. In describing their irritation with public reactions, Marge commented:

The staring didn't bother me as much because I decided not to see anyone. And even to this day when we go shopping, Ed sees everybody we know. I never see anybody. And it's not because I'm ignoring them. It's terrible, I just never see anybody. Even if we don't have the kids, I just don't see other people. I had to train myself to do that. Ed only went shopping with us once a month, if that much. He just isn't into shopping. Whereas I was out all the time. I always had the kids with me. And my biggest thing was I had Robb in braces walking around, and he would tell people he was a genius when they'd talk to him, because he looked like he was two and here he was four or five. So he could handle his own game. Will was usually in casts.
[Was it mostly adults or children that would stare?]
Oh, adults are the worst ones.

Both Robb and Will have been aggressive in their achievements in school and in developing work opportunities. Both have been proficient in repairing cars since their mid-teens. Most of their training came from auto-shop courses at school. Cars and trucks in varied states of repair line the driveway and street in front of the Macklins's house.

Ed: Robb has about six projects going. He's got that master cylinder off, the wheel cylinder off, the brake lining off, and the speedometer cable apart. He's also doing major body and fender work. He was out there with his hat and goggles drilling away.
Marge: He went out and rented a huge hydraulic machine on that rainy, stormy day. Here are these two little guys on crutches. My Mom went out and was looking through the window, and she said "Oh, that's pitiful." I said, "It's not at all. Those are two boys who are learning to do body work that we can't do!" Finally, I went out and asked if I could help, but they said, "We've got it all fixed."

Robb arranged for his first job when he was twelve years old. Marge remembered this vividly:

Robb said, "I want a paper route." I said, "Paper route?" And my mother said, "You can't let him do that." My father said, "There's no way he could do it!" And I said, "Well, we know that, but he doesn't, so let him find out." So Ed drove him over and got him out of the car. He went over to the man. All the little boys were lined up, and there's Robb shorter than everyone and on crutches, and he says, "I want a paper route." I guess the guy was shocked beyond words because he didn't say anything. They hired him, and they gave him the route that was one of the main streets here, which is all the stores and the businesses. That was good because it's just up one side, then down the other. We'd have to bring the papers in because they were too heavy for him to carry, and then I'd go back to bed and he would kind of fold those papers, and it would take forever. I used to feel bad, but I thought, "No, I'm not going to feel guilty enough to get up and take away his full responsibility. I finally would get up to take him out in the car and he threw the papers.

Robb thereafter talked his way into many jobs, often conquering the doubts of potential employers about his physical abilities.

Robb's popularity was first publicly manifested in his being chosen as the speaker at his junior-high-school graduation. His mother commented that he was a "mouth piece: that kid has got mouth." Robb always verbalized extremely well.

Robb attended a school for the handicapped during the sixth grade because he needed physical therapy. He then was mainstreamed into a regular junior-high-school program for half a day and then for full days. When he entered the city high school, he knew a large number of students because he had attended two junior high schools. He was very popular in high school and was elected vice-president of his senior class. He also attended school dances regularly and danced every dance. For short periods he could stand without his crutches, moving his head and body. Said Marge: "Oh yes, he gets out there. He does all the fast dances. He doesn't hold anybody, but you don't have to these days."

Robb also excelled in wrestling, a sport enjoyed and safely engaged in by many dwarf children and young adults. Diastrophics often ambulate on crutches and may build particularly strong shoulders in this manner. Wrestling allows them to benefit from this strength. Ed described Robb's wrestling technique:

He lays his crutches down, and he can barely walk without his crutches. He just hobbles out there, and the crowd just gets so quiet you could hear a pin drop. Because he's just barely standing there, they think, "Is this guy going to break in two if you touch him?" And then the guy drops the handkerchief or whatever he does to start. Robb goes immediately to his knees, which is not a take-down. Now a take-down is where you get the other guy down. So they usually can take him down, but you can't turn him over. They can never pin his shoulders down. So that's why he doesn't lose by someone pinning him. Actually, he helps the team out because a lot of times another team will have a weight class they forfeit; if they don't present a guy, they take a loss. Robb can go in and he's almost a guarantee when he goes in there, because he's never pinned. Nobody of his weight can pin him.

Will, however, was always quieter and less aggressive at making friends. Nonetheless, he found that with his necessity to be in a wheelchair at school following surgeries, other children would run out to help him for transfers or for any complications with his wheelchair.

Robb frequently utilized a wheelchair for mobility on his geographically dispersed high-school campus. At home and for social situations he ambulates with metal crutches. Will typically uses crutches at all times, rather than a wheelchair. Robb, an adventurous and ambitious doer, through the research period was always busy making plans, for example, to buy a motorcycle, for car repairing, and later even for small real-estate investments. Will, on the other hand, is a characteristically silent, orderly, and deliberate young man and was often in his room reading or looking at his stamp and coin collections. Even when young, Will was a quiet, thoughtful, and complex child.

Marge: We used to try to analyze Will a lot. Some mornings he would wake up and he wouldn't speak to us.

Ed: I think Will was more angry at his situation than Robb was.

Marge: Without knowing why, from the time he was born even.

Ed: This has got to be something inner. From the time he was born—"I am in this footcast." At two days old he was in a cast. So here's this young kid with no social training, trapped in this cast, and he just couldn't stand it. He cried for five years straight. Robb would more or less go along with it.

Robb and Will showed little interest in LPA until recently. Robb's interest in LPA began with his graduation from high school, when he began to think seriously of LPA as a resource for dating. He then began his participation in local, regional, and national meetings. Will's pattern of active participation appears to be following this same course. Robb has become one of the eligible young bachelors of LPA on the national scene and has a busy correspondence with many young women around the country, some of whom have visited him and stayed in the Macklins' home.

Parents' Attitude Toward Their Sons' Dwarfism

The Macklins' attitude toward their sons' dwarfism and toward life in general has been largely determined by their strong and encompassing faith:

Ed: Our basic approach is that every single individual has intrinsic worth. He doesn't have a worth because he's able to do something or he looks a certain way. He has worth of the God who has created him in the image of God. . . . It kind of boils down to a choice factor. You can choose to be bitter or better. Faith is a choice factor. It is not a commodity we take in a bottle or anything else. Every man chooses. If we hadn't made the choice, we would be a problem for society in that we would have been very bitter and stopped working so hard and even gone on public assistance.

Marge: Once I spoke at a women's club I belong to, and people came up afterward and said, "I never knew you had any problems." They were just amazed. And I consider that really great that they have not picked up that I was wanting to cry on their shoulder.

Ed: Self-pity is really something that we like to wallow in as human beings.

Marge: And it doesn't mean just in the relationship to the boys. Because usually it comes out in some other place. You know, whether it's, "I don't have a new couch, and I wanted one," or some other dumb thing, but it all stems back not to the boys as much as just I'm not being treated with preferential treatment like I think I should be.

Ed: Self-pity leads to depression and anger. If we were involved in self-pity or anger, what we're doing is telling the world, "World, I'm unable to handle this problem, so I have to resort to self-pity and anger." And so what we've done is admitted that we can't handle it from the beginning, but God can. There's no shame in admitting your weakness. But in admitting your weakness and trusting God, then you use God's strength.

[What kind of philosophy have you tried to give your kids, and what kind of philosophy *have* you given them?[

Ed: We've tried to give them truth. The proven test would be if you could read one of Lisa's letters from college. I would consider how she relates back to us in her letters as a real success. Also Lisa has a really good grasp on the truth—that all problems are opportunities. And that we have to translate them from problems to opportunities. You know, you just don't have to live with them as problems. I'm trusting my faith with our boys. Our philosophy is life and wisdom. The Bible says that people without understanding are ruined. And so I've tried to be understanding to my kids. The main thing is that if they screw up, I'm not going to reject them.

Marge: I think that families are able to handle the problems of their children's dwarfism not just because of LPA or because of dogged determination but because of a spiritual realm. . . . It's not that we had to leave and marry someone else and try to start a new life, nor did I have to make a trip to Hawaii to get away from the problem. Instead, during this problem, we can have peace of heart, which I think is what everyone's looking for.

The Macklins have developed a no-nonsense pragmatic approach to their children's physical differences and limitations, viewing these as challenges to be continually encountered and met through life.

Ed: Once in kindergarten Robb came home and said, "A kid down the street called me a dwarf." I think our philosophy starts to come through when we say, "So what? You are a dwarf. That kid's got a good set of eyeballs." Later on, he would answer, "I'm just as big to me as you are to you." We see the truth, and we're not going to let the world put a negative tag on truth. We don't have to let linguistic symbols rattle our beads. See, I think at that point if we had gotten indignant or something like that or put a negative connotation to it, it would have been bad. We've met some LPs that have gotten indignant. That's where we've differed. I think that we approach the fact that our sons are dwarfs as a matter of fact, and I think it's helped them to think like they're normal. They know they have some physical problems . . . but they have an attitude that I'm a dwarf—so what?

Marge: I've always said to Robb since he was really little, being six foot is not going to solve any problems you might have, so don't use that as an excuse. And this is true. I mean none of us are whole people.

Ed: Do you know what it means when you're six foot six? It means you're six foot six. And that's all it means. It doesn't mean you are honest or lovable.

Marge: I think that's helped him get over some barriers. And one time he even told this Rotary Club that he spoke at that he even was kind of glad that he was a dwarf.

[Does he use the term "handicapped?"]

Marge: Yes, and we try to use that because so many people take offense at "handicap," or "dwarf," or "midget" or all these things. I decided, "Hey, if the world is going to use those terms, then we do, too." The kids call themselves "crips." Their friends call them "crips," too. It depends who says it.

The Macklins have consistently attempted to impart their philosophy to their children. They have given them an unswerving and positive statement of their value as worthy, talented persons, a value that cannot be threatened by their short stature. Ed and Marge also emphasize that benefits of special strength may develop because of their physical difference.

Ed: Our children think highly of themselves. We've treated them as people of worth, and loved them constantly, and have been open about their condition. "You are crippled, you are dwarfs." We have not attached a negative connotation to it, and their friends like to be around them, because they can see that they're inspired. When the average person becomes crippled or something like that, he feels like his worthiness has decreased. But the reality of it is that these boys' worth has increased. Because they are, at this point in their life, able to encourage a lot of other people who suffer in other ways. And encouragement is worth a lot these days.

Marge: We've pointed out to them, too, that everyone is handicapped in some way and to be personality handicapped is the worst. Or emotionally handicapped would be greater because you can't handle what is going on. When Robb was in junior high, we had a talk because he was feeling he wanted to be in some sports. He said, "Mom, if I wasn't handicapped, I could be the best football player there is. I know every play." He would tell me about how he knew in his mind he could play football or basketball if he just wasn't crippled. And I said, "I know you really want to get into sports, but you have an advantage." I was thinking fast. I said, "You have a real advantage. Most kids are going to spend all their time in little league in baseball and football and all that stuff. Then they're going to get to college and go away from home, and they're going to have to deal with life's problems, thinking and working out their personalities and all." This isn't always totally true, but it is true in a lot of cases. I said, "To think you have had so much to go through already. You've had to deal with each surgery; you've had to know who you are; you've had to deal with being handicapped and how to overcome that with your friends, and you are so far ahead of them that when it gets to college time, man, you are going to be head and shoulders above anybody. Because in college or out in the world how many businessmen sit around and talk about how many ballgames they won in high school? That's just a nothing experience, and you'll forget that experience!"

In the midst of a conversation about their sons, Ed pointed to Will across the room and said partially to him as well as to the researcher: "Like this guy here. He has no problems. He has the world by the tail. He's a good student; he's good-looking; he's got a lot of things going for him. If he ever bellyaches about one thing, I'll kick him right in the rump. He's got more going for him than most people. He has no cause to bellyache but has much to be thankful for, like us all."

Ed and Marge are very proud of the accomplishments of their three children. They often speak of the differences in personality between the three. They feel that normal sibling relationships exist between their children despite the inordinate number of medical experiences that the family has undergone. They sometimes speculate about the importance of these for Lisa.

[How is Lisa's relationship with Robb (brother closest to her age)?]

Marge: I would call it normal because we've never picked up any guilt that she's carried. I know this has happened in some families.

[Did you have to give him enough special attention as he was growing up that it may have caused some early resentments?]

Marge: Well, so much of it was time, and I know that an important commodity was given to him just going to the hospital. She was dragged along. She's only twenty months older. So here, just at the time when as a cute little two year old she was walking and all that stuff, she should have had a lot of attention, and I look back now, and of all the things, I see her time was spent in the hospital. Sometimes it was every day. At least twice a week we went for cast changes, and he would scream and holler, and she'd sit in the waiting room. I think that she's really come away pretty much unscathed. Because of the person she is perhaps. She's a very strong individual, and now she is training to be a nurse. Whether she's a strong person because of growing up with two handicapped brothers or not, I don't know. But when I see them fight, or argue—and they've done this all their life—I'm thrilled to death, because I feel like that's a normal part of growing up. I didn't invent the idea, but it's my feeling, and I've adopted it. If kids are raised in a family where they don't have sibling rivalry or fighting among themselves, they're not going to know how to handle the world outside. And I think that kids, if they fight a lot when they're younger, learn how to deal with people; they learn how to bargain, how to get out of situations without fighting. So that when they get into school, they know how to negotiate. I don't like the word "manipulate" because I think that's a negative side. But negotiating is good, and I've seen that happen with them. Robb irritates her some, but I think that's good. I don't want her feeling sorry for him, and I've never picked that up. In fact, she went with me when I spoke one time at a church group. She said, "You know, it's so funny to hear that story because I don't really think about them being handicapped."

Working out a life style rewarding for all the members of the family has been a major concern for Marge and Ed. So much of the Macklins' life style has been shaped by the exigencies of their boys' condition that it would be extremely difficult to attempt to assess the importance of dwarfism in their life.

We always had the idea when we first married, being athletic type of people, that we were going to do backpacking and lots of camping and horseback riding and all kinds of things. And we have not been able to do that. Lisa's very athletic, an excellent tennis player and all, and we've not done those sorts of things with her because we don't want to neglect the boys. And so we've tried to pick activities that have been family oriented. We've done a lot of camping. We can swim, and we make trips. Once we threw the kids in the Volkswagen bus and went to New York City, camping along the way. And all of us slept in the car, and we ate in grocery stores instead of restaurants. We didn't have extra money to go, but we found it, and I think that's been something that's held us together. We have the same philosophy of life that experiences are priceless, and you never have extra money for an experience, so you might as well just do it. You know, put it on the charge card or something. Do without something else.

The chief social support that the Macklins have had has come from Marge's parents and their church friends. Marge's parents have helped sit with the children during some of their many doctor and hospital visits, and they made many hospital visits with them. Marge said they also have helped with "spiritual and emotional strength." Other support came from their Christian friends in the way of prayers and hospital visits. They were also helped financially by their church with a substantial money contribution from a collection when Will was born.

The siblings of both Marge and Ed live in other parts of the country, busy with their own growing families. Family members on both sides of the Macklin family are unusually tall, with most being over six feet. Robb and Will enjoy family occasions with their taller cousins, and their height is often an issue of joking. Marge notes that Robb tells his friends: "If you don't do so and so, I'll get my [six-foot] cousin to come out and pound you into the ground."

At the close of the research period Ed had worked for the same carpentry contractor for more than twenty years. Marge had held a number of part-time jobs. Lisa had become a nurse and was married. Following a year of post-high-school education, Robb held a good job in a high-technology field, and Will was in college working on a liberal-arts degree. Marge and Ed's constant cheerfulness belies their years of medical problems and financial sacrifices. Their positive philosophy toward life and pragmatic attitudes have helped their sons deal with their physical problems and develop solid, healthy self-images. The three children interact with love and respect for one another. The Macklins represent a family who have adapted in an unusually vital and positive manner to a potentially disruptive and severe physical difference.

Chapter 10
Conclusion

"When you're a little person it's not like you're really handicapped; you're just sitting there between the two worlds."
Mother of dwarf child in "Little People" (Krawitz and Ott, 1982)

FAMILY ADAPTATION

Families with dwarf children must adapt not only to a physically different child, but to a mythic stereotype and the accompanying complexities of having a dwarf for their "real life" son or daughter. The parents in this study had seen few, or in some cases, no dwarfs before the birth of their child. Thus, they had no idea of what their child's life would be like or what would be the implications of having a dwarf as a family member. An initial major task for many was the work of normalization and demythicization—to learn if and how their child would fit society's expectations. Once they determined that their child could lead a "normal" life, their anxieties about their child's difference notably diminished. Many parents also wondered if *they* could deal with a lifetime of potentially problematic societal responses to their child. These are substantial burdens for new parents. The situation was understandably more difficult for first-time parents because of their inexperience in the normal and expected routines of child rearing.

Becoming parents involves the taking on of new roles and role behaviors— assuming the tasks of parenthood and learning the knowledge base attached to these roles. All persons in our society become partially socialized into these roles through absorbing common understandings of appropriate behavior and watching role models in the persons of their own parents, siblings, friends, and characters in the media. Thus, at the time of birth expectant parents are at least partially prepared for parental roles; however, these roles are as parents of the child who fits our normative standards and expectations. Ordinarily, we have no preparation for the tasks of parenting different or exceptional children, and adaptation to this role may be fraught with a resistance to the novel and unexpected, as well as to the realistic logistics of the situation.

Families respond to the challenge of raising a dwarf child in keeping with features of the individuals involved and of the family system. Some of these features are the individual personality characteristics of spouses and other children, the relationship between spouses, the value system of the family, the period in the life cycle of the family, the ordinal placement of the child, the sex of the child, and the specific physical condition of the child and its attendant considerations.

Extreme shock was the universal initial response of parents when informed about the birth. Mothers tended to react more emotionally than fathers. The initial shock and related extreme distress lasted in some cases weeks, in others months. In a few cases the distress lasted for several years. Four circumstances tended to mediate, diminish, or even end the shock and distress/depression: (1) prior first-hand experience with physically or mentally different children; (2) a very practical problem-solving orientation, usually held by both parents; (3) a strong religious or spiritual ideology; and/or (4) introduction and exposure to LPA.

In two cases mothers said they had had first-hand experience with children with severe differences, which provided them not only with an introduction to the practical problems faced by such children and their parents, but also with the knowledge that such children can thrive and lead meaningful lives with appropriate attention and treatment. This kind of experience constituted a form of elementary socialization to the role of "parent of a dwarf child."

A practical problem-solving orientation may transfer the energies of parents from negative emotional reactions or paralysis to an active constructive and concrete search for answers to problems and the motivation to proceed on the basis of these answers.

A strong religious or spiritual ideology may provide a theory about the cause of the birth, which makes it more understandable and acceptable to the parents and may interpret the situation for them in a manner that provides a philosophy for dealing with it. Such a philosophy might also be the basis for a practical, no-nonsense problem-solving approach. For example, the Macklins' strong religious belief system carried with it a formula for dealing with their children's dwarfism similar to that employed by the Lawrences.

Initial shock and distress occurred with the same severity among assertive problem solvers as among less assertive and effectively managing parents. In some cases this shock and distress lasted for months, but when the distress was replaced by action, the management of the continuing challenges in the dwarf child's life was carried out very efficiently and with enthusiasm. For example, many of these assertive problem-solving parents are energetic leaders in LPA

Parents' Groups across the country. A mother whose initial reaction was almost as severe as that of Leigh Harkins is now a prime resource for other parents on the national level of LPA.

A circumstance which assisted family adaptation was parents' contacts with LPA. Meeting individual adult dwarfs and other parents through LPA and participation in Parents' Group activities were major factors in parents' acceptance and understanding of their child's condition and future possibilities. Because most parents had no knowledge of dwarfism or the life style of dwarf individuals, they had urgent reality questions to be addressed. Solid and constructive answers to parents' immediate questions about the social future of their child greatly assisted in allaying their anxieties and contributing to a positive adaptation experience.

Certain individual personality characteristics of parents, such as basic insecurity, poor self-image, lesser problem-solving capacities, value systems that reject the dwarf child offhand, or basic disagreements between spouses may serve to hinder realistic acceptance of the child and his/her condition and the chances for rapid or successful adaptation for parents. In extreme cases these characteristics may even preclude adaptation throughout the parents' lifetime.

AMBIGUITY AND MYTH SURROUNDING DWARFISM

In the case of dwarfism, a physical difference carries with it historical and cultural baggage that has created a mythic stereotype. My work suggests that much of the ambivalence and problematic behavior exhibited by parents, medical personnel, the general public, and by dwarfs themselves is caused by a confusion generated by having to reconcile realistic similarities and differences, mythic stereotypes, and cultural images. Dwarf characters popularized on television, in films, and in children's games present dwarfs as creatures in caves, exotic "sidekicks," or persons with special or magical abilities. Smallness in size is a disvalued characteristic in our society, and may carry with it expectations of persons who are perennially childlike. The fact that dwarfs are ordinary persons with normal intelligence who work, play, and manage families and the business of daily life is less known to the general public. Likewise, this fact is less known to new parents of dwarf infants who must adjust to the generic issue of physical difference and to the specific issue of having a dwarf child as a family member.

Ambiguities surround the dwarf child. His difference may be interpreted in widely varying manners. He/she is different, yet not *so* different. Although profoundly smaller than their peers, the potential of dwarfs in most aspects of life is the same. Although physically very divergent, dwarfs typically are not mentally impaired, nor are they severely disabled or limited in their activities. A major contradiction surrounds an individual whose physical person is dramatically different, yet who shares the same dreams, joys, and goals as others in our society. Julie Rota, a member of LPA, eloquently articulated this dilemma: "We are a contradiction in packaging, for encased in our small bodies are not small minds, not small needs and desires, not small goals and pleasures, and not small appetites for a full and enriching life" (quoted in Ablon, 1984, frontispiece).

The ambiguities inherent in the condition and status of "dwarf" in American society foster ambivalences and multiple perceptions and understandings for both child and parents in terms of daily life experiences and adaptation. These ambiguities are played out in various areas of the child's career. Some of these are in parental response at the time of birth, in parents' perceptions of their child as a dwarf and in relation to their other children, in child's and parents' perceptions of their child in relation to "handicapped" status, and in the child's social life.

Ambiguity is created and nurtured by doctors and nurses at the time of birth through their mode of presentation of the child and the child's condition. Sometimes parents had to wait long hours or even a day to see their infant. Communications typically contained awkward and negative messages about the child's condition and future: "She's going to be short," or "she'll have short arms and legs, but she's going to be all right." What does this mean to a new mother? Once parents were told they had a dwarf baby, their hunger for information to resolve their immediate questions was satisfied in more cases through contacts with LPA than through communications with professionals.

Many parents expressed their ambivalences about their child's dwarfism in their statements surrounding their consciousness of the child's differences. After saying they are "never" or rarely aware of the child's dwarfism, many then immediately verbalized ways in which the difference is highlighted. Parents were often unaware of the simultaneous and conflicting character of their statements. Others pinpointed practical issues that bring the child's identity to their awareness. Some said that this occurred rarely, and others identified circumstances that would have to occur regularly not only in the everyday life experiences of their own child, but in those of the other children in the study as well. This suggests a differential incorporation of this switching phenomenon as a sometimes conscious, yet unconscious occurrence in families.

Related to this issue is the perception of parents regarding whether they treat their dwarf child differently from their other children. Many said no but then almost immediately said yes. Again, some parents pinpointed the differences in their behavior as hinging on realistic differences in the dwarf child's ability to engage in specific activities or to carry out certain tasks around the house. Most parents would prefer to think they do not treat their dwarf child differently, thus asserting the basic normalcy of the child. Parents who are comfortable with their child's dwarfism appear to have adopted a "different but not special" philosophy which is espoused by Little People of America. Essential physical differences must be recognized, then the logistics and social implications of these differences at home and at school must be carefully thought out and negotiated. More ambiguity surrounds the endeavor in the case of dwarfs than in the case of persons with many other conditions whose limitations are more definitive.

Another area of ambiguity and ambivalence for parents is around the issue of "handicapped" status. Although parents do not hesitate to put their children into special schools or courses to their advantage, in most cases they do not think of these children as "handicapped." The use of facilities for the handicapped tends to be expedient without involving a self-labeling process for children or in labeling by parents of their children. The near normalcy of dwarfs appears to preclude this labeling, even when children are primarily enrolled in courses or facilities for the handicapped.

The popularity of many dwarf children constitutes a complex area for exploration. In point of fact, dwarf children are often very outgoing and have many friends. They are widely known. In some cases this may be due to their ready identifiability and some of the mystique around dwarfism. They have employed "mascotism". Psychologists have also suggested that for a variety of reasons many achondroplastic dwarfs appear to be happy and jolly. For example, Money stated: "One is tempted to believe that whatever it may be that produces achondroplasia also produces a 'happiness hormone.' Almost without exception achondroplastic persons are endowed with the personality traits of chronic cheerfulness, optimism and confidence" (1967, p. 136). Other researchers have taken issue with Money's findings (for example, Brust et al., 1976; Ablon, 1984). Far from being caused by a "happiness hormone," this style of social adaptation, allied perhaps to that stereotype of the "jolly fat person," may well be another dimension of the mascot syndrome. Many children are quick to learn that their difference can be mediated by an extra-pleasant personality. As one father was noted to say:

I have often thought how Bob might be different if he weren't a dwarf. . . . Bob is a very nice guy. I wonder if he weren't a dwarf, maybe he wouldn't be so nice.
[What do you mean?]
He wants to be liked. You know, it's not typical of these teen-agers to say, "I'm a nice guy. I want you to like me. What can I do to make you like me?" That's not what these kids are like. Bob has always been this way. He's overcompensated very well for his size. He's very outgoing.

Some parents have tried to raise their dwarf child as any other child, in some cases to the point of denying the child's dwarfism. In those instances some children have been normalized to the degree of making their stature a very minor consideration. Those children may be popular in spite of their dwarfism and, in fact, without using it. However, both types of children, those who have used it and those who have denied it, encounter severe difficulties when time for dating comes, despite their former popularity and continuing same-sex popularity even in the teen or dating years. At that time no difference is a "special" one, exempt from the demands of social conformity.

SOCIAL SUPPORT SYSTEMS

During the last decade, clinicians and researchers from varied disciplines have emphasized the significance of social support systems for the emotional and physical health of individuals. Caplan, a psychiatrist, defined a support system as "an enduring pattern of continuous or intermittent ties that play a significant part in maintaining the psychological and physical integrity of the individual over time" (1974, p. 7). The most common support systems are made up of family and friends. Support systems may function in a variety of ways, helping in practical matters and offering emotional support. Support systems buffer individuals against stresses and "negative feedback" in their environments. If individuals do not receive systematic and positive cues about their behavior or signals enabling them to anticipate the friendliness or hostility of others, they will not feel safe and valued and are more at risk for illness. Support systems protect individuals from physiological and psychological consequences of exposure to stressful situations (Cassell, 1974; Pilisuk and Parks, 1986). For persons with special or unusual circumstances or conditions such as dwarfism, the naturally occurring support systems—relatives, friends, church groups—may not be able to offer the specialized support services needed. Literally thousands of self-help organizations, today commonly called "support groups," have been created for persons with special needs.

Many researchers have pointed out the advantages for parents of physically or mentally different children of joining self-help or support groups or in other ways gaining access to other parents "in the same boat" (Katz and Bender, 1976; Lieberman and Borman, 1979). Featherstone (1980), from her own experiences as a parent and as a professional and from the experiences of others, discussed the value of support groups in which parents can candidly express their feelings about their problems:

They become actors instead of victims. The chance to meet other parents with the same concerns and problems, the shared work and sense of accomplishment, the opportunity to give and receive help, all chip away at loneliness. . . . Catherine Lederman, reflecting on her time in our mothers' group concluded that this was the one setting that freed her to describe her feelings with total honesty. To the rest of the world she played a role. "I was acting, starring in a movie about myself." In a small group of other stricken parents, with the encouragement of a social worker who shared their fate as mothers of handicapped children, she could be herself. In different words, other parents echoed her feelings: The rest of the world does not really want to hear about your problems; even if you tell them, they will not understand what it is really like. Here in the group you can be honest, expose your sorrow to others who share it, and receive comfort (p. 66).

Featherstone noted that some parents are too exhausted from caring for their own families to join groups or work for larger entities. Others do not believe in talking about personal problems with strangers. However, Featherstone noted that any sort of contact with other parents can help parents with their feelings of isolation.

Darling (1979) stated that a very large number of the parents of handicapped children whom she studied had established friendships with other parents of handicapped children. Some of these belonged to parents' groups and others met outside of groups. Darling observed that parents were particularly helped by knowing they were not alone and by also seeing other children who had even worse problems than their own child. Parents learn how to solve problems more effectively as they gain by the example of others. Darling noted that as a result of their group interaction, some parents changed physicians or explored various treatment modes even against the advice of professionals.

Darling interpreted the friendship of parents of children with widely differing conditions to mean that societal reactions are similar for a variety of medical conditions. Parents of dwarf children rarely join parents' groups for other physically different conditions. Dwarfism appears to be sufficiently specialized in both practical and symbolic terms that parents are able to receive the assistance that they want and need from LPA. This may likewise reflect the fact that parents do not think of their children as handicapped in any general sense of this term.

I have elsewhere (1984) described the ways that LPA serves important social, psychological, and educational functions for its adult dwarf members. The Parents' Groups also serve important functions that allow parents and children to realize that dwarfs can have rich and fulfilled lives and that parents can cope successfully with problems that initially may have seemed unique and unconquerable. Parents learn about medical and social problems and how to deal with these, and both children and parents are provided with comfortable and comforting communities of peers.

Why do only a fraction of families with dwarf children belong to LPA? Many families have never heard about LPA. Until the past decade little was known about LPA by the lay public or even by professionals. Individuals and families found their way to LPA primarily through chance encounters with someone who had heard about the organization or through infrequent media coverage (Ablon, 1984). Today LPA is a well respected resource, and doctors, nurses, genetic counselors, and social workers in many metropolitan areas routinely refer to LPA. In rural or less-populated areas where there are fewer members and chapters, the organization is less known.

Why do families who learn about LPA not come? My conversations with health personnel who see the general population of these families suggest those who do not come fall into one or more of the following categories:

1. Families who deny their child's dwarfism and his/her differences. These families resist seeing other dwarfs because they cannot face up to the image of what their child will look like as he/she grows older. If they were to join LPA, they would be admitting their child's dwarfism and, in their perception, resigning their child to a community of little people.

2. Families who are members of ethnic minorities with strong cultural or language barriers. These families do not feel comfortable in a largely white middle-class group and may not expect to receive help from such a group. They are less likely to attend any mainstream voluntary organizations.

3. Families who live in small, often rural or suburban communities where they are well accepted and their child is protected from curiosity or other types of responses common to exposure in large urban populations. Adult dwarfs who grew up in such protected milieus describe relatively secure early lives in these contexts (Ablon, 1984).

4. Some very large families who may be able to surround the child with a cushion of normalcy, emphasizing that he/she is treated like everyone else. In this immediate environment the difference of dwarfism might be lost; however, the child still must deal with schoolmates and the larger world. This model of protection is more successful in a small rural community.

5. Families who are not joiners and will avoid any group. These families are determined to make it on their own in relation to all problems.

6. Pathologically maladjusted families who might keep their children at home as much as possible. This type of family tends to make an unhappy loner of their child.

Denial of the child's dwarfism would appear to be the most frequently mentioned and obvious reason that parents would choose not to come to LPA or to other support services. Indeed, denial is a common and familiar response of those with dwarfism and their intimates. Most adult dwarfs whom I have interviewed characterized their lives before coming to LPA as years of denial. Basic social needs, often extreme loneliness, finally brought them to LPA, some sooner and some later, after they had learned about the organization (Ablon, 1984). It may well be that parents who do not come to LPA know so little about dwarfism that they cannot clearly perceive what the needs of their child *are*, even if the parents *themselves* do not feel the need for assistance.

Members of Parents' Groups sometimes talk about the period between the time they heard about LPA and the time they contacted the organization. Some of these parents also were hesitant to see other dwarfs, yet once they had gained this window to their child's future, they were greatly relieved and felt extremely fortunate to have found LPA. The benefits reported by parents in Chapter 8 have allowed them to feel that they have prepared themselves in the very best way possible to cope with the special challenges of child rearing and to assist their child in the most informed manner. Parents of dwarf children who do not participate in LPA cannot anticipate what these challenges might be; decision making about health, school, and social issues that will arise for any dwarf child are made in a void of information.

To consider health issues alone, appropriate specialty care is necessary for diagnosis and such treatment as corrective surgery. Members of LPA are provided with access to the best medical care in the country and often without charge. They benefit from a highly sophisticated informational network constituted by professional opinions and parents' experiences. Whatever fears and concerns they have about their child's health, they can at least feel they are doing the very best to help him/her. The advantages of LPA for other areas of the child's life are mirrored in this dimension of health.

INTERACTIONS WITH PHYSICIANS

Dwarf children and their parents, like most others in our society, seek out medical attention with a need to ask questions, receive treatment, and to feel generally cared for with dignity. Medical science has made major strides in improving the general health and mobility of dwarf individuals. However, many dwarfs and their families have yet to find satisfactory interpersonal relationships with medical personnel commensurate with the technical excellence of the field.

Most families in this study who described the circumstances around the birth of their child expressed considerable anger at physicians who typically proclaimed that the parents had a normal baby and then had to reverse their statements later, and at physicians who they felt were abrupt, awkward, and insensitive when they informed the parents about their dwarf child. Sometimes doctors kept parents waiting for many hours or even days to see their babies. Darling (1979), Featherstone (1980), and DelCampo et al. (1984) discussed the dissatisfaction and anger experienced by parents of physically or mentally different children with physicians. Featherstone (1980) stated:

The medical profession is the largest single target of parental anger. Parents complain, first of all, about the manner in which their doctor (or doctors) presents the initial diagnosis. "Hardly anyone," writes Janet Bennett," is pleased with the way she found out about her child's handicap" (1974). Parents complain about the doctor's reluctance to believe them and to respect their burning desire to know what is really wrong. Parents complain about cowardice and equivocation. They complain that doctors swing from one infuriatingly unrealistic extreme to the other. They complain that hospital staffs treat them without tact, consideration, or even common humanity. I could cite instances from nearly every volume I have read (p. 36).

However, Featherstone also suggested that parents are extremely sensitive at this time and may be taking out their shock, dismay, and guilt at handy targets: "Personal experience has taught me that anger is not always proportional to the crime. I can remember flashes of irritation that seemed unjust to me even at the moment I experienced them" (p. 38).

DelCampo et al. (1984) stated that twelve of fourteen families in their study reported negative experiences around diagnosis and the feeling that the doctors were "cold and insensitive." For example, one mother reported that her doctor's initial statement in discussing the diagnosis was: "You know the dwarfs that you see in a circus, well that's what your child will be like" (p. 81). The authors observe that parents are undergoing stress and anxiety when they see doctors about their children's growth problems. Because of this, they may be listening "selectively" and only hear seemingly insensitive aspects of the doctor's remarks.

The authors suggest that medical personnel should be aware of this possibility and be more cautious in their contacts.

Stace and Danks (1981a), reporting on an Australian sample of parents, noted that twenty-two of seventy-six parents were dissatisfied with the "abrupt and inadequate" manner in which they were given their children's diagnoses. The authors stated: "It is recognized that persons receiving bad news can transfer their negative feelings onto the newsbearer, but not withstanding this, several parents seemed to have genuine cause for complaint. Some doctors appeared tohave projected their own negative feelings towards dwarfed people in their counseling" (p. 169).

The accounts of parents of dwarf children are remarkably similar to those given by parents of other different children. For example, Darling's account (1979) of a sample of parents' experiences at the births of their physically different children describes instances of procrastination at showing mothers their babies, avoidance of the mother and baby by doctors and nurses, telling parents about their child in a highly awkward and evasive manner, and cryptic minimization of the child's differences. Said two mothers in Darling's study:

I remember very vividly. The doctor did not say anything at all when the baby was born. Then he said, "It's a boy," and the way he hesitated, I immediately said, "Is he all right?" And he said, "He has ten fingers and ten toes," so in the back of my mind I knew there was something wrong. . . . [In the morning] he didn't come up with the other babies, and I kept saying, "Where's my baby?" When I think back on it, everyone was hush-hush, saying "There's nothing wrong, he'll be up."

He was born on Tuesday, and by Thursday, I was suspicious. Nurses would come in and ask to see pictures of my first child; then they would leave quickly. . . . The baby wasn't eating well, and once when a nurse came in after a feeding, I told her I was worried. She said, "It's all due to his condition." I asked, "What condition?" but she just walked out (p. 129).

The parents in Darling's study indicated that the greatest interactional difficulties they experienced around their children were with doctors and other medical personnel. Darling stated: "Doctors' technical competence was questioned less often than their lack of compassion, concern, and understanding of parents' feelings" (p. 152).

As one component of her study, Darling (1979) interviewed fifteen pediatricians about their attitudes toward treating children with birth defects. Darling's interviews with doctors produced responses that clearly supported the parents' views. For example, almost all of the doctors stated they did indeed procrastinate in telling parents the truth initially because they were uncomfortable with the situation. Some felt that parents were not ready to hear the truth:

"Birth is a traumatic experience. For 24 to 48 hours after birth the mother has not returned to a normal psychological state, so I just say everything is O.K., even if it isn't."

"Mothers are too emotionally wrought up, they don't understand or listen anyway" (p. 205).

Darling stated that doctors appear to share similar attitudes toward physically and mentally different persons as do the lay public in this society.

The pediatricians' responses presented by Darling provide a very congruous and illuminating perspective on the kinds of negative behavior that was reported by parents of dwarf children. The parents in my study have few complaints about actual treatment or surgery procedures, and in fact, the technical aspect of medical treatment is rarely criticized. Parents' complaints center around the social-relationship aspect of medical care or the area that in the past was called "bedside manner." Parents frequently feel that they and their children are treated impersonally and sometimes experimentally.

There is no doubt that parents experience considerable anxiety around their medical encounters and also have feelings of frustration at medical sciences' inability to "cure" dwarfism or deal with some of its more serious problems. Some of this anxiety and frustration may be contained within the negative feelings toward medical personnel, who in many cases are able to do little to help dwarf children.

In general, families have had the most positive medical experiences with physicians who are the most knowledgeable about dwarfism. For example, members of the LPA Medical Advisory Board typically are personally interested and cordial in their relationships with parents and children. Many of these physicians see patients regularly for examinations and consultations at no charge at the annual convention. Likewise, contacts with staffs of these physicians' institutions are positively evaluated. This opportunity for physicians and patients to come to know one another within a special context helps to produce an exemplary style of interpersonal relations. Ideally, a model of health care could be developed that would incorporate the same dimensions of sensitivity and personalization outside of the convention context, a context that is not available or feasible for the great number of doctors in our population who see persons with physical differences.

IMPLICATIONS FOR CLINICAL CAREGIVERS

Although medical science cannot "cure" profound short stature, it is possible to avoid unnecessary additional trauma for patients and their families. A number of implications for reducing trauma became apparent in statements from interviews and from Parents' Group discussions:

1. The manner of the physicians' first informing parents of the birth of a physically or mentally different child is of the *utmost* importance in alleviating or escalating the level of trauma parents will experience. A general sensitivity toward and tolerance for difference maintained by physicians allow them to give crucial initial and subsequent communications in a straightforward and constructive manner. Parents should be provided with security about the future of their child in this first disclosure.

2. Most physicians see few or no dwarfs in the course of their careers. They have received no specialized training in treating them. Thus, in most instances doctors should refer families immediately to specialty physicians and hospitals to ensure that dwarf patients receive accurate diagnosis and appropriate treatment. Some types of dwarfism require a scheduling of surgeries that may begin at infancy. Determining the correct diagnosis at the earliest possible time is essential for children's good health and mobility.

3. Physicians at specialty centers should encourage more sensitive and effective modes of communication with patients and families, who often are especially sensitive and vulnerable at the time of contact. Parents repeatedly reported that the specialists who examined their child spoke primarily to their teaching associates in the parents' presence and essentially ignored parents and children and their anxieties. Parents feel they are considered almost irrelevant to their child's condition or future. Families often left examinations knowing little more than when they came except that they had provided yet another body and set of X-rays and test results for the clinical and research sciences. This situation resulted in feelings of exploitation or the "guinea pig" syndrome. More effective communication would also include the explanation of specific reasons for a physician's advocacy of a certain procedure. Parents could then deal with conflicts of professional opinions in a more informed and less emotional manner.

4. General pediatric facilities and specialty centers should build into their programs social workers or other types of counselors or therapists sensitive to, even if not greatly knowledgeable about, problems families and individuals face related to short stature. Counseling is particularly crucial when families face decision making or crises concerning serious surgeries or other life-or mobility-threatening events. Counselors could also act as coordinators or troubleshooters to facilitate families' access to ongoing necessary clinical, psychological, or social services that may be needed.

5. Physicians and other professionals should refer families to Little People of America, The Human Growth Foundation, and/or to other relevant available support organizations at the earliest opportunity. The assistance provided by group participation and through personal contact or telephone peer counseling is consistently reported as a critical source of help and education for parents confronting the experiences of rearing a dwarf child.

IN CLOSING

All societies establish cosmetic prescriptions for conformity to positively valued appearance and "beauty." In our society few compromises are allowed in meeting these prescriptions. Those persons who do not fit societal expectations in any major regard may anticipate a lifetime of challenges.

Families with dwarf children confront the fact of the enormous importance of height as a symbol and augur of social and economic success in our society. From the moment of their child's birth and on, families are given messages from medical personnel, relatives, friends, teachers, classmates, and a curious and sometimes ridiculing public that there is something gravely discordant about their child. Beyond the practical issues that attend profound short stature, parents and children must cope with special meanings and attitudes that surround dwarfism. These meanings and attitudes are rooted in our cultural values and institutions—social, educational, and medical—and in our tendencies to rely on stereotypes in attempts to pigeonhole or categorize people and qualities. Understanding these cultural dynamics and their implications for daily life may assist professionals in working with families and aid parents in planning more effective coping strategies for themselves and their children.

Appendix A
The Sample

Twenty-five families from across the country who were members of LPA Parents' Groups were interviewed about their initial responses to the birth of their child and various topics relating to the physical and social development of the child, medical problems, and aspects of family life associated with the presence of a dwarf child as a family member; approximately two-thirds of the children in these families were achondroplastic, and the remaining one-third were diastrophic or other less common types of skeletal dysplasias. The ages of the dwarf child or children in these families ranged from less than one year to twenty-one years. A subsample of six families who have participated regularly in Parents' Group functions were interviewed repeatedly over a six-year period, from 1977 to 1983. Two-thirds of the children in these families were achondroplastic, and one-third less common types. The dwarf children in the six families at the time of the first interviews ranged from five years to sixteen years of age. My discussions with the twenty-five families suggest that the experiences of these six families are very typical. These six families would be classified as spanning "middle class" by definitions of residence, occupation, education, and life style. All lived within their same respective pleasant suburban neighborhoods during the six-year period they were followed. Five families were interviewed three times or more and one family two times. Interviews occurred in their homes and characteristically lasted four hours or longer, often over the dinner table. Family happenings were also followed through conversations with family members at ongoing LPA events during the interview period and for several years afterward. The families were always cordial in responding to my requests for interviews and were open and thoughtful in answering questions. Both parents were interviewed in each family contact. Spouses were not hesitant to disagree over specific issues, but in most cases it was apparent that they had made compatible and consistent adjustments in working out a common or joint pattern of family management.

Appendix B
Impact of Child Disability and Physical Difference on the Family

RESPONSE TO THE BIRTH

During the past twenty years, a large and significant literature has developed on family—typically parental and, even more frequently, mothers'—responses to childhood disability. The following presents a sampling of this literature. Particular attention has been given to family reaction to the birth and diagnosis of the handicapped neonate. Mori (1983) summarized much of this literature. He observed that for expectant parents the birth of the perfect child is their gift to each other and the symbol of their love and marriage. If the child is less than their expectation for perfection, they may be psychologically devastated.

Cummings et al. (1966) noted that most parents are profoundly affected by the attributes of their children. Variations in physical or mental characteristics that are considered "deficiencies" or "handicapping" conditions may seriously influence parents' perceptions of their own identity and self-worth, bringing forth expressions of anxiety, loss, and depression. Parents' own fulfillment and evaluations of themselves thus may be at stake in the persons of their children and the normalcy for the family. Individual studies have explored parental reaction in a myriad of physical and mental handicapping conditions. Survey articles (see, in particular, Power and Orto, 1980; Zucman, 1982; Mori, 1983; and Fortier and Wanlass, 1984) have lumped together for generalization purposes such conditions as blindness, mental retardation, or congenital deformations ranging from cleft palate to congenital heart disease, even though the degree of disability and adhering stigma may range widely between conditions.

Solnit and Stark (1961), in an early classic article, described the grieving process of parents who are confronted with the loss of the perfect child. Bristor (1984) reviewed the subsequent literature on this subject and detailed a more recent grieving model. Documenting the sequences of such common parental responses such as grief, shock, and fear has been one area of preoccupation in the literature. Many authors noted similarities between the stages of individual response to disability first postulated by Wright (1960) and response to imminent death as classically proposed by Kubler-Ross (1969). Sequences of stages of parental responses have been proposed by Hay (1951); Koegler (1963); Grays (1963); Gordon and Kutner (1965); Kirk et al. (1968); Steinhauer et al. (1974); Buscaglia (1975); Drotar et al. (1975); Pearse (1977); Menolascino and Egger (1978); and Marion (1981). The stages proposed vary as to number, names, sequence, and precise nature of parental concerns. Power and Orto (1980) suggested the following synthesis of reactive patterns from the previously mentioned literature:

$$\text{Trauma} \rightarrow \text{Shock} \quad \begin{array}{c} \text{Denial} \\ \\ \text{Grieving} \end{array} \quad \rightarrow \text{Depression} \rightarrow \text{Adjustment}$$

Rosen (1955) presented a series of behaviors rather than emotions exhibited by parents. These are awareness of the problems, recognition of its nature, search for a cause, search for a cure, acceptance, and others.

Several models have been proposed to study the family system of newborns and their families (Belsky, 1981; Belsky and Tolan, 1981; Skrtic et al., 1983).

In a remarkable study of the mothering of thalidomide children, Roskies (1972) presented a psychosocial working model for the presentation and analysis of her data. Stated Roskies:

We formulated, then, a working model in which, basically, we hypothesized that the birth of an obviously defective child could create a very specific type of crisis. The essence of the crisis lies not only in the narcissistic injury to the parent, or the need to mourn the wished-for normal child (Solnit and Stark, 1961), but also in the fact that the existing child embodies a basic contradiction. To put it in its crudest terms, living children are taken home, cared for, loved, and identified with, while dead children are buried. The child who is living but defective is an unknown combination of the two. Thus, immediately, the mother is confronted by the dilemma of deciding whether her child is normal enough to induce the mutuality of mother and child, or whether he is so defective that he no longer arouses the emotions and responses habitually aroused by a child. In practical terms, this conflict may be expressed in the decision to attempt to integrate the child within the family, institutionalize him, or kill him.

Unlike many other forms of family crisis, however, we hypothesized that this particular form is usually neither resolvable through time, nor terminable by a single decision. Unless the mother is able to kill the child, or consider him as totally dead, she is faced by a growing and developing child who is partly normal and partly abnormal.

In common with mothers of all children, the course of development exacts a continuous process of adaptation and readaptation of a changing mother to a changing child. In this sense the rearing of a disabled child resembles the rearing of a normal child. But for the mother of the disabled child, the normal developmental crises are intermingled with an additional continuous crisis. The unclear and constantly changing amount of normality and abnormality embodied in the handicapped child makes the mothering of such a child an adventure in two different cultures. At times, the rules of the culture of normality are more relevant, while at other times the rules have to be taken from the culture of abnormality. Often it is difficult to predict in advance which would be most relevant. And frequently the choice involves an overt conflict between two equally valid but incongruent possibilities (pp. 20–21).

Roskies offered a sensitive, insightful, and moving description and analysis of mothers' adaptation to limb-deficient children.

Many researchers have noted that problems begin with the initial anger of parents being told in awkward or negative ways about the physical or mental differences of their child (Buscaglia, 1975; Darling, 1979; Featherstone, 1980). Buscaglia interviewed hospitals about their routine procedures for informing parents of their child's condition. He found in almost every case that there was no routine procedure. Zucman (1982) used the term "violence of disclosure" to refer to the insensitive way the disability of an infant or child is often revealed by professionals to parents. Zucman stated that feelings of isolation, guilt, and anger typically follow this disclosure. Buscaglia (1975) noted that although disabled infants have the same emotional needs as other infants, they may be emotionally and physically separated because of their physical problems, thus complicating the development of early relationships with parents.

Vash (1981) observed that in cases where the disability of the individual begins in childhood, the primary issue in adaptation is the extent to which parents can both emotionally and intellectually accept the fact of the disability. She proposed that this issue will determine all family relations. The acceptance of the child's disability may depend on the self-esteem of all family members and their tolerance for disruption.

Coping patterns evolve in keeping with family patterns that had already formed at the time of the child's birth or diagnosis. Drotar et al. (1975) noted that studies in the literature at the time of his writing had paid much less attention to *adaptive* aspects of parental attachment to the exceptional child than to pathological responses.

ONGOING RESPONSE

Schell (1981) and Marion (1981) pointed up a variety of factors that influence parents' responses to their child: the severity of the child's handicap and the degree of its visibility, the social acceptability of the handicap, the socioeconomic level of the family, the manner in which the parents are informed of the condition, and the age when the diagnosis is made.

In the case of a childhood disability, the family viewing the future faces major long-term treatment responsibilities that may result in complex reactions of anger, guilt, and grief. Power and Orto (1980) list a variety of factors bearing on family coping patterns that have been proposed by researchers:

1. The age of the child and the child's ordinal placement;
2. Family size and structure;
3. How the sick child understands the condition;
4. The complexity of demands on the family caused by the particular illness;
5. The visibility of the defect;
6. The religious beliefs of the family;
7. The degree of financial burden and availability of community resources;
8. The stage in the family cycle when the child is born or develops a disability.

Families face personal, practical, logistic, and financial problems around the special child. For example, Moroney (1981) discussed such problems as financial hardships, extraordinary demands on time for personal care of the child, social isolation, diminished time for sleeping and recreational pursuits, actual or perceived stigma, and feelings of pessimism.

Roos (1979, 1982) explicated ways in which having a handicapped child intensified common generic anxieties of parents:

1. Parents' hopes and dreams for the child diminish;
2. Parents sense the loss of a chance of achieving intimacy with the child;
3. The occurrence demonstrates how little control people have over their own destiny and how fragile life is;
4. Parents question fairness in life and ask, "Why me?";
5. The "wise guide" and other normative parental roles are curtailed;
6. The future of the child seems bleak and full of failure and rejection;
7. The handicap threatens the symbolic sense of immortality that children bring.

The normal quality of the mother–child bond is intensified in the case of the handicapped child (Zucman, 1982). Because of the significance of this inter-relation for the molding of personality and socialization of the child, there is potential for warping of the child's personality. The child may be perceived as weakly endowed, highly vulnerable, and not measured by normative expectations (Mori, 1983).

Zucman (1982), in a major review of international literature dealing with disability and the family, noted that the daily lives of mothers and couples are as upset by the real constraints they face and the way society regards them as they are by their emotional reactions to the disabling condition. Such mundane activities as feeding, dressing, and toileting the handicapped child pose special problems. Mothers tend to bear the brunt of emotional disturbance and logistic problems. Related to the stress of taking care of the handicapped child, mothers display problems in their health and also in their professional lives (Zucman, 1982). Few studies document the impact of the child's handicap on the father. (Examples are Cummings, 1976; Gallagher et al., 1981.) Fathers share similar worries, although sometimes differing emotions (Gumz and Gubrium, 1972).

THE MARITAL RELATIONSHIP

The birth and presence of a different child has the potential to wrench asunder even relationships that appeared to be solid joint endeavors before the advent of the child. Severe emotional responses may encompass deep individual and marital unhappiness. Featherstone (1980) commented on the metaphorical significance of the health of children for the family:

We integrate important events into our lives by investing them with meaning.... [A] child's disability may subtly shift each parent's perception of the marriage. At the magical and metaphorical level where so much of the emotional life is lived, a child's disability calls the union into question. Practical reality reinforces the tendency to confuse the health of the children and the health of the marriage, for the disability touches most what parents do together: it influences the circumstances of sleep, work, mealtimes, outings, and so forth. If a handicap constricts a couple's life at every point, the marriage becomes a prison (p. 91).

The vitality of healthy children reassures parents about their marriage as well as about themselves. Children are tangible, lovable symbols of their joint undertaking. In thriving they bless a parent's choices—the choice of spouse, the decision to have children, the style of parenting. When a child's development goes seriously awry, it calls the whole enterprise into question (p. 102).

The presence of a handicapped child has been demonstrated by some studies to have serious effects on marital couples in many dimensions of their lives. In a study conducted by Lonsdale (1978), in 40 percent of the cases parents acknowledged that the disability added a burden to their life as a couple. In 8 percent of the cases the marriages ended. However, the divorces reported in many studies are difficult to analyze. Zucman (1982) noted that divorces should be viewed as the crystalizations of conflicts in couples prior to the birth of their disabled children. Said Zucman (1982): "We maintain that a child's disability acts not as the 'provocateur' but as the 'revealer' of potential abilities as well as difficulties in his familial milieu: creativity or fragility of the mother; solidity or split in the couple; social ability or withdrawal—all are reinforced for better or worse after the birth of a disabled child" (p. 34).

Other researchers have reported little negative impact on the family. Darling (1979) stated that in her experience most families appear to adjust to the difficulties caused by the presence of handicapped children and she noted that a number of studies report family life is not significantly different for these families than for those in the larger society (Salk, 1972; Birenbaum, 1970, 1971; Voysey, 1975). While some studies reported marital breakdown related to the presence of a severely handicapped child (Walker, 1971; Freeston, 1971; Korn et al., 1978; Tew et al., 1974), others reflected no difference in divorce rates between such families and the general population.

In general, most parents in Darling's sample reported that their child's situation had made their family unit more cohesive. While the nuclear family worked together positively around their problem, the reaction of extended kin was variable. When relatives reacted negatively, they were generally dropped from the family's "reference set" rather than being allowed to influence attitudes in a negative manner. Supportive friends and neighbors sometimes were substituted for those dropped.

SIBLINGS

A number of recent studies have explored the impact of the presence of handicapped children on their siblings. These studies likewise report uneven findings. Most identified patterns in role behavior and such emotions as guilt, anger, and jealousy in the nonaffected siblings (for example, Featherstone, 1980). However, many studies do not include comparison samples; therefore, assessing how different these families are from those of the general population is difficult to determine. Also, studies tend to focus on negative features rather than positive coping and adaptation skills. Since most studies focus on one period in time, there is no way to capture the developmental career of families. Mori (1983) noted that much of this research has been carried out in families in which the disabled child was retarded. He stated, "It may be assumed that many of these findings apply to siblings of any handicapped child" (p. 30). This assumption is open to question.

Siblings may be at considerable risk for emotional problems and increased demands for doing errands, household tasks, and so forth. Parents and professionals alike often ignore the needs and concerns of these siblings. Vadasy et al. (1984) reviewed a number of studies of siblings, the majority being siblings of retarded children or adults. They stated that not enough is known about how the type and severity of a child's handicap influences the child's siblings, and they acknowledged that most studies have been done within the population of retarded persons. The authors reviewed variables that appear to be significant in a number of studies: age, sex, and birth order. McCullough (1981) interviewed families in which the disabled children were so severely affected that they would not be able to live independently as adults. He questioned parents and siblings about the future of the affected child. These two groups disagreed about future plans. While 41 percent of parents thought that nonhandicapped siblings would assume at least partial care of the handicapped child, 68 percent of the siblings thought they would assume some responsibility for care. Parents had not prepared their children to care for the handicapped sibling nor made financial arrangements for them.

While some authors unequivocally described siblings of retarded children to be at high risk (Mori, 1983), others did not find this to be the case. In fact, Zucman (1982) stated that internationally reports on this subject are contradictory. She stated the reason may be the diversity of authors who do not speak the same language and the fact that there is an absence of theoretical and clinical knowledge of the dynamics of siblings in general. Zucman stated that parents have a tendency to deny that problems among siblings exist, while professionals say that such problems indeed do exist. Some reports stated that siblings feel left out, they are not given enough attention, and they may experience many emotional responses, such as anxiety, anger, guilt, and frustration. They have a great need for communication with their parents (Mori, 1983).

Collections of papers that deal with family and disability have been edited by Power and Orto (1980) and Earhart and Sporakowski (1984).

WORKS OF SPECIAL INTEREST

Two important works in the literature dealing with physical difference, Featherstone's *A Difference in the Family* (1980) and Darling's *Families Against Society* (1979), are of special interest. Featherstone, who wrote from the dual perspective of a parent with a severely disabled son and of a professional teacher, presented a very sensitive exploration and analysis of parental and sibling emotional responses to physically and mentally different children. She candidly and poignantly related personal statements of parents and detailed feelings and experiences, which she categorized under headings of fear, anger, loneliness, guilt, and self-doubt. Darling focused on the nature of attitudes developed and maintained by parents of severely handicapped children and the relation of these attitudes to the children's self-esteem and the interactional adaptations of parents. Darling presented an extensive review of the literature of stigma and its relationship to attitudes, self-esteem, and behavior, and of varied other issues affecting parents' responses.

Darling presented a comprehensive discussion of sources of parental attitudes toward different children that have been proposed in the literature. Psychoanalytic studies have tended to focus on prior personality traits of the parents. Other studies have examined the relationship between parental acceptance and social class, religion, age of children, parents' self-acceptance, prior experience of the parents with children in general, the stability of the marital relationship, and age of parents. Darling (1979) noted that all of these variables would be expected to influence parents' definitions, values, and norms regarding children. Yet, as Darling and others demonstrated, parental attitudes also change through interactions and situations following the birth of children.

Darling (1979, 1983) examined the significance of meaning to parents. She proposed that the early problems of parents are exacerbated by the frequent occurrence of denial of children's deviant conditions and the avoidance of giving straight, early information by professionals. Parents are enveloped in a condition of meaninglessness or an anomic (lack of norms) situation for which they have had no prior socialization.

Darling in another work (1980) traced the career of the family from birth through "seekership" (Lofland and Stark, 1965), a period during which parents begin the search for realistic definitions and solutions. Darling reported that the seekership phase is often a continuing status. Parents leave the seekership role when they have obtained satisfactory medical, educational, social, and other needed services for their children.

THE RESPONSIBILITY OF THE MOTHER

Both Featherstone and Darling discussed the primacy of mothers in shouldering both "blame" and responsibility for children who are different. Children are a projection of mothers' and fathers' hopes, dreams, and self-images. However, in our society the mother is most closely associated with the child and his/her successes and failures. If the child is less than perfect, the mother feels the brunt of the blame. Mothers' identification with their children is forged and mirrored in the many hours of the day most of them spend with infants or small children. Even when mothers work or have other interests, their priority for concern and the area that is most closely associated with their own sense of self-esteem and success or failure is their performance as mothers. Featherstone (1980, pp. 71, 72, and 122) clearly made this point:

The whole culture supports a mother in the opinion that her children are what she has made them. Whether from upbringing, Freud, or *Family Circle*, most women learn this lesson thoroughly by the time they are grown. . . .

The traditional family set-up, in which a man works full-time while his wife assumes primary responsibility for their children, offers a man the opportunity to spend many of his waking hours in a world untouched by private tragedy, however good or bad that world may be in other respects. The diagnosis of a child's disability may reshape his vision of the world, but it rarely changes the way the world sees him; his on-the-job responsibilities continue as before. A job allows both an escape from the child's problems and a setting that helps to establish continuity in life. Outside work helps people to avoid defining themselves exclusively in terms of a child's disability. . . .

While the father of a handicapped child usually recognized the practical problems of care, his wife's suffering, and his own sadness, embarrassment, rage, and even despair, he is less attuned to the possibility that his own self-confidence has suffered. And maybe it has not: in the eyes of the world, a man's major accomplishments are outside the family.

In keeping with this view of the father being enveloped in outside pursuits, Darling (1979) reported that a major complaint of wives in her study was that husbands sometimes left all the seekership chores to their wives. Darling stated that a few mothers reported experiencing a breakdown during their children's infancy as a result of their bearing total responsibility for their children. Their situation improved once they became part of a parents' group or other kind of supportive network. For example, said one mother: "[My husband] buried himself in his work, and I had nothing. I wanted to run away. I was with Debbie all the time. I was isolated and lonely. I felt smothered" (p. 163).

Both Darling and Featherstone wrote excellent discussions of parents' problems with the medical world. Their accounts of parents' difficulties bear a great semblance to accounts of difficulties experienced by families of dwarf children. See Chapter 10 of this book for a summary and comparison. Darling (1983) presented an insightful analysis of the conflict in world view and philosophy that comes into play in physician–patient/family interactions and expectations.

Appendix C
The Literature on Short-Statured Children

The clinical complexities of abnormal short stature have been widely explored in the medical literature with emphasis given to endocrine and orthopedic concerns. In contrast, the literature dealing with the psychosocial dimensions of short stature is much smaller, particularly in regard to persons with skeletal dysplasias. The literature is disparate and often uneven, chiefly summarizing observations, interviews, and/or results of psychological tests administered to patients, usually children, in various hospital and clinical caseloads. The papers report on intelligence, developmental and emotional problems, interpersonal relationships and personality characteristics of their subjects, and the varying coping styles subjects have developed to confront their lives as profoundly short individuals.

Many sweeping generalizations have been extended to all dwarfs from the results of studies in the literature. In fact, if distinctions are made, they tend to be made only between hypopituitary dwarfs and achondroplastic dwarfs, despite the fact that there are more than one hundred types of dwarfs differing widely among themselves and in some cases even within types. The studies in the literature are on discrete types of short-statured persons from heterogeneous samples, with each population exhibiting very different physiognomies and accompanying height and health expectations, not to mention the diverse family milieus of subjects.

HYPOPITUITARY AND OTHER PROPORTIONATE SHORT-STATURED CHILDREN

The majority of clinical papers have focused on hypopituitary children. The classic, most frequently cited papers appeared in the late 1960s, chiefly from clinicians at Johns Hopkins, which has had the greatest specialty interests in dwarfism. Other more recent papers reported on cases as far afield as Poland, Israel, and Canada. Early papers acknowledged that the intelligence of dwarfs characteristically is normal (for example, Pollitt and Money, 1964; Money et al., 1967; Drash et al., 1968). Money and Pollitt (1966) focused on the immaturity of their subjects, hypopituitary children, noting that they lagged behind in psychomaturation. The authors early on defined the complementary relationship that existed between the degree of psychomaturity achieved by the children and the success of their parents and other adults in treating the children in accordance with their *age* and not their *size*. They described the effect of silhouette and visual gestalt in determining immediate social response, a process later termed by Drash (1969) as "the concept of complementarity of pathology":

All who come in contact with a dwarf, whether professional people, parents, relatives, or strangers, find that impulsively and intuitively they gear their reactions and expectancies of the dwarf first to his size and not his age. It is only on second thought, or through habituation, that allowance is made for age and social maturity. . . .

All dwarfs are obliged to deal with some degree of babying in their social-behavioral and personality development as a result of the silhouette effect. One expects a complementary relationship between being babied and responding immaturely. This relationship is also a matter of degree; that is, the more a dwarf is babied, the greater is the immaturity or lag in social-behavioral and personality development (Money and Pollitt, 1966, p. 381).

The authors noted that the dwarf's smallness also confers on him "an index of recognizance—an animadversion index—so that without any effort on his part, he becomes widely known in his community and school. This notoriety places another burden of sorts on the dwarf, either as an instrument of mortification to him, on account of its origins, or as an instrument of popularity and friendship" (Money and Pollitt, 1966, p. 388). Thus, clinicians in even the earliest works on the psychosocial characteristics of their subjects identified the greatest danger to the personality of dwarf children as infantilization, a typical response of average-sized persons, relating age and maturity to size. Children will develop behavioral characteristics in keeping with responses to them, and a circular pattern of development and behavior emerges.

Money (1967) and Drash (1969) discussed various responses of dwarf children to their treatment by others, such as "behavioral infantilism," "denial," "mascotism," "overcompensation," and "the use of humor." These authors emphasized the importance of beginning growth hormone therapy while children are young, parental treatment by age rather than size, and psychotherapy for children and/or parents when needed. When these conditions are met, positive outcomes appear more certain for their subjects.

The literature from areas other than Johns Hopkins tended to present a bleaker picture, portraying a common syndrome of immaturity, depression, low self-esteem, and lack of aggressive behavior. Even in cases in which the subjects have grown significantly through the utilization of human growth hormone, the mind set of short stature had so negatively impressed the subjects at early ages that depression and poor self-image still dogged their footsteps when they had achieved a relatively normal height at maturity (Money and Pollitt, 1966; Obuchowski et al., 1970; Kusalic et al., 1972; Kusalic and Fortin, 1975; Spencer and Raft, 1974; Shurka and Laron, 1975; Rotnem et al., 1977). Studies of adult male sexuality likewise portrayed depression and behavioral problems, with a chronic treatment of dwarfs, even in their adult years, as juveniles by parents, fellow students, and strangers (Money, et al., 1980).

However, several recent papers in the literature challenged the negativity of earlier studies. For example, Drotar et al. (1980) questioned the validity and reliability of previous studies on the basis of differing methodologies employed by researchers. On the basis of their standardized tests comparing hypopituitary children with a matched sample of "physically healthy peers," these recent papers argued that the psychological adjustment of the short-statured children compared favorably with that of control groups. Stabler and Underwood (1977) reported no difference in anxiety or locus of control among samples of hypopituitary, physically healthy children, and a chronic-illness control group. Drotar et al. (1980) found that the only psychological variable that differentiated hypopituitary children was their reaction to frustration. These children were less adaptive in finding solutions to problems and emphasized obstacles rather than solutions. The authors contended that hypopituitary children have experienced continued frustrations because of physical environmental problems and their relationships with their peers. As noted by earlier researchers, they tend to withdraw and hold in resentments. Drotar et al. (1980) suggested, as did the early Johns Hopkins researchers, the importance of anticipatory guidance for these children and their parents in achieving adaptive solutions to their problems and in dealing with the expected frustrations. The authors further suggested that clinical attention and research be constructively directed toward problem solving rather than toward the definition of children's "deficits."

Gordon et al. (1982) compared a sample of children of constitutional short stature with a comparison sample of children of normal height. The short-statured children displayed significantly more behavior problems and less self-esteem. They were socially withdrawn and aloof. Parents indicated poorer communication and cooperation among family members. The authors commented that although discrepant results between their study and those of Drotar et al. (1980) and Stabler and Underwood (1977) might be due to methodological differences, they might also represent differences in the psychological characteristics of children on growth hormone and constitutionally delayed children. For example, the former, who see medical personnel regularly, may have greater opportunity to express their anxieties about their height. Also, their parents, who are able to rely on treatment for their children, may be more at ease. The authors highlighted the need for recognition of possible difference between short-statured populations, noting that it would be unwise to generalize from hypopituitary children because they represent less than 1 percent of all short-statured children.

A landmark collection of papers prepared for a symposium on psychosocial aspects of growth delay in 1984 (Stabler and Underwood, 1986) explored varied factors and nuances of personality and behavior of children and treated adults with a variety of types of proportionate short stature, such as hypopituitary dwarfism, Turner syndrome, constitutionally short, and abuse dwarfism. In these papers a diversity of issues, such as academic performance, aspects of cognitive functioning, social competence, self-esteem, and adult outcomes, were explored.

Two papers of special interest are those of Young-Hyman and Rotnem. Young-Hyman's study (1986) illustrates the importance of family environment in mediating social behavior. Cognitive abilities were valued independently of height and physical competence. The author suggested that family membership in a socioeconomic class that values cognitive abilities and intellectual pursuits over sports allows children who excel in cognitive areas to maintain good self-esteem and social competence. Compensatory strategies of children in managing their social relationships were discerned. The author concluded that psychological intervention might best be focused on family attitudes and compensatory areas of mastery.

Rotnem (1986), from her research with hypopituitary children, explored the complexities of psychosocial adaptation of short-statured children and their parents. Regarding short stature as a chronic health condition, she discussed phases and emotions of parental adaptation, as well as developmental problems faced by the child. She described fundamental parenting dilemmas as a basis for the development of coping strategies and proposed family and school interventions. Rotnem suggested that treatment outcomes should be measured more in terms of the degree of social integration attained in adulthood rather than just physical growth. Rotnem presented in this work a sensitive and valuable discussion of significant family concerns.

ACHONDROPLASTIC DWARFS

Fewer works deal with achondroplastic children, no doubt because they have less need than hypopituitary children to come regularly to clinics and thus do not constitute a captive sample for mental-health researchers. Researchers from Johns Hopkins again have provided the major statements available. Money (1967), for example, presented a broad generalization of the "happy achondroplastic." The author discussed "mascotism" as a common situation created by and for dwarf children in which the children capitalize on their small size and define positive roles for themselves in the social structure. Money noted that the ability to do this requires considerable self-confidence:

It is quite possible that some people simply have more of it [self-confidence] than do others. This certainly seems to be the case in achondroplastic dwarfs as compared with other types. One is tempted to believe that whatever it may be that produces achondroplasia also produces a "happiness hormone." Almost without exception achondroplastic persons are endowed with the personality traits of chronic cheerfulness, optimism and confidence. If one judges from the paintings of the old masters, these traits were capitalized upon in the era of the court jester, for apparently all the dwarfs who held this position were achondroplastics (p. 136).

Drash et al. (1968) also reported on the chronic cheerfulness of achondroplastic child subjects in comparison to hypopituitary, Turner's syndrome, and deprivation-syndrome subjects. The clinicians' discussion and explanation of possible differential responses to differing types of dwarfism were clearly colored by the cosmetic values of this society in relation to body form:

ACHONDROPLASTIC DWARFISM. The proverbial cheerfulness of the achondroplastic dwarf was evident in the majority of the nine children in the present group. In contrast to the hypopituitary dwarfs, some of whom were shy and inhibited, the achondroplastic children were relatively extroverted and outgoing in personality. They were unexpectedly accepting of their situation, optimistic and generally happy with life. Despite the rather grotesque appearance with which some were afflicted, they did not appear "crushed" by their predicament. The psychomaturational lag characteristic of many hypopituitary dwarfs was not evident among the achondroplastic children. . . .

The achondroplastic dwarfs, by contrast, are constantly active, sociable, jovial and cheerful sometimes to the point of euphoria. The hypopituitary group feel the sting of their shortness and resent it. They would like to ignore it and do, in fact, deal with many problems by "sweeping them under the rug," that is, they are selectively inattentive and have a penchant for inhibitory personality mechanisms in dealing with problems. . . .

Although achondroplastic dwarfs are as short as most hypopituitary dwarfs, if not shorter, there is little possibility that the bystander will simply mistake them for being much younger than they are. He will perceive their bodily disproportion and respond perhaps with curiosity, pity, ridicule, or even fear, together with a knowledge that something is wrong. These responses will temper any tendency toward treating the achondroplastic dwarf as a young child. The cheerful and optimistic reaction of the achondroplastic may be in part a basic temperamental trait and in part a tendency to capitalize on this trait as a behavioral compensation for that which he lacks in physical attractiveness (pp. 574–79).

FAMILIES WITH DWARF CHILDREN

Only a few rare works are available that focus specifically on families with a dwarf child. Stace and Danks (1981 a,b,c) conducted a study of all persons with bone dysplasias whom they could contact through a variety of outreach endeavors in Victoria, Australia. Parents of seventy-four dwarf children were included in this study (1981a). In all cases parents responded that doctors did not give them any idea of the prognosis for the child at the time of diagnosis:

In many cases the parents' imaginations, hunts through library books, or heresay from friends gave them a very black picture and sent them into a state of fear, disbelief or deep depression. Many doctors did not arrange follow-up appointments to discuss with the parents their immediate concerns and to allow them to express their feelings about the diagnosis.

The parents most satisfied with how they first received the news had been given some information at the initial meeting. Even if the diagnosis was uncertain, parents still found nonspecific information about dwarfing to be helpful—e.g. being told that their child would be shorter than the average because his bones were not growing in the normal way and that mental retardation was unlikely (when this reassurance was appropriate). Parents were pleased to be given a chance to ask questions that immediately came to mind and to have a follow-up appointment made within a few days.

Those who had received counselling in this way showed a lesser degree of depression and rarely the development of denial, both of which proved so detrimental to many of the other families (p. 168).

Several parents complained about the dearth of information about social aspects of their child's life and future. They felt "many unnecessary 'off the cuff' and poorly considered comments had been made, e.g. 'he'll be a clown in a circus' " (p. 169).

Overall, forty-two parents were quite satisfied with how they had been told, three were indifferent, and twenty-two were dissatisfied because of the physician's abrupt manner, the lack of time for discussion and follow-up, and inadequacy of information. Stated the authors: "It is recognized that persons receiving bad news can transfer their negative feelings onto the newsbearer, but not withstanding this, several parents seemed to have genuine cause for complaint. Some doctors appeared to have projected their own negative feelings towards dwarfed people in their counseling" (p. 169).

Parents differed widely in how they would have preferred to be told about such a matter. Thirteen preferred to be told as soon as possible; others preferred a later time. The authors noted that the variety of opinions expressed by parents make it difficult to set a specific time for the telling. They recommended that the needs and cultural background of parents be considered.

Parents varied widely in their reactions. Eight couples adjusted quickly and showed little emotional reaction. Eighteen were upset initially but stated their lives were not disrupted. Some said that after they "had a good cry and scream," they pulled themselves together. Four couples stated they were very upset over a prolonged period. Six others were given medication or psychiatric help. Of these, some had severe negative reactions to the extent of wishing their child dead. Two parents denied their situation over a long period and after acceptance went into deep depression. In twenty-one couples one spouse had a more severe reaction than the other, and some "poor" marital relationships deteriorated further as a result of the birth.

Thirty-one parents considered their child's health to be worse than average, while twelve stated their child's health was better than average. Every parent was concerned about their child's future emotionally, socially, and concerning employment.

Stace and Danks noted that the most depressing feature of the study was the high incidence (50 percent) of the families who reported prolonged emotional or mental disturbance. They suggested that the dwarf individual and often other family members may need episodic or continuing psychological and emotional support.

Stace and Danks in another component of their study (1981b) talked to parents of seventy-five children who had twenty-one kinds of dwarfing conditions. The children most affected displayed delay in reaching early milestones in motor development and physical skills. Disproportionate short stature produced complications in toilet training, dressing, mobility, and accommodating comfortably to furniture at school. Parents attempted to assist their children with physical therapy and special training for hygienic matters, obtaining special clothes and shoes with easier modes of opening, obtaining boxes and stools that allowed the children to sit more comfortably or reach things, and lowering pulls and switches. Bicycles allowed many children greater independence and mobility. Although most children were of average or above intelligence, more than 27 percent were a year older than the average for their grades (as opposed to 17 percent in the general population), and most of these had repeated grades in primary school.

Stace and Danks reported delayed emotional maturation for almost all of the "severely dwarfed" children and a close correlation with physical dependency. Because children were often treated in relation to their size rather than their age, they were babied and overprotected. Children often received a lot of attention, causing "friction" in the family. These children were often the class or team mascot and "reveled" in the attention. Some twenty-five parents of children who were old enough to interact with peers felt their child's dwarfism affected the number and closeness of friends. Twenty-five others felt that instead, the child's "personality" was the determining factor. There seemed to be a definite pattern of popularity and its waning. Stated the authors:

The general pattern for all the children was great popularity in the early years of school, with invitations to parties and outings. By the time the child had reached high school, popularity, and with it, close friends of their own age, had dropped away markedly, and the younger teenager often found himself lonely, or seeking the company of older or much younger peers. They rarely went out, and were afraid and withdrawn. Although sexual development was normal, emotional maturation was slower. At this stage they often became more dependent on their family. In reaction, the parents showed a tendency to want to hide them away, to protect them from the harsh world of stares and comments, because of their own feelings of shame or rejection welling up again.

With his peers, the dwarfed person could no longer gain acceptance by being the mascot or the comedian. Fashionable clothes couldn't be bought, and dating was rare (pp. 174–75).

The authors further comment on the "crisis of adulthood": " 'Crisis' is not too strong a word to describe the impact of the dwarfed person's 'growing up', on himself and his family. It was obvious from interviews that both parents and dwarfed teenagers were coming to realize the permanent nature of the dwarfing and its probable consequences for work and social relationships" (p. 175).

Parents' attitudes toward the desire and value of meeting other little people and their families were mixed:

There were 33 families who had had some contact with other dwarfs, some through the Little People's Association of Australasia (L.P.A.A.). Some parents found they felt differently at different stages, sometimes wishing they had never met other dwarfed people, feeling embarrassed or even repulsed. Mostly, something positive was gained— contact helped the parents plan more realistically; gave a boost to confidence in managing their child; and, especially, helped them to see that things were not as bad as they had imagined. The parents often said that they were relieved to talk with other parents in a similar situation.

There were 42 parents who had never met another dwarfed person. Six of these parents were anxious to make contact, as they thought it would be helpful to themselves, and good for their child to see "he's not the only one". The remaining 36 parents said they definitely did not want to meet other dwarfed people, for a variety of reasons—it would only mirror their child's handicap; they did not want their child to become dependent on other dwarfed people; they did not want to mix with others who they thought had more problems; and their child had to be brought up to cope with the normal-sized world (p. 175).

The authors noted that 64 percent of the families in this study exhibited a physical, mental, or behavioral disturbance in one or more of its members outside of the dwarfism. This frequency of disturbance is higher than that of the general population and prompted the authors to suggest that more investigation on the impact of dwarfism on the family is needed to be able to provide sound emotional support for all family members.

DelCampo et al. (1984) studied a sample of fourteen families in which six children had treatable, five had nontreatable and three had undiagnosed growth disorders. They obtained the sample through the Human Growth Foundation and Little People of America. The children varied from five to sixteen years of age.

Twelve of the fourteen families reported negative initial experiences with medical persons surrounding their learning about their child's growth problems. In every family the diagnosis was made only after parents persistently pursued doctors to find out why the child's growth was delayed. Parents reported a lack of sensitivity on the part of the doctors who gave them the diagnosis:

There were a few parents who were positive about the way their physicians handled the situation, but the prevailing feeling was indignation toward the physician for the coldness and insensitivity that was displayed. In one case, a mother reported that the physician's initial statement in discussing her two-year-old's diagnosis was: "You know the dwarfs that you see in a circus, well that's what your child will be like." A more dramatic example was when a pediatrician walked into the hospital room of a primiparous mother whose child was two days old and said, "You're the mom of the child with all of the problems. Hope you won't hide him in the closet!" (p. 81).

The authors speculated that the parents' anxiety may have resulted in selectively hearing only the seemingly insensitive portions of doctors' remarks. Also they posited that the lack of knowledge most doctors have about dwarfism led them to be evasive and thus defensive as parents pursued their questioning. Thus, a situation was created that resulted in negative perceptions and remembrances on the part of the parents. The authors suggested that it would be logical for physicians to be especially cautious in such situations.

The authors reported two themes that emerged in extended-family response to the birth of the dwarf child. Extended family members tended to ignore the problem, and grandparents in particular tended to deny that the problem existed. Secondly, every family reported that relatives treated the dwarf child as special by being more indulgent toward him/her. While parents attempted to encourage children to be independent, these efforts were undermined by relatives and persons who treated the child in relation to his size, not age, and babied him.

Children experienced minimal stress in early peer relations with children who knew them well. Parents reported that teasing by peers became progressively more frequent as children got older and the size difference became more noticeable. The preadolescent years were the most difficult as children encountered new children in larger schools who did not know them.

Parents urged others to accept their child's condition and then work to facilitate their child's acceptance. They said that parents should talk matter-of-factly about the child's condition with him and other family members. Eight of the families stated that working through the growth crisis of their child brought them a newfound sense of closeness.

The road to acceptance was very similar to the stages people go through in accepting other crisis situations such as death or divorce. Long periods of depression, family disorganization and bitterness were experienced by parents who found it more difficult to accept the condition. Yet parents had to accept the situation within themselves first before they could begin to be effective in helping their children. Some turned to a stronger faith in God during this process, but by far, the most distinctive coping mechanism in working toward acceptance was comparing the child to other children with problems. As one parent put it, "When I would get down, I'd say if I think I have it bad, just look around. My child can see, hear and has all of his mental facilities; it could be lots worse" (p. 83).

Parents who were effective in building self-worth in their child devoted time exploring various areas in which the child could excel.

The authors emphasized the importance of acceptance by parents and the promotion of openness and communication about the child's problems and their implications. They suggested the value of specialized services, such as those offered by the Human Growth Foundation and Little People of America, and other sources of assistance, such as family therapists familiar with the psycho-social aspects of short stature, informational meetings with medical personnel, and self-help networks of parents.

Two studies were carried out recently with parents by Ference and Ricker, both professional educators who are also parents of dwarf children. The purpose of Ference's study (1984) was to determine the perceptions and needs of parents who are raising a dwarf child. The author sent a mail survey to one hundred parents in a district of LPA on the East Coast. The categories of data she collected included a parents' profile, developmental characteristics, medical treatment, school experiences, helpful organizations, and special needs and experiences. The parents were of higher educational level than the national norm. The majority of children were achondroplastic and ranged in age from infancy to twenty-two years. These parents reported that relationships with professionals were strained and that information given to them was often in-adequate and insensitive. Parents reported that they treated their dwarf children in much the same manner as average-sized siblings but different child rearing was practiced in areas in which physical ability differed, such as in dress, riding a bike, and so forth. Weight control was stressed. Two thirds of parents felt they had unique problems. These were educating peers to the child's problems; needing to communicate with other parents of a dwarf child; and needing community education about dwarfism. Fifty-eight percent reported attendance at some educational program geared to dwarfism.

Ricker's study (1984) explored issues related to stress in seventy-five mothers who were members of the Human Growth Foundation. Mothers of daughters estimated significantly lower stress for diagnosis of childhood and adult shortness. Perceptions of stress of treatment correlated significantly with stress of diagnosis and childhood shortness. Stress for adult shortness showed significant relation-ships with stress of diagnosis and type of recent treatment. Nearly all parents whose children had hormonal treatment said the family experienced stress. Previously experienced highly stressful events did not affect perceptions of stress. Mothers rated growth-related events significantly lower than death of spouse or child and divorce, but not significantly lower than other deaths, illnesses, or separation.

GENERAL READING

A very readable and useful work on general problems of short people is *Growing Up Small: A Handbook for Short People*, by Kate Gilbert Phifer. This book contains material on the physiology of growth, human genetics, and practical suggestions for dealing with the daily problems of life encountered by short-statured children and adults. There is a chapter in this book on dwarfism and LPA.

Appendix D
Professional Resources for Dwarfism

THE MEDICAL ADVISORY BOARD OF LITTLE PEOPLE OF AMERICA

The Medical Advisory Board of LPA is composed of distinguished professionals with expertise in varied areas of growth-related problems:

Charles I. Scott, Jr., M.D., Chairman
Director of Department of Genetics
Alfred I. Du Pont Institute
P.O. Box 269
Wilmington, Delaware 19899

Arthur S. Aylsworth, M.D.
Genetics Counseling Program
Division of Genetics and Metabolism at Chapel Hill
306 Biological Sciences Research Center, 220H
Chapel Hill, North Carolina 27514

Betty Elder, Ms.
5007 Sweet Air Road
Baldwin, Maryland 21013

Clair Francomano, M.D.
Division of Medical Genetics
The Moore Clinic
Johns Hopkins Hospital
600 North Wolfe Street
Baltimore, Maryland 21205

Judith A. Hall, M.D.
Clinical Genetics Unit, UBC
Salvation Army Grace Hospital
4490 Oak Street
Vancouver, British Columbia, Canada V6H 3V5

William A. Horton, M.D.
Medical Genetics Clinic
Department of Pediatrics
University of Texas Health Science Center
P.O. Box 20708
Houston, Texas 77025

Thaddeus E. Kelly, M.D.
Department of Pediatrics, Box 201
University of Virginia Medical Center
Charlottesville, Virginia 22908

Steven E. Kopits, M.D.
St. Joseph Hospital
7620 York Road
Towson, Maryland 21204

Leonard O. Langer, M.D.
Department of Radiology
Midway Hospital
1700 University Avenue
St. Paul, Minnesota 55104

Victor A. McKusick, M.D.
University Professor of Medical Genetics
Johns Hopkins Medical Institutions
Johns Hopkins Hospital
600 North Wolfe Street
Baltimore, Maryland 21205

Richard M. Pauli, M.D.
Clinical Genetics Center
University of Wisconsin
1560 Highland Avenue
Madison, Wisconsin 53706

Cheryl Reid, M.D.
Department of Pediatrics
Cooper Hospital
University Medical Center
Plaza 3 Haddon Avenue
Camden, New Jersey 08103

David L. Rimoin, M.D.
Department of Pediatrics
Medical Genetics–Birth Defects Center
Cedars-Sinai Medical Center
Los Angeles, California 90048

Ms. Katherine K. Smith
Division of Medical Genetics
The Moore Clinic
Johns Hopkins Hospital
600 North Wolfe Street
Baltimore, Maryland 21205

Joan O. Weiss, LCSW
Division of Medical Genetics
The Moore Clinic
Johns Hopkins Hospital
600 North Wolfe Street
Baltimore, Maryland 21205

PROFESSIONAL ORGANIZATIONS FOR INFORMATION AND REFERRALS

National Center for Education in Maternal and Child Health
38th and R Streets Northwest
Washington, D.C. 20057
(202) 625–8400

National Society of Genetic Counselors, Inc.
c/o Bea Leopold
233 Canterbury Drive
Wallingford, Penn. 19086

American Society of Human Genetics
9650 Rockville Pike
Bethesda, Maryland 20814

Appendix E
Organizational Resources for Dwarfism

LITTLE PEOPLE OF AMERICA

For general information on Little People of America or for publications, contact:

Little People of America
P.O. Box 633
San Bruno, California 94066

Districts and Chapters of LPA

For information about the districts or chapters below contact:

Little People of America
P.O. Box 633
San Bruno, California 94066

District 1—Maine, New Hampshire, Vermont, Connecticut, Rhode Island, Massachusetts
    No specific chapter, district activities only.

District 2—New York, Pennsylvania, New Jersey
    The Islanders Chapter, New York
    Mets Chapter, New York
    Alburn Chapter, New York
    Hudson Valley Chapter, New York
    Garden State Chapter, New Jersey
    Pennsylvania Dutch Chapter, Pennsylvania
    Philadelphia Chapter, Pennsylvania
    Western Pennsylvania Chapter, Pennsylvania

District 3—Delaware, Washington, D.C., Maryland, Virginia, North Carolina, South Carolina
    Del-Marva Chapter, Maryland, Delaware, Virginia, Washington, D.C.

District 4—Mississippi, Alabama, Georgia, Florida
    North Georgia Chapter, Georgia
    South Florida Mini-Gators Chapter, Florida
    Central Florida Mini-Gators Chapter, Florida

District 5—Indiana, Michigan, Ohio, Kentucky, Tennessee, West Virginia
    Northern Ohio Chapter, Ohio
    Cincinnati Tri State Chapter, Ohio
    Indianapolis Chapter, Indiana
    Mid-Michigan Chapter, Michigan
    Detroit Chapter, Michigan

District 6—Wisconsin and Illinois
    Milwaukee Chapter, Wisconsin
    Central Illinois Chapter, Illinois

District 7—Kansas, Oklahoma, Missouri, Arkansas
    St. Louis-Gateway Chapter, Missouri
    Kansas City Chapter, Missouri
    Oklahoma City Chapter, Oklahoma

District 8—Louisiana and Texas
    Dixie Lil High Chapter, Louisiana
    Dal-Worth Chapter, Texas
    Houston Area Chapter, Texas
    San Antonio Chapter, Texas

District 9—South Dakota, North Dakota, Nebraska, Minnesota, Iowa
    Twin-Cities Chapter, Minnesota
    Des Moines Chapter, Iowa

District 10—Utah, Colorado, Arizona, New Mexico
    Denver Chapter, Colorado
    Phoenix Chapter, Arizona
    Salt Lake City Chapter, Utah
    Albuquerque Chapter, New Mexico

District 11—Washington, Oregon, Idaho, Montana, Wyoming, Alaska
    Ever Gems Chapter, Idaho
    Puget Sound Chapter, Washington
    Portland Chapter, Oregon
    Central Oregon Chapter, Oregon

District 12—California, Nevada, Hawaii
  Los Angeles Chapter, California
  San Francisco Chapter, California
  San Diego Chapter, California
  Orange County Chapter, California

LITTLE PEOPLE OF CANADA

LITTLE PEOPLE OF CANADA
P.O. Box 453
Abbotsford, British Columbia
Canada V2S5Z5

OTHER ORGANIZATIONS THAT FOCUS ON GROWTH AND RELATED ISSUES

Human Growth Foundation
4720 Montgomery Lane
Bethesda, Maryland 20814
(301) 656–7540

The MPS (Mucopolysaccharidoses) Society, Inc.
17 Kraemer Street
Hicksville, New York 11801

Osteogenesis Imperfecta Foundation, Inc.
P.O. Box 14807
Clearwater, Florida 34629–4807
(516) 325–8992

Osteogenesis Imperfecta-National Capitol Area, Inc.
Box 941
1311 Delaware Avenue South West
Washington, D.C. 20024
(202) 265–1614

References

Ablon, Joan. 1982. The Parents' Auxiliary of Little People of America: A Self-Help Model of Social Support for Families of Short-Statured Children. *Prevention in Human Services* 1:3.

———. 1984. *Little People in America: The Social Dimensions of Dwarfism*. New York: Praeger Publishers.

Ainlay, Stephen C.; Becker; Gaylene, and Coleman, Lerita M. 1986. *The Dilemma of Difference: A Multidisciplinary View of Stigma*. New York and London: Plenum Press.

Becker, Gaylene. 1980. *Growing Old in Silence*. Berkeley: University of California Press.

Belsky, J. 1981. Early Human Experience: A Family Perspective. *Developmental Psychology* 17:3–23.

Belsky, J., and Tolan, W. J. 1981. Infants as Producers of Their Own Development: An Ecological Analysis. In *Individuals as Producers of Their Development: A Life-Span Perspective*, eds. R.M. Lerner and N.A. Busch-Rossnagel. New York: Academic Press.

Bennett, J. 1974. Proof of the Pudding. *Exceptional Parent* (May/June):7–12.

Bierman, Jessie M.; Siegel, Earl, French, Fern E.; and Connor, Angie. 1963. The Community Impact of Handicaps of Prenatal or Natal Origin. *Public Health Reports* 78(10):839–855.

Birenbaum, A. 1970. On Managing a Courtesy Stigma. *Journal of Health and Social Behavior* 11:196–206.

———. 1971. The Mentally Retarded Child in the Home and the Family Cycle. *Journal of Health and Social Behavior* 12:55–65.

Bray, N.; Coleman, J.; and Bracken, M. 1981. Critical Events in Parenting Handicapped Children. *Journal of the Division for Early Childhood* 3:26–33.

Bristor, Martha W. 1984. The Birth of a Handicapped Child—A Wholistic Model for Grieving. *Family Relations* 33:25–32.

Brues, Alice M. 1977. *Peoples and Races*. New York: Macmillan.

Brust, James S.; Ford, Charles V.; and Rimoin, David L. 1976. Psychiatric Aspects of Dwarfism. *American Journal of Psychiatry* 133:160–64.

Buscaglia, L. 1975. *The Disabled and Their Parents: A Counselling Challenge.* New York: Slack.

Camera, G., and Mastroiacovo, P. 1982. Birth Prevalence of Skeletal Dysplasias in the Italian Multicentric Monitoring System for Birth Defects. In *Skeletal Dysplasias: Proceedings of the Third International Clinical Genetics Seminar Held in Athens, Greece May 9–13*, ed. C. J. Papadatos and C. S. Bartsocas.

Caplan, Gerald. 1974. *Support Systems and Community Mental Health.* New York: Behavioral Publications.

Caplan, Gerald, and Killilea, Marie, eds. 1976. *Support Systems and Mutual Help.* New York: Grune & Stratton.

Caplan, M. E. and Goldman, M. 1981. Personal Space Violations as a Function of Height. *Journal of Social Psychology* 114(2): 167–171.

Cassel, John C. 1974. Psychiatric Epidemiology. In *American Handbook of Psychiatry*, vol. 2, ed. Gerald Caplan. New York: Basic Books.

Centerwall, Willard, and Centerwall, Seigried. 1986. An Introduction to Your Child Who Has Achondroplasia. Redmond, Wash.: Medic Publishing.

Christianson, Roberta E.; van den Berg, Bea J.; Milkovich, Lucille; and Oechsli, Frank W., 1981. Incidence of Congenital Anomalies among White and Black Live Births with Long-Term Follow-Up. *American Journal of Public Health* 71:1333–1341.

Cleveland, Martha. 1980. Family Adaption to Traumatic Spinal Cord Injury: Response to Crisis. *Family Relations* 29:126–33.

Cooper, R. R.; Ponseti, I.V.; and Maynard, J. A. 1973. Pseudoachondroplastic Dwarfism. A Rough-surfaced Endoplasmic Reticulum Storage Disorder. *Journal of Bone and Joint Surgery* 55A:475–84.

Cummings, S. T. 1976. The Impact of the Child's Deficiency on the Father: A Study of Fathers of Mentally Retarded and of Chronically Ill Children. *American Journal of Orthopsychiatry* 46:246–55.

Cummings, S. Thomas; Bayley, Helen C.; and Rie, Herbert E. 1965. Effects of the Child's Deficiency on the Mother: A Study of Mothers of Mentally Retarded, Chronically Ill and Neurotic Children. Paper presented at the Annual Meeting of the American Orthopsychiatric Association, New York.

———. 1966. Effects of the Child's Deficiency on the Mother: A Study of Mothers of Mentally Retarded, Chronically Ill and Neurotic Children. *American Journal of Orthopsychiatry* 36:595–608.

Darling, Rosalyn Benjamin. 1979. *Families Against Society.* Beverly Hills, Calif.: Sage Publications.

———. 1983a. The Birth Defective Child and the Crisis of Parenthood: Redefining the Situation. In *Life-Span Developmental Psychology.* New York: Academic Press.

———. 1983b. Parent-Professional Interaction: The Roots of Misunderstanding. In *The Family With a Handicapped Child*, ed. M. Seligman. New York: Grune & Stratton.

Darling, Rosalyn Benjamin, and Darling, John. 1982. *Children Who Are Different.* St. Louis: C.V. Mosby.

Deck, L. P. 1968. Buying Brains by the Inch. *Journal of the College and University Personnel Association* 19:33–37.

DelCampo, Robert L.; Chase, Teresa; and DelCampo, Diana S. 1984. Growth Disorders in Children: The Impact on the Family System. *Family Relations* 33:79–84.

Dorland, William Alexander Newman. 1981. *Dorland's Illustrated Medical Dictionary.* 26th ed. Philadelphia: W.B. Saunders.

Drash, Philip W. 1969. Psychologic Counseling: Dwarfism. In *Endocrine and Genetic Diseases of Childhood,* ed. Lytt Gardner, pp. 1014–22. Philadelphia: W. B. Saunders.

Drash, Philip W.; Greenberg, Nancy E.; and Money, John. 1968. Intelligence and Personality in Four Syndromes of Dwarfism. In *Human Growth,* ed. D. B. Cheek, pp. 568–81. Philadelphia: Lea & Febiger.

Drillien, C. M., and Drummond, M. B. 1977. *Neurodevelopmental Problems in Early Childhood.* Oxford, England: Blackwell Scientific Publications.

Drotar, D., Baskiewicz, A.; Irvin, N.; Kennell, J.; and Klaus, M. 1975. The Adaptation of Parents to the Birth of an Infant with a Congenital Malformation: A Hypothetical Model. *Pediatrics* 56:710–17.

Drotar, Dennis; Owens, Ruth; and Gotthold, Jacqueline. 1980. Personality Adjustment of Children and Adolescents with Hypopituitarism. *Child Psychiatry and Human Development* 11:59.

Earhart, Eileen, and Sporakowski, Michael J., eds. 1984. Special Issue: The Family with Handicapped Members. *Family Relations* 33(1).

Edgerton, Robert. 1967. *The Cloak of Competence.* Berkeley: University of California Press.

Emery, A. E. H., and Rimoin, D. 1983. Nature and Incidence of Genetic Disease. In *Principles and Practice of Medical Genetics,* vol. 1, eds. Alan Emery and David Rimoin, pp. 1–3. New York: Churchill Livingstone.

Estroff, Sue E. 1981. *Making It Crazy: An Ethnography of Psychiatric Clients in an American Community.* Berkeley: University of California Press.

Featherstone, Helen. 1980. *A Difference in the Family.* New York: Basic Books.

Ference, Rita Helen. 1984. A Survey of the Perceived Experiences and Unique Needs of Parents Who Are Raising a Dwarf Child: Implications for Parent Education. Ph.D. thesis, University of Pittsburgh.

Fine, B. A.; Greendale, K.; Holladay, K.; and Carey, J. C. 1982. *Trisomy 18: A Book for Families.* Omaha, Nebraska: Southeast Nebraska Chapter, March of Dimes Birth Defects Foundation.

Folstein, Susan E., Joan O. Weiss, Francine Mittelman, and Deborah J. Ross. 1981. "Impairment, Psychiatric Symptoms, and Handicap in Dwarfs." *The Johns Hopkins Medical Journal* 148:273–77.

Fortier, Lauria M., and Wanlass, Richard L. 1984. Family Crisis Following the Diagnosis of a Handicapped Child. *Family Relations* 33:13–24.

Freeston, B. M. 1971. An Inquiry Into the Effect of a Spina Bifida Child Upon Family Life. *Developmental Medicine and Child Neurology* 13:456–61.

Gallagher, J.; Cross, A.; and Scharfman, W. 1981. Parental Adaptation to a Young Handicapped Child: The Father's Role. *Journal of the Division for Early Childhood* 3:3–14.

Giele, Janet Zollinger. 1984. A Delicate Balance: The Family's Role in Care of the Handicapped. *Family Relations* 33:85–94.

Gillis, J.S. 1982. *Too Tall Too Small,* Champagne, I.L.: Institute for Personality and Ability Testing.

Goffman, Erving. 1963. *Stigma. Notes on the Management of Spoiled Identity.* Englewood Cliffs, N.J.: Prentice-Hall.

Gordon, Michael; Crouthamel, Carol; Post, Ernest M.; and Richmann, Robert A. 1982. Psycho-social Aspects of Constitutional Short Stature: Social Competence, Behavior Problems, Self-Esteem and Family Functioning. *Journal of Pediatrics* 101:477–80.

Gordon, N., and Kutner, B. 1965. Long-term and Fatal Illness and the Family. *Journal of Health and Human Behavior* 6:190–96.

Grays, C. 1963. At the Bedside: The Pattern of Acceptance in Parents of the Handicapped Child. *Tomorrow's Nurse* 4:30–34.

Gumz, E., and Gubrium, J. 1972. Comparative Parental Perceptions of a Mentally Retarded Child. *American Journal of Mental Deficiency* 77:175–80.

Gunderson, E. K. 1965. Body-Size, Self-Evaluation and Military Effectiveness. *Journal of Personality and Social Psychology* 2:902–06.

Hall, Judith G. 1986. *Summary of the First International Conference on Human Achondroplasia.* Newsletter, Little People of British Columbia Association, 4(3).

Hay, W. 1951. Mental Retardation Problems in Different Age Groups. *American Journal of Mental Deficiency* 55:191–97.

Hinckley, E. D., and Rethlingshafer, D. 1951. Value Judgments of Heights of Men by College Students. *Journal of Psychology* 31:257–62.

Human Growth Foundation. 1979. Growth Hormone Deficiency. Chevy Chase, Md.: Human Growth Foundation.

Isaacs, Jennie, and McElroy, Mary Richter. 1980. Psychosocial Aspects of Chronic Illness in Children. *Journal of School Health* 50:318–21.

Johnston, Francis E. 1963. Some Observations on the Roles of Achondroplastic Dwarfs Through History. *Clinical Pediatrics* 2:703–8.

Kaplan, S. L.; Underwood, L. E.; August, G. P.; Bell, J. J.; Blethen, S. L.: Blizzard, R. M.; Brown, D. R.; Foley, T. P.; Hintz, R. L.; Hopwood, N.J.; Johansen, A.; Kirkland, R. T.; Plotnick, L. P.; Rosenfeld, R. G.; and VanWyk, J. J. 1986. Clinical Studies with Recombinant-DNA-derived Methionyl Human Growth Hormone in Growth Hormone Deficient Children. *Lancet* 8483:697–700.

Katz, A. H., and Bender, E. I. 1976. *The Strength in Us: Self-Help Groups in the Modern World.* New York: New Viewpoints.

Kelly, Thaddeus E.; Robinow, Meinhard; Johanson, Ann; Janku, Patricia; Kaiser, Fran; and Fleet, W. Shep. 1978. *Short Stature: Definition and Estimate of Short Stature in U.S. Population.* Report to the Human Growth Foundation.

Keyes, Ralph. 1980. *The Height of Your Life.* New York: Warner Books.

Kirk, S.; Karnes, M.; and Kirk, W. 1968. *You and Your Retarded Child: A Manual for Parents of Retarded Children.* Palo Alto, Calif.: Pacific Books.

Koegler, S. 1963. The Management of the Retarded Child in Practice. *Canadian Medical Association Journal* 89:1009–14.

Korn, S. J.; Chess, S.; and Fernandez, P. The Impact of Children's Physical Handicaps on Marital Quality and Family Interaction. In R. M. Lerner and G. B. Spanier (Eds.), *Child Influences on Marital and Family Interaction.* New York: Academic Press, 1978.

Krawitz, Jan, and Ott, Thomas. 1982. *Little People.* Little People of America documentary film.

Kubler-Ross, E. 1969. *On Death and Dying.* New York: Macmillan.

Kusalic, Maria, and Fortin, Claire. 1975. Growth Hormone Treatment in Hypopituitary Dwarfs: Longitudinal Psychological Effects. *Canadian Psychiatric Association Journal* 20:325–31.

Kusalic, Maria; Fortin, Claire; and Gauthier, Yvonne. 1972. Psychodynamic Aspects of Dwarfism: Response to Growth Hormone Treatment. *Canadian Psychiatric Association Journal* 17:29–34.

Langer, L. O., Jr. 1965. Diastrophic Dwarfism in Early Infancy. *American Journal of Roentgenology* 93:399–404.

Langness, L. L., and Harold G. Levine, eds. 1986. *Culture and Retardation.* Dordrecht, Netherlands: D. Reidel Publishing.

Lavigne, John V., and Ryan, Michael. 1979. Psychologic Adjustment of Siblings of Children With Chronic Illness. *Pediatrics* 63:616–27.

Lieberman, Morton A.; Borman, Leonard D.; and Associates 1979. *Self-Help Groups for Coping with Crisis: Origins, Members, Processes, and Impact.* San Francisco: Jossey-Bass Publishers.

Little People of America. 1979. National Membership Roster. Owatonna, Minnesota: Little People of America.

Lofland, J., and Stark, R. 1965. Becoming a World Saver: Theory of Conversion to a Deviant Perspective. *American Sociological Review* 30:862–75.

Longo, Diane C., and Bond, Linda. 1984. Families of the Handicapped Child: Research and Practice. *Family Relations* 33:57–66.

Lonsdale, G. 1978. Family Life with a Handicapped Child: The Parents Speak. *Child Care, Health and Development* 4:99–120.

MacMillan, D. L. 1982. *Mental Retardation in School and Society.* 2nd ed. Boston: Little, Brown.

March of Dimes. 1986. Facts. White Plains, N.Y.: March of Dimes Birth Defects Foundation.

Marion, R. L. 1981. *Educators, Parents, and Exceptional Children.* Rockville, Md.: Aspen Systems Corporation.

Maroteaux, Pierre. 1979. *Bone Diseases of Children.* Translated from the French and adapted by Herbert J. Kaufmann. Philadelphia: J. B. Lippincott.

Martel, Leslie F. and Biller, Henry B. 1987. *Stature and Stigma.* Lexington, Mass.: Lexington Books, D. C. Heath and Co.

Mattsson, A. 1972. Long-Term Physical Illness in Childhood: A Challenge to Psychosocial Adaptation. *Pediatrics* 50:801.

McCullough, M. E. 1981. Parent and Sibling Definition of a Situation Regarding Transgenerational Shift in Care of a Handicapped Child. Doctoral dissertation, University of Minnesota.

McIntosh, R.; Merritt, K. K.; Richards, M. R.; Samuels, M. H.; and Bellows, M. T., 1954. The Incidence of Congenital Malformations: A Study of 5,964 Pregnancies. *Pediatrics* 14:505–22.

McKusick, Victor A. 1986. *Mendelian Inheritance in Man.* 7th ed. Baltimore: Johns Hopkins University Press.

Menolascino, F., and Egger, M. 1978. *Medical Dimensions of Mental Retardation.* Lincoln: University of Nebraska Press.

Mitchell, R. G. 1977. The Nature and Causes of Disability in Childhood. *Neurodevelopmental Problems in Early Childhood,* eds. C.M. Drillien and M. B. Drummond. Oxford, England: Blackwell Scientific Publications.

Money, John. 1967. Dwarfism Questions and Answers in Counseling. *Rehabilitation Literature* 28:134–38.

Money, John; Clopper, Richard; and Menefee, Jan. 1980. Psychosexual Development in Postpubertal Males with Idiopathic Panhypopituitarism. *Journal of Sex Research* 16:212–25.

Money, John; Drash, Philip W.; and Lewis, Viola. 1967. Dwarfism and Hypopituitarism: Statural Retardation Without Mental Retardation. *American Journal of Mental Deficiency* 72:122–26.

Money, John, and Pollitt, Ernesto. 1966. Studies in the Psychology of Dwarfism, II. Personality Maturation and Response to Growth Hormone Treatment in Hypopituitary Dwarfs. *Journal of Pediatrics* 68:381–90.

Mori, Allen A. 1983. *Families of Children With Special Needs*. Rockville, Md.: Aspen Systems Corporation.

Moroney, R. 1981. Public Social Policy: Impact on Families with Handicapped Children. In *Understanding and Working with Parents of Children with Special Needs*, ed. J. L. Paul. New York: Holt, Rinehart and Winston.

Obuchowski, K.; Zienkiewicz, H.; and Graczykowska-Koczorowska, A. 1970. Psychological Studies in Pituitary Dwarfism. *Polish Medical Journal* 9:1229–35.

O'Donnell, Mary 1977. *The Idea Machine*. Little People of America Foundation.

Patterson, Joan M., and McCubbin, Hamilton I. 1983. The Impact of Family Life Events and Changes on the Health of a Chronically Ill Child. *Family Relations* 32:255–64.

Pearse, M. 1977. The Child with Cancer: Impact on the Family. *The Journal of School Health* 3:174–78.

Phifer, Kate Gilbert. 1979, *Growing Up Small: A Handbook for Short People*. Middlebury, Vermont: Paul S. Eriksson.

Pilisuk, Marc, and Susan H. Parks. 1986. *The Healing Web: Social Networks and Human Survival*. Hanover, N.H.: University Press of New England.

Pollitt, Ernesto, and Money, John. 1964. Studies in the Psychology of Dwarfism, I. Intelligence Quotient and School Achievement. *Journal of Pediatrics* 64:415–21.

Power, Paul W., and Orto, Arthur E. Dell. 1980. General Impact of Child Disability/Illness on the Family. In *Role of the Family in the Rehabilitation of the Physically Disabled*, ed. P.W. Power and A. E. Dell Orto. Baltimore: University Park Press.

Ricker, Margaret Dow. 1984. Application of the Double ABCX Model to Predict Changes in Perception of Stresses Associated with a Child's Growth Problem. Ph.D. thesis, University of Maine.

Rieser, Patricia, and Underwood, Louis E. 1986. *Growing Children: A Parents' Guide*. San Francisco: Genentech, ®.

Rimoin, David L. 1979. International Nomenclature of Constitutional Diseases of Bone with Bibliography. In Birth Defects Original Article Series 20(10). White Plains, N.Y.: March of Dimes Birth Defects Foundation.

Rimoin, D. L., and Lachman, R. S. 1983. The Chondrodysplasias. In *Principles and Practice of Medical Genetics*, vol. 2, eds. Alan Emery and David Rimoin, pp. 703–35. New York: Churchill Livingstone.

Rogers, John G. and Weiss, Joan. 1979. In *My Child is a Dwarf*. 2nd edition. Little People of America.

Roos, P. 1979. Parents of Mentally Retarded Children—Misunderstood and Mistreated.

In *Parents Speak Out: View From the Other Side of a Two Way Mirror*, eds. A. Turnbull and R. Turnbull., Columbus, Ohio: Charles E. Merrill.

———. 1982. Special Trends and Issues. In *Mental Retardation: From Categories to People*, eds. P. T. Cegelka and H. J. Prehm. Columbus, Ohio: Charles E. Merrill.

Rosen, L. 1955. Selected Aspects in the Development of the Mother's Understanding of Her Mentally Retarded Child. *American Journal of Mental Deficiency* 59:522.

Roskies, Ethel. 1972. *Abnormality and Normality: The Mothering of Thalidomide Children.* New York: Cornell University Press.

Roth, Hy, and Cromie, Robert. 1980. *The Little People.* New York: Everest House.

Rotnem, Diane L. 1986. Size Versus Age: Ambiguities in Parenting Short-Statured Children. In *Slow Grows the Child: Aspects of Growth Delay*, eds. Brian Stabler and Louis Underwood. Hillsdale, N.J.: Lawrence Erlbaum Associates.

Rotnem, D.; Genel, M.; Hintz, R. L.; and Cohen, D. J. 1977. Personality Development in Children with Growth Hormone Deficiency. *Journal of the American Academy of Child Psychiatry* 16:412–26.

Salk, L. 1972. The Psychosocial Impact of Hemophilia on the Patient and His Family. *Social Science and Medicine* 6:491–505.

Schell, G. C. 1981. The Young Handicapped Child: A Family Perspective. *Topics in Early Childhood Special Education* 1:21–27.

Scott, Charles I., Jr. 1977. Medical and Social Adaptation in Dwarfing Conditions. In *Birth Defects Original Article Series* 18(3C):29–43. March of Dimes Birth Defects Foundation.

Secord, Paul F., and Jourard, Sidney M. 1953. The Appraisal of Body Cathexis and the Self. *Journal of Consulting Psychology* 17:343–47.

———. 1954. Body Size and Body Cathexis. *Journal of Consulting Psychology* 18:184.

Shapiro, Sam; Ross, L. J.; and Levine, H.S. 1965. Relationship of Selected Prenatal Factors to Pregnancy Outcome and Congenital Anomalies. *American Journal of Public Health* 55:268–282.

Shurka, Esther, and Laron, Zvi. 1975. Adjustment and Rehabilitation Problems of Children and Adolescents with Growth Retardation, I: Familial Dwarfism with High Plasma Immunoreactive Human Growth Hormone. *Israel Journal of Medical Science* 11:352–57.

Skrtic, T. M.; Summers, J. A.; Brotherson, M. J.; and Turnbull, A. P. 1983. Severely Handicapped Children and Their Brothers and Sisters. In *Severely Handicapped Young Children and Their Families: Research in Review*, ed. J. Blacher. New York: Academic Press.

Solnit, A. J., and Stark, M. H. 1961. Mourning and the Birth of a Defective Child. *Psychoanalytic Study of the Child* 16:523–37.

Spencer, Roger F., and Raft, David D. 1974. Adaptation and Defenses in Hypopituitary Dwarfs. *Psychosomatics* 15:35–38.

Spranger, J. W., and Langer, Jr., L. O. 1970. Spondyloepiphyseal Dysplasia Congenita. *Radiology* 94:313–22.

Spranger, J. W.; Langer, Jr., L. O.; and Weidemann, H. R. 1974. *Bone Dysplasias: An Atlas of Constitutional Disorders of Skeletal Development.* Philadelphia: W.B. Saunders.

Stabler, Brian, and Underwood, Louis. 1977. Anxiety and Locus of Control in Hypopituitary Dwarf Children. *Research Related to Children Bulletin* 38:75.

————, eds. 1986. *Slow Grows the Child: Psychosocial Aspects of Growth Delay*. Hillsdale, N.J.: Lawrence Erlbaum Associates, Publishers.

Stabler, Brian; Whitt, J. K.; Moreault, D. M.; D'Ercole, A. J.; and Underwood, L. 1980. Social Judgment in Children of Short Stature. *Psychological Reports* 46:743–46.

Stace, Lucille, and Danks, David M. 1981a. A Social Study of Dwarfing Conditions, I: The Reactions and Questions of Parents of Children with Bone Dysplasias. *Australian Paediatric Journal* 17:167–71.

————. 1981b. A Social Study of Dwarfing Conditions, II: The Experience of Children with Bone Dysplasias, and of Their Parents. *Australian Paediatric Journal* 17:172–76.

————. 1981c. A Social Study of Dwarfing Conditions, III: The Social and Emotional Experiences of Adults with Bone Dysplasias. *Australian Paediatric Journal* 17:177–82.

Steinhauer, P. D.; Mushin, D.; and Rae-Grant, Q. 1974. Psychological Aspects of Chronic Illness. *Pediatric Clinics of North America* 21:825–40.

Tew, B.; Laurence, K.; and Samuel, P. 1974. Parental Estimates of the Intelligence of Their Physically Handicapped Child. *Developmental Medicine and Child Neurology* 16:494–500.

UNICEF. 1980. *Childhood Disability: Its Prevention and Rehabilitation*. Report of Rehabilitational International to the Executive Board of UNICEF, March 26:8.

United States Department of Commerce, Bureau of the Census. 1986. Statistical Abstract of the United States. 106th ed.

United States National Center for Health Statistics Percentiles. n.d. *Boys: 2–18 Years Physical Growth*. Genentech, ®.

————. n.d. *Girls: 2–18 Years Physical Growth*. Genentech, ®.

Vadasy, P. F.; Fewell, R. R.; Meyer, D. J.; and Schell, G. 1984. Siblings of Handicapped Children: A Developmental Perspective on Family Interactions. *Family Relations* 33:155–68.

Vash, Carolyn L. 1981. *The Psychology of Disability*. New York: Springer.

Venters, Maurine. 1981. Familial Coping With Chronic and Severe Childhood Illness: The Case of Cystic Fibrosis. *Social Science and Medicine* 15A:289–97.

Voysey, Margaret. 1972. Impression Management by Parents with Disabled Children. *Journal of Health and Social Behavior* 13:80–89.

————. 1975 *A Constant Burden: The Reconstitution of Family Life*. London: Routledge and Kegan Paul.

Walker, J.H. 1971. Spina Bifida—and the Parents. *Developmental Medicine and Child Neurology* 13:462–76.

Weinberg, Martin S. 1968. The Problems of Midgets and Dwarfs and Organizational Remedies: A Study of the Little People of America. *Journal of Health and Social Behavior* 9:65–71.

Weiss, Joan O. 1977. Social Development of Dwarfs. In *Proceedings of a Conference on Genetic Disorders: Social Service Intervention*, eds. W. T. Hall and C. L. Young. University of Pittsburgh: Graduate School of Public Health.

Wolfsenberger, W. 1967. Counseling the Parents of the Retarded. In *Mental Retardation: Appraisal, Education, and Rehabilitation*, ed. A.A. Baumeister. Chicago: Aldine.

Wright, Beatrice A. 1960. *Physical Disability—A Psychological Approach*. New York: Harper and Row Publishers.

Wynne-Davies, Ruth; Hall, Christine M.; and Apley, A. Graham. 1985. *Atlas of Skeletal Dysplasias*. Edinburgh, Scotland, and N.Y.: Churchill Livingstone.

Young-Hyman, Deborah. 1986. Effects of Short Stature on Social Competence. In *Slow Grows the Child: Aspects of Growth Delay*, eds. Brian Stabler and Louis Underwood. Hillsdale, N.J.: Lawrence Erlbaum Associates.

Zucman, Elizabeth. 1982. *Childhood Disabilty in the Family: Recognizing the Added Handicap*. Monograph no. 14. New York: World Rehabilitation Fund.

Index

acceptance of dwarfism, 61, 109, 171–72. *See also* denial

achondroplasia: case studies of, 107–23; cause of, 11; characteristics of, 11; and childbearing, 68; and developmental tasks, 31–32, 118; incidence of, 11–12; medical problems of, 34; and personality, 141, 166–67; psychosocial characteristics of, 166–67. *See also* hydrocephalus

adaptation: to dwarfism, 155–57; of environment to dwarf, 33; of family through LPA, 139; of mother to different child, 8

adolescence: dwarf experience, 55, 84, 169; jobs during, 84, 129. *See also* dating; social life

ambiguity, culture of, 8, 139–41; negotiation of, 8

ambivalence of parents, 75–78, 140

anger as parental response to dwarfism, 36, 155

anxiety: of parents, 3, 153, 156; about dwarf's academic achievement, 46, 119; about dwarf's attractiveness, 51; about dwarf's occupation, 66–67; about dwarf's social acceptability, 46, 47, 117; about dwarf's social role, 27–28, 137; about mental retardation, 26, 28

awareness of dwarfism by parents, 61, 120

birth defects: prevalence of, 1–2; visibility of, 57

birth order of dwarf child, 58–59. *See also* siblings

blame: for birth of dwarf, 22, 29–30; of mothers, 160; of physicians by parents, 145; of self, 26; of social factors, 48

childbearing and dwarfs, 67, 85, 122

children's hospitals, 4

clothing, 33–34, 84

coping: anger, 51; dwarfs' skills in, 83; of family, 155–56; hypersensitiveness of parents, 64; with negative social response, 49–56; Parents' Group advice, 73; religion, 57, 126; variables in, 57. *See also* denial; humor; support systems

cure, parents' search for, 34–35, 36

dating: and dwarfs, 28, 55–56, 79, 81, 84, 131, 141, 169. *See also* adolescence

denial of dwarfism: by child, 50, 56; by family, 171; by parents, 141, 144, 159, 171. *See also* self-identity

About the Author

JOAN ABLON is Professor of Medical Anthropology, Departments of Epidemiology and International Health and Psychiatry, at the University of California at San Francisco. Ablon received her Ph.D. from the University of Chicago in social anthropology. She has carried out field research in urban and rural areas of the United States and in Mayan villages of southern Mexico. She has primarily focused on social and health issues within American society. Her first major research projects in this country concerned patterns of urban adaptation of relocated American Indians and, later, Samoan migrants to metropolitan areas.

As a medical anthropologist, Ablon has studied and written about subjects little explored by anthropologists: contemporary middle-class family life; alcoholism and the family; and since 1976, dwarfism and its influence on individual self-image, life style, and family behavior. Ablon has also studied the dynamics of nonprofessional therapeutic self-help groups and social support systems as they function to help members of stigmatized populations. She has worked extensively with Al-Anon Family Groups and, more recently, with members of Little People of America and its Parents' Groups. Ablon has published numerous articles and chapters in clinical and scholarly journals and books. Her first book on dwarfism, *Little People in America: The Social Dimensions of Dwarfism*, also published by Praeger, chronicles the life experiences of adult dwarfs and the impact on their lives of Little People of America, a peer support group for profoundly short-statured persons.